Hostiles?

HOSTILES?

*The Lakota Ghost Dance
and Buffalo Bill's Wild West*

Sam A. Maddra

University of Oklahoma Press : Norman

Library of Congress Cataloging-in-Publication Data

Maddra, Sam.
    Hostiles? : the Lakota ghost dance and Buffalo Bill's Wild West / Sam A.
Maddra.
        p. cm.
    Includes bibliographical references and index.
    ISBN 0-8061-3743-6 (alk. paper)
    1. Ghost dance—South Dakota. 2. Teton Indians—Rites and ceremonies.
3. Buffalo Bill's Wild West Show. 4. Teton Indians—Cultural assimilation.
5. Teton Indians—Government relations.   I. Title.

E99.T34M33 2006
978.004'975244—dc22   2005053854

1 2 3 4 5 6 7 8 9 10

CONTENTS

ILLUSTRATIONS

FIGURES

Following page 111

MAP

PREFACE

This book has grown out of an interest that was first sparked in 1994, when I became aware of a repatriation request for a Ghost Dance shirt that reportedly had been removed from a body in the aftermath of the Wounded Knee massacre. The shirt, which was then owned by Glasgow Museums, had been acquired more than one hundred years before from George C. Crager, who was in Glasgow as the Lakota interpreter with Buffalo Bill's Wild West. I researched the shirt's provenance and in so doing, learned of the visit to my hometown in 1891–92 by Buffalo Bill's Wild West. Among the performers in William F. Cody's exhibition were a number of Lakota Ghost Dancers who had formerly been prisoners at Fort Sheridan.

After the successful repatriation of the Ghost Dance shirt to the Wounded Knee Survivors Association in 1999, my focus shifted toward the Wild West show's tour of Britain. I uncovered source material that appeared to question the dominant interpretation of the Lakota Ghost Dance. The involvement of personnel from Buffalo Bill's Wild West and the suppression of the Ghost Dance in South Dakota have often been mentioned in passing in the secondary literature, but have rarely been examined in depth. It became clear that by focusing on this interaction, much could be learned about the actions and motivations of Lakota men and women at this significant time in their history.

I would like to extend my gratitude to all the institutions that have supported my work by providing funds for specific research trips or for more general purposes: University of Glasgow Postgraduate Scholarship, Faculty of Arts, University of Glasgow; Phillips Fund for Native American Research, American Philosophical Society; Garlow Memorial Fund, Buffalo Bill Historical Center; Glasgow Educational and Marshall Trust Schemes, Glasgow; Marcus Cunliffe Short Term Travel Award, British Association of American Studies; Research Support Award, Graduate School of Arts and Humanities, University of Glasgow; Financial Assistance for Postgraduate Students, School of History and Archaeology, University of Glasgow; the Principal, Professor Sir Graeme Davies, Discretionary Fund, University of Glasgow; the Vice-Principal, Professor Drummond Bone, University of Glasgow; the Department of History, University of Glasgow; the Andrew Hook Centre for American Studies, University of Glasgow; the Dean of the Faculty of Arts, University of Glasgow.

I also extend grateful thanks to those who have assisted me in my research in the following archives: Archives II, Maryland; Art Gallery and Museum, Kelvingrove, Glasgow; British Library Newspaper Library, Collindale, London; Buffalo Bill Museum and Grave, Lookout Mountain, Golden, Colorado; Denver Public Library, Western History Collection, Denver, Colorado; Federal Archives and Record Center, Kansas City, Missouri; Glasgow Room, Mitchell Library, Glasgow; National Archives and Record Administration, Washington, D.C.; South Dakota State Historical Society, Pierre, South Dakota; Wyoming State Archives, Cheyenne, Wyoming. I am grateful to Paul Fees, Lynn Houze, and all the staff in the McCraken Research Library, Buffalo Bill Historical Center, Cody, Wyoming. I thank Antonia Lovelace and Mark O'Neill of Glasgow Museums, and Marcella Lebeau of the Wounded Knee Survivors Association, who were instrumental in supporting and encouraging my work in its initial stages.

I am indebted to Simon Newman, Phillips O'Brien, and Marina Moskowitz, who have been unstinting in their support and advice, and to Ray DeMallie, Alison Phipps, Laura Peers, and Tricia Denholm. Many colleagues and friends have given support and advice over the years, which has been invaluable and greatly appreciated. I also owe great thanks to my copyeditor, Lys Ann Weiss, and all those at the University of Oklahoma Press who have helped bring this project to completion, most notably Charles Rankin, Alessandra Jacobi, and Steven Baker. Last but by no means least, for their patience, understanding, and constant support I would like to thank my family, Rob, Rosie, and Tricia.

HOSTILES?

INTRODUCTION

In the winter of 1889–90, Short Bull and Kicking Bear led a party of ten Lakota delegates to Nevada to see the Indian prophet Wovoka. Upon their return, the delegates introduced Wovoka's religion to their kinsmen, and the Ghost Dance briefly flourished on the South Dakota reservations. However, by the end of 1890 the U.S. government perceived the Ghost Dance as being a threat to its programs of assimilation, and the Lakota Ghost Dancers as being hostile. At the close of the military suppression of the religion in South Dakota, which culminated in the infamous Wounded Knee Massacre, Short Bull and Kicking Bear were among twenty-seven Lakota Ghost Dancers incarcerated at Fort Sheridan, Illinois. Twenty-three of the Fort Sheridan prisoners were eventually released into the custody of Col. William F. Cody (Buffalo Bill), and in April 1891 they accompanied a further forty-two Lakota Indians across the Atlantic to Europe to perform in Buffalo Bill's Wild West exhibition. The show spent the summer of 1891 touring provincial England before traveling to Glasgow for a five-month winter stand. When Cody decided to return home for a break, the exhibition hired a group of thirty Africans to cover his absence. In January 1892 Kicking Bear welcomed the Africans to the exhibition in the East End of Glasgow. "My heart is glad to see you today, and I shake your hand. Long ago, we had plenty of land, but civilisation has driven us from it. Make better treaties, and see they are kept."[1] Kicking Bear's words of welcome were particularly pertinent, and illustrated the Lakotas' perception of the problems that faced them at the close of the nineteenth century. Having nomadically followed the vast buffalo herds of the northern Plains during the first half of the century, the Lakota had flourished as a formidable warrior society. However, the encroachment of Euro-Americans and their railroads through valuable hunting grounds, coupled with such fateful events as the Battle of the Little Bighorn, resulted in a steadily diminishing land base. Herded onto reservations, by the 1890s the Lakota were almost completely dependent on the federal government for subsistence. Such dependency was in stark contrast to the independent life of pre-reservation days, and many Lakota shared Kicking Bear's belief that it was the loss of invaluable land that lay at the root of their problems.[2]

This book considers both the Lakota Ghost Dance of 1890 and Buffalo Bill's Wild West exhibition in the years 1890–92, exploring the nature, significance, and consequences of their interaction at this particularly crucial time in Native American history. It demonstrates that the traditional interpretation of this aspect of Native American history has given a limited or overly generalized picture. Historical evidence reveals the complex subtleties involved in the actions of the protagonists, underlining the messiness of history and its refusal to fit into clearly defined compartments.

Examining the association of Cody's Wild West with the Lakota Ghost Dance offers a new insight into the religion in South Dakota. It reveals some of the tactics employed by the Lakota to deal with the demands of the dominant society at the close of the nineteenth century. The Ghost Dance and the Wild West shows presented the Lakota with various alternatives to the dependency that the government's Indian policy had brought about, while also enabling them to retain their Indian identity. In consequence, the architects of the government's Indian policy viewed both the Ghost Dance and the Wild West shows as a threat to their programs of assimilation, which they believed to be the only option for the Indians to achieve independence.

At the close of the nineteenth century, with the Indian nations having been militarily pacified, the U.S. government decided to impose "total assimilation" upon its Indian "wards."[3] A consensus of politicians and philanthropic Indian campaigners agreed that the only way for Indian survival was the complete absorption of Indians into American society. Taking confidence from the scientific racial theories that proved popular with the majority of the dominant society and that appeared to reinforce the concept of white racial superiority, they saw the tribal culture of the Indian nations as preventing their elevation from "savage" life to one of "civilization."[4] Reforms were introduced to prepare the Indians for citizenship by means of individual allotment of communally owned tribal lands, the passing of laws prohibiting traditional religious and cultural practices, and a fundamental commitment to educational programs.[5]

The motivations of reformers for embracing American Indians' entry into mainstream society might appear somewhat contrary to the predominant racism in America at the close of the nineteenth century. During the same period American blacks were facing increased persecution and legally sanctioned segregation, as evidenced by the infamous *Plessy v. Ferguson* Supreme Court decision of 1896.[6] We could argue that the government's "civilizing" programs conformed to the prevailing philanthropic beliefs that America owed the Indians for a century of land grabbing, therefore providing a moral justification for attempts to "civilize" the Indians. However, the main motivation was more likely the desire to end the Indians' dependency on the government for their subsistence, which was proving to be a significant financial burden.[7] Having been released from chattel slavery at the close of the Civil War, blacks were not dependent upon either white society or the government for subsistence, and therefore there was no financial incentive to "elevate" and incorporate them into mainstream society. Perhaps more significant, in the aftermath of the Civil War the "Indian question" proved to be "politically neutral" and therefore posed no threat to national unity and only "the smallest threat to existing social relationships."[8]

Recent historiography has shown that American Indian responses to the assimilation policies of the U.S. government were both individual and complex. Yet it appears clear that whether individuals embraced total assimilation, employed selective accommodation or resisted all assimilation policies, their major motivation was survival. To those who chose resistance or selective accommodation, the maintenance of an Indian identity was paramount.[9]

How individual Lakota chose to respond to the perceived crisis that faced them during the early assimilationist period reinforced the ongoing factionalism within the community.[10] Such factionalism, which was by no means specific to the Lakota, has generally been described as the "progressive-traditional dichotomy." However, David Rich Lewis has shown how limiting such definitions can be. Lewis argues that "this growing factionalism, based on what agents perceived as a progressive-traditional dichotomy running along band lines, was in fact individualistic, fluid, and issue- and economics-orientated." Therefore, "equating *progressive* with change and *traditional* with resistance sacrifices individually complex behavior, diminishing our understanding of Native Americans' rationales and responses."[11]

Nevertheless Lewis also acknowledges that such definitions can be useful "as academic shorthand for issue-specific situations," and it is with this in mind that I use the terms *traditional* and *progressive* with regard to individual Lakota reactions to the government's assimilation programs.[12] To clarify, when I describe Short Bull as a "traditionalist," I do not wish the reader to interpret this as "closed" or "fixed." As this book will show, Short Bull was open to both innovation and accommodation, while at the same time being determined to defend the Indians' right to their own identity.

At the heart of the 1890 Ghost Dance religion was Wovoka, a Paiute spiritual leader and weather prophet. He was born in about 1856 near Yerington, Nevada, and at the time of the Ghost Dance was more commonly known as Jack Wilson. In the late 1880s Wovoka had experienced a religious revelation wherein he died and went to heaven. While there he received from God instructions for a dance and a message of peace to share with all people. Later, Wovoka received emissaries from different Indian nations who had traveled to Nevada to learn all they could about the new religion. He prophesied that if they lived peacefully, did not lie, worked hard, and performed the Ghost Dance, dead friends and relatives would return and all would live together in the traditional way with plentiful game. In the fall of 1889 ten Lakota men set out to visit the Paiute prophet. They were gone all winter, and when they returned in the spring of 1890, they brought with them the Ghost Dance, a new religious practice that appeared to promise renewed hope for the Lakota people.[13]

The Ghost Dance of the Lakota was performed around a central tree, a practice borrowed from the Sun Dance, which had been the principal religious ritual of the Lakota until it was banned in the 1880s. The dancers circled around with hands clasped, swinging their arms back and forth, and chanting Ghost Dance songs. This ritual would be repeated over a period of hours. If fortunate, the dancers would fall into unconsciousness and experience visions in which they might meet and talk to dead friends and relatives. Ghost Shirts were worn by the dancers as an important part of the religion, and the Lakota imbued the shirts with protective qualities by means of decoration and ceremony.[14]

The dominant interpretation, for both contemporary observers and subsequent historians, accuses the leaders of the Lakota Ghost Dance of perverting Wovoka's doctrine of peace into one of hostility, characterized by the introduction of impenetrable Ghost Dance shirts. Writing in 1891, having investigated the religion in Nevada, army first lieutenant Nat P. Phister observed that "the doctrine has been much perverted and distorted in its transmission to the Sioux, Cheyennes, Arapahoes and other tribes."[15] This sentiment was echoed five years later by James Mooney in his enormously influential publication, *The Ghost Dance Religion and the Sioux Outbreak of 1890*, in which he commented, "Among the powerful and warlike Sioux . . . the doctrine speedily assumed a hostile meaning."[16] In his book *The Last Days of the Sioux Nation* (1963), Robert Utley concurred with his nineteenth-century predecessors, noting that "other Ghost Dancing tribes adopted the Ghost shirt, but only the Sioux invested it with bulletproof qualities. . . . The Sioux apostles had perverted Wovoka's doctrine into a militant crusade against the white man."[17]

In recent years, this interpretation has been questioned. Raymond DeMallie, for example, has argued in "The Lakota Ghost Dance: An Ethnohistorical Account" that "the historical record does not support the accusation that the Sioux 'perverted' the ghost dance doctrine of peace to one of war." But as DeMallie himself commented, "this is a minority viewpoint in the literature," and subsequent publications have continued to argue that the Lakota were responsible for "distort[ing] the true Ghost Dance religion."[18]

DeMallie's analysis was based on the ethnohistorical approach of symbolic anthropology, comparing "epistemological and philosophical bases for action from the perspective of the different cultures involved."[19] So far there has been no systematic examination of why the dominant interpretation has been that the Lakota "perverted" Wovoka's doctrine of peace into one of hostility, and the possible flaws in this interpretation. Most significant, there has never been a methodical analysis of the five Short Bull narratives recorded between 1891 and 1915, the most complete and authoritative of the surviving accounts of a Lakota Ghost Dancer. These documents undermine the traditional view, and give new insights into the Lakota interpretation of the Ghost Dance and the events in South Dakota during this critical time. All five accounts are reprinted in the appendix to this book.

Chapter 1 presents the historical background and biographical context. The following two chapters take issue with the longstanding belief that the Lakota Ghost Dancers "perverted" Wovoka's doctrine of peace into one of hostility. A reexamination of the primary historical sources as well as the secondary literature reveals that the dominant interpretation of the Ghost Dance in South Dakota is based on accounts of the religion given by those who actively worked to suppress it. As such these sources give a very narrow interpretation of the Lakota understanding of the religion and only a partial view of the unfolding events in South Dakota during the winter of 1890–91. Sources originating with the Lakota Ghost Dancers themselves illustrate that the message brought back by the Lakota delegates was the same as Wovoka's original teachings, and give a fuller and more complex reading of the religion in South Dakota.

To the Lakota, the religion offered hope in a time of great transition when their very identity was under attack; it gave them a sense of direction that was both familiar and new. To the U.S. government, which remained relatively ignorant of the religion throughout its suppression, the Ghost Dance represented an obstacle to be overcome, a shift backward toward pagan ways and thus a rejection of the assimilation programs it was attempting to impose on the Plains Indians. When government agents reported a loss of control over the Lakota, the response of federal authorities was to reassert that control as swiftly as possible. And reassert it they did: the U.S. military's massacre of almost 300 Lakota men, women, and children at Wounded Knee Creek was the most "hostile" and aggressive element of the Ghost Dance troubles. It was not the Lakota who perverted Wovoka's doctrine of peace into one of war, but rather those who gained from its brutal suppression.

One of many groups to benefit from the religion's military suppression, though indirectly, was Buffalo Bill's Wild West. Chapters 4 and 5 explore the significance of the repression to the continued success of William Cody's famous Wild West show. While the Ghost Dance was sweeping across the Indian reservations of the American West, a controversy had erupted in the eastern press over Cody's treatment of his Indian employees, while touring in Europe. The affair resulted in a ban on Indian employment in Wild West exhibitions.

When Cody and his Indian performers returned to America to refute the allegations of mistreatment, they became embroiled in the suppression of the Lakota Ghost Dance. Cody himself was asked by General Miles to arrest Sitting Bull, but the plan was thwarted and the mission never completed. The returning Indian showmen, however, worked for the government in various capacities, such as Indian police, scouts for the army, and peace negotiators. Cody was subsequently able to illustrate that, contrary to the assertions of his critics, the Wild West shows encouraged the government's assimilation programs, and that the experience of touring with his outfit was beneficial for Indians and whites alike.

If the management of Buffalo Bill's Wild West had not been forced to return the Indian performers, neither Cody nor the Wild West personnel would have become involved. Touring with Cody's Wild West offered the Indian performers independence from government control, as well as regular food and a reliable income. These advantages compared favorably with the poverty and monotony of reservation life. Therefore, the involvement of some of the Wild West's Indian personnel in the suppression of the Ghost Dance needs to be viewed in the context of the ban on their employment in Wild West shows and their desire to overturn it. Furthermore, without the military suppression of the Lakota Ghost Dance, Buffalo Bill's Wild West undoubtedly would have evolved into something very different. By disarming the arguments of the reformers opposed to Indian employment in Wild West shows, Cody and his Lakota performers secured for themselves and other Indians the right to work at a job of their own choice.

The events in South Dakota enabled Cody to turn the situation to his advantage to such an extent that in February 1891, when he applied to hire seventy-five Lakota performers, the government granted permission. To crown this success, twenty-three of the Ghost Dancers who had been removed to Fort Sheridan at the close of the military suppression of the Lakota Ghost Dance were released into his custody to travel abroad as performers in his Wild West exhibition. The campaign against Cody's Wild West that had been launched by the Indian Rights Association was thus seriously disarmed. Not only was the organization unable to prevent Cody employing Indian performers, it could not stop him adding the Fort Sheridan prisoners to the ranks of the Indians he was taking to Europe.

The 1891–92 tour was Cody's second visit to Britain with his Wild West show. In the many biographies of Buffalo Bill's Wild West, most authors have tended to write in more detail about the first visit, in 1887. However, the second tour was significantly different on two counts. First, the presence of the Fort Sheridan prisoners gave rise to considerable excitement. The general public regarded with great interest these participants in the last great Indian rebellion. Second, on this tour the exhibition traveled to the provincial towns of England and made its first visit to Wales and Scotland, thus bringing Cody's image of the American West to a much larger British audience. Chapters 6, 7, and 8 focus on the 1891–92 tour of Britain. Chapter 6 explores how Cody used and presented the Fort Sheridan prisoners in the context of his narrative of the conquest of America. British perceptions of the Lakota Ghost Dancers, and the influence of Buffalo Bill's Wild West on their views of the Indians as "the Other," are examined in chapter 7. Finally, looking through the lens of the Indians' experiences on the tour, chapter 8 analyzes how the allegations of mistreatment, leveled against Buffalo Bill's Wild West the previous summer, affected Cody's treatment of his Indian employees.

By taking the Lakota prisoners on tour with the Wild West, Cody and the government hoped to force the "hostiles" to experience the power and might of white civilization so that they would never again rebel. While on tour with Buffalo Bill's Wild West, the Fort Sheridan prisoners openly mingled with the other Indian performers and with American and European whites. They showed a keen interest in white culture and religion, gaining an expanded view of the world and knowledge that would be of benefit in future dealings with whites. Significantly, they stayed true to their beliefs, often continuing to practice the Ghost Dance years later.

At the close of the winter stand in Glasgow, the majority of Ghost Dance prisoners who were still with the exhibition decided that they had had enough of show business and asked to be returned home. The final chapter examines what happened to the Fort Sheridan prisoners once they returned to America, and explores whether their time with Cody had the hoped-for effect. The evidence clearly demonstrates that, for Kicking Bear and Short Bull at least, their journey across the Rocky Mountains to Nevada had a much greater influence on them than their visit to Europe. Both men maintained their belief in the Ghost Dance.

This book draws not only on British newspapers, clipping books, and Wild West programs but also on the records of the U.S. Office of Indian Affairs and of the Secretary of the Interior, in addition to materials from many different archives. Such documentation allows the book to offer a rich and detailed account of the Indians' experiences on the tour and a unique record of the British perception of Buffalo Bill's Wild West and its Indian performers.

The use of archival sources, such as newspapers and Indian narratives, can pose potential problems of reliability. Generally, newspaper articles comply with the overall editorial stance of the paper and present only a specific political viewpoint. Although the credibility of the newspaper stories can sometimes be questionable, it is still possible to glean facts from them when supported by corroboration. As newspapers would normally reflect the beliefs and attitudes of their readership, they can also be particularly good for assessing perceptions, and this makes them an especially useful source. By examining newspapers that cut across the broad spectrum of the political agenda, a researcher can cover all angles and access a variety of points of view.

Narratives can also pose problems of credibility, not least when it comes to translations, and this is particularly true for one of the key sources for this book, "As Narrated by Short Bull" (see the appendix). No Lakota version of the text exists to confirm the accuracy of the translation, as George Crager both transcribed and translated the narrative himself.[20] Despite such difficulties, Indian narratives are invaluable in giving a more complete picture of Indian agency and motivations than can otherwise be obtained. As long as they can be substantiated by other sources, documents such as Crager's can provide a wealth of valuable information. For example, the document "As Narrated by Short Bull" provides us with perhaps the only surviving eyewitness account of events in the Badlands stronghold during the tense impasse between the Lakota Ghost Dancers and the U.S. military. It illustrates in greater detail than any other text Short Bull's own understanding of the Ghost Dance and what Wovoka had told him. I believe this document is the single most significant source on the experiences of the Lakota delegates who journeyed west to see Wovoka, and those of the Lakota Ghost Dancers during the winter of 1890–91.

Drawing on this wide variety of sources adds significantly to our knowledge of the Lakota Ghost Dance and to the importance and consequences of the interaction of Buffalo Bill's Wild West with the suppression of the religion in South Dakota. The sources illustrate how individual Lakota utilized various forms of accommodation, both through adherence to the Ghost Dance and by seeking employment with Buffalo Bill's Wild West, at this significant transitional time in their history. In various ways, the Ghost Dance and the Wild West shows presented the Lakota with the chance to resist the dependency that the government's Indian policy had created, while allowing them to retain their Indian identity.

The sources also clearly show that the Lakota were not rebellious, but were interpreted as such by those who wished to reassert control over the Ghost Dancers. The closest the "hostiles" got to rebellion was *playing* hostile Indians in the Wild West arena. This in turn reinforced the onlookers' perception of them as "savages" and ultimately helped justify, in the minds of their white European audience, the suppression employed by the U.S. government. The peaceful religion's endurance is the best demonstration that the Lakota Ghost Dance was not an uprising by hostile Indians, but a religious movement that preached peace and accommodation, and that thus survived long after its ruthless suppression.

CHAPTER ONE

LAKOTA CULTURE
IN AN ERA OF CHANGE

The Lakota, also referred to as the Teton Sioux, are the most westerly group originating from the Seven Council Fires, which in the six- teenth century had established itself on the headwaters of the Mis- sissippi.[1] The Lakota themselves were also divided into seven different subtribes or *ospaye*: Brule, Oglala, Minneconjou, Sans Arcs, Two Kettles, Blackfeet, and Hunkpapa.[2] Each of these tribes was divided into two or more bands or *tiyospaye*, "which were commonly composed of ten or more bilaterally extended families."[3]

Band leaders could command the respect and loyalty of their *tiyospaye* by their lifelong commitment to the four fundamental Lakota virtues of bravery, generosity, fortitude, and wisdom, but ultimately they had little or no real decision-making authority. They were esteemed as the guardians of their bands, and withdrawal of support served to curb a leader's conduct. Dissatisfied individuals could leave their *tiyospaye* and join that of a proven leader, or on some occasions, they might form an entirely new band. Therefore, pre-reservation Lakota society "was fluid and dynamic, character- ized by the recurrent fusion and fission of bands."[4]

The Lakota people were accomplished at adjusting to changing circumstances. They had been forced to adapt to a new environment during the eighteenth century, when they moved westward onto the Great Plains. They did so with such success that they prospered as a formidable warrior society. At the beginning of the nineteenth cen- tury the nomadic Lakota bands that traversed the open prairies on

horseback, following the vast buffalo herds and engaging in successful territorial and raiding wars against neighboring enemy tribes,
were perhaps the most successful Indian nation of the region. However, throughout the nineteenth century the encroachments of whites,
who first crossed and then settled the Great Plains, meant that this
also would be a period of great transition for the Lakota. Initially, the
U.S. government requested territorial negotiations, a process in
which the Lakota appeared to fare somewhat better than many other
Indian nations. But insatiable desire for Lakota tribal lands eventually led to more demands by the U.S. government, accompanied by
enforced restrictions. Primarily these limitations applied to decisions
about where the Lakota people could live and hunt, with the introduction of the reservation system, but in the latter part of the century
the dominant white society began to apply constraints to all aspects
of Lakota life and culture.

Policymakers of late nineteenth-century America believed that the
only way for American Indians to survive was by a process of assimilation. They felt that Indians needed to discard their traditional culture and tribal affiliations, and instead be absorbed into American
culture and society as independent individuals or "Indian Americans."[5] One of the significant consequences for the Lakota was that
two distinct groups emerged. The progressives concurred, often
reluctantly, with the dominant society and concluded that their
group's survival relied upon their embracing white culture. In contrast, the traditionalists believed that the only course for Lakota survival was staying true to their traditional ways, and resisting the
government's attempts to assimilate them. However, responses to
the government's assimilation programs were often issue-based and
depended on individual circumstances, and both progressives and
traditionalists might accommodate and adapt to the dominant society, in order to survive.

In line with the assimilation program, Hiram Price, the commissioner of Indian affairs, forwarded a directive on 10 April 1883 defining a number of "Indian Offences"; the order was designed to stamp
out practices that he felt were "demoralizing and barbarous." This
was a direct attack on Lakota religious and cultural practices. Price's
directive made it an offense to hold feasts and dances, including the

Sun Dance, the principal religious ceremony of the Lakota. It out-
lawed such well-established practices as polygamy and the "purchase" of a wife by leaving property at the father's door. All practices
of medicine men, both medicinal and religious, were forbidden, and
the willful destruction of property—the traditional way of showing
grief over the death of a relative—became an offense.[6] The persistent
attacks on their culture were deeply felt and bitterly resented by the
Lakota, but the disappearance of the buffalo and other game through
indiscriminate hunting by white men left the Lakota and neighboring Indian nations reliant on the U.S. government for subsistence, "a
dependency that was nearly absolute."[7] In 1903 Red Cloud astutely
commented, "The white men try to make the Indians white men
also, it would be as reasonable and just to try to make the Indians'
skin white as to try to make him act and think like a white man. But
the white man has taken our territory and destroyed our game so we
must eat the white man's food or die."[8]

These attacks on traditional Lakota culture were part of a larger
government strategy designed to solve the perceived "Indian problem." Thomas J. Morgan, the incoming commissioner of Indian
affairs, stated in his annual report of 1889 that "the logic of events
demands the absorption of the Indians into our national life, not as
Indians, but as American citizens. . . . The Indians must conform to
'the white man's ways,' peaceably if they will, forcibly if they must."[9]

Some of the Lakota people had already chosen to follow this path
and had made attempts to embrace the white American way of life,
while others saw no benefit in it and determined to stay loyal to traditional Lakota culture. As with most Indian tribes, these divisions
had begun to emerge during the earliest dealings with the American
government, but it wasn't until the government decided to intervene
in Lakota culture and "civilize" the Indians that the distinct camps of
progressives and traditionalists arose. Such notable Lakota leaders
as Red Cloud (Oglala) and Sitting Bull (Hunkpapa) clung resolutely
to traditional Lakota ways and resisted all attempts of the government to forcibly change their society and culture. Their primary
motivation appears to have been their belief that the survival of their
people "demanded uncompromising devotion to time-tested val-
ues." Such leaders as these were perceived by the government to be

the biggest obstacle to the process of "civilizing" the Lakota, and government officials therefore decided to dismantle their authority and destroy tribal relationships.[10]

When the Office of Indian Affairs sent out instructions to knock down the chiefs, their intention was to do away with uncompromising traditionalist chiefs. As a result of this policy, factions further divided the Lakota. Those known as progressives usually cooperated with their agent, and as a consequence did not suffer the full force of the government's attack, which was reserved for the traditionalists. However, as the traditionalist chiefs often remained more powerful, the government was repeatedly inconsistent in following its own policies. When circumstances arose that necessitated Indian cooperation, the traditionalist chiefs were the ones to whom the government would reluctantly turn.

The Indian agents working at the individual reservations were also inconsistent, and often their assaults on chieftainship were attacks on specific traditionalist chiefs whose power and influence they resented. Robert Utley noted that "to accomplish anything they had to work either through real chiefs who happened to be progressive or through progressives promoted to chieftainship by the agent."[11] Such inconsistency by the government led inevitably to confusion on the part of the Lakota, so that even those who wished to do the government's bidding were sometimes left perplexed as to what was required of them.

The rifts between the progressive and traditionalist groups of Lakota were reinforced and exaggerated by the Sioux Act of 1889, which was introduced to open up more Lakota land to white settlers. In his annual report of 1890 Commissioner Morgan reemphasized the government's policy of assimilation: "It has become the settled policy of the Government to break up reservations, destroy tribal relations, settle Indians upon their own homesteads, incorporate them into the national life, and deal with them not as nations or tribes or bands, but as individual citizens. The American Indian is to become the Indian American."[12]

In accordance with this policy, and in light of the General Allotment Act of 1887 (Dawes Act), Congress had hurried through a bill applying to the Great Sioux Reservation.[13] The Sioux Act of 1888, however, was slightly different from the Dawes Act, in that it called for negotiations with Indians to buy the surplus land before surveys had been run and allotments made to the Indians. The Lakota were called upon to cede 9 million acres of land, which the federal government deemed surplus to its needs. In return for surrendering their right to "joint undivided occupancy" of the Great Sioux Reservation, the Lakota would gain title to six separate reservations coinciding with the existing agencies, and would receive allotted payment as settlers took up homesteads in the opened district.[14] In keeping with the Fort Laramie Treaty of 1868, the act could not take effect without the consent of three-fourths of all Lakota adult males. A commission was appointed to obtain the required signatures, but it was met by an almost completely unified Lakota stand against the proposed land agreement.

The following year the Republicans were returned to power in the national elections. The new administration was firmly committed to breaking up the Great Sioux Reservation. Further stimulus came with the passage of the Omnibus Bill in February 1889, which provided for the admission to statehood of North and South Dakota later that year. To open the Lakota homeland, Congress enacted two measures. The Indian Appropriation Act (1889) authorized the president to assign another commission to "negotiate the best agreement possible," and the Sioux Act of 2 March 1889 laid out "new terms of an agreement that the Indians must accept or reject as a whole." The commission was instructed to present the second act to the Lakota, and only if it was rejected were they to engage in negotiations.[15]

Again, the Lakota had resolved to resist all coercion. But this time, under the experienced hand of Gen. George Crook, the commissioners adopted a different approach and worked behind the scenes to entice individuals away from the influence of their chiefs. This technique proved successful, for the commissioners eventually departed with more than the required signatures, but they left behind a divided people.[16] The progressive and traditionalist dichotomy, which had existed since the government's initial attempts to "civilize" the Lakota, was now more sharply defined than ever, and there was deep enmity between the two factions.[17] American Horse recalled: "I signed the bill and 580 signed with me. The other members

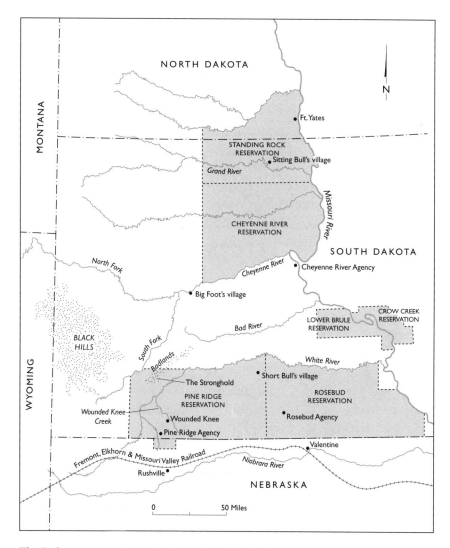

The Lakota reservations in the wake of the 1889 agreement that split the Great
Sioux Reservation into six separate smaller ones: Standing Rock, Cheyenne
River, Lower Brule, Crow Creek, Rosebud, and Pine Ridge

of my band drew out and it divided us, and ever since these two parties have been divided."[18]

One of the most heated disagreements between the traditionalist and progressive groups concerned the rations furnished by the government. The commissioners had been repeatedly forced to promise the Lakota that acceptance of the agreement would in no way influence the amount of food issued thereafter. But the fear that the government would cut rations once it had obtained the desired land had not abated, and the traditionalists predicted a reduction in rations. The progressives were certain that even the whites could not be that foolish, and they confidently dismissed the idea. As it turned out, they did not have long to contest the issue. Only two weeks after the commissioners had departed, the order came to substantially reduce the beef ration. Utley noted that "by the same Indian Appropriation Act under which the Sioux Commission was appointed, Congress in an economy move had cut the appropriation for subsistence and civilization of the Sioux."[19]

Hugh D. Gallagher, the agent at Pine Ridge, reported that "when it became generally known that the reduction was really going to be made, it caused intense feeling against the Sioux Commission among those who had signed the bill." Nonsigners derided the progressives for being so foolish, and the signers quickly lost prestige and status among their people.[20]

It was during this critical period that the Lakota first heard of the existence of an Indian redeemer located in the West. The factionalism that existed on the Lakota reservations at the time shaped reactions to this new religion. Significantly, the Lakota were once again turning to traditional chiefs and medicine men for leadership, and personal enmity between progressive and traditional Lakota dictated acceptance or dismissal of the Ghost Dance. The Lakota sources traditionally used by historians to suggest that the Lakota Ghost Dancers corrupted the religion into an antiwhite armed rebellion, originated among progressive Lakota who, along with government officials, viewed the Ghost Dance as being contrary to assimilation.

In 1889 numerous letters were received from tribes in Utah, Wyoming, Montana, and Indian Territory, all talking about the advent of a new messiah.[21] Capt. George Sword of the Pine Ridge

Indian Police later stated that the first people who knew about the messiah "were the Shoshoni and Arapaho." Sword went on to say that "in 1889 Good Thunder with four or five others visited the place where the Son of God [was] said to be."[22] This small delegation seems to have been the first Lakota group to travel west and investigate the new religion.[23] In the fall of 1889 in a private council on the Pine Ridge Reservation, a larger delegation was appointed to visit the western agencies to find out more about the new messiah.[24] A messenger took a letter to Rosebud, and the Brule Lakota selected an additional two delegates.[25]

Short Bull, one of the delegates selected at the council at Rosebud, was one of ten Lakota who traveled west to visit Wovoka during the winter of 1889–90. He became one of the Ghost Dance leaders of the Brule Lakota, and has been portrayed by both contemporary and historical critics as one of the most hostile of the Lakota Ghost Dancers.[26] However, this image of Short Bull is completely at odds with the perceptions of those people who actually met him. For example James R. Walker, the agency physician at Pine Ridge, described Short Bull as "an open, generous and kind-hearted man who attends with diligence to his own business, frequenting public places only when . . . necessary, and remaining quietly at home most of the time. He is one of the few chiefs remaining . . . and in all respects in which it could be expected of him he proves himself a real gentleman. His face always wears a smile, telling unmistakenly that nature made him gentle and benevolent."[27]

It is likely that Short Bull (Tatanka Ptecela) was born c.1847 in Nebraska's Niobrara River country.[28] Before reservation days he had been a notable warrior and had taken part in numerous skirmishes with such traditional Lakota enemies as the Crow, the Flatheads, and the Pawnee.[29] By 1889 Short Bull had become a well-respected medicine man in the Wažáže (Osage) band of the Brule Lakota. His commitment to traditional Lakota culture and religion is illustrated by events in 1879, when Cicero Newall, the new Rosebud Reservation Indian agent, threatened to prohibit the Sun Dance. Short Bull, along with Two Heart, led a group of Brule off the reservation with the intention of joining Sitting Bull in Canadian exile. They were pursued by the U.S. Army and were returned to their reservation on 15 October 1879, after having been captured and put on a steamboat.[30]

In the fall of 1889 Short Bull was working as a freighter for the government, transporting goods between Valentine, Nebraska, and the Rosebud Agency, when he and Scatter were chosen at a council meeting to go "on a great mission."[31] Short Bull later recalled, "I was called by Jocko Wilson [Wovoka] to go and I went to see him. . . . He wanted a man who would be straight and would not lie."[32] In addition to Short Bull and Scatter, eight others were selected by the Lakota as delegates: Kicking Bear, He Dog, Flat Iron, Yellow Knife, Brave Bear, Twist Back, Yellow Breast, and Broken Arm.[33] On his return in the spring of 1890, Short Bull was questioned by the Rosebud agent and admonished not to practice the new religion. But by October the Ghost Dance was in full swing on the Rosebud Reservation, having been started by Scatter, and after "occasionally visiting the dances," Short Bull finally participated, "becoming in time a 'regular' dancer—day and night."[34]

Throughout his life, Short Bull kept a pictorial record of past events, known as a winter count, and a record of his life by means of images, both painted and carved.[35] He was interviewed on several occasions by people who were interested in traditional Lakota culture and more specifically the Ghost Dance. He became perhaps the single most significant source of information coming directly from the Lakota Ghost Dancers. Short Bull's longest and most detailed account of the Ghost Dance, narrated in the summer of 1891, came about through his brief involvement with Buffalo Bill's Wild West. His engagement as a performer in the exhibition was mutually beneficial both to himself—in that it released him from incarceration at Fort Sheridan—and to the exhibition's figurehead, Buffalo Bill, who was thereby enabled to continue presenting genuine participants of recent western history to his audiences.

William Frederick Cody (Buffalo Bill) had risen to national fame as an Indian scout and buffalo hunter, but it was his role as a showman with Buffalo Bill's Wild West that brought him international renown.[36] The inaugural performance of Buffalo Bill's Wild West was given in May 1884 in St. Louis, Missouri. Within the exhibition, Cody presented an image of the West as a place of excitement and danger, based loosely upon his own personal experiences. He proved to be an incisive judge of public taste, and found a combination that appealed universally to audiences both in the United States and in Europe. The exhibition portrayed the "heyday of the West as a glorious period, based around the adventures of cowboys and Indians."[37] The shows included such stock acts as bronco busting, horseback riding, trick shooting, roping, hunting, shootouts, and exciting skirmishes with Indians. Frontier life was presented as being dramatic and exciting, appealing to the nostalgic spirit of the time, and set piece acts such as "Custer's Last Stand" served to reinforce western myth as reality and greatly influenced public perceptions of the American West.

One of Cody's most fortuitous decisions was to take on as a partner Nate Salsbury, whose expertise in business and showmanship contributed greatly to the exhibition's unrivaled prosperity.[38] John M. Burke, who had worked with Cody during his early theatrical tours, became the Wild West's tireless press agent and general manager. Burke devoted his life to the promotion of Cody and his Wild West show, becoming the exhibition's most vigorous advocate, and was immensely influential to its widespread appeal.[39]

After a shaky start, the shows grew in popularity, attracting almost 200,000 visitors in one week alone in New York.[40] People from all walks of life wanted to see Buffalo Bill's Wild West and, more important, be seen to be there. The displays began to adopt a format that was to remain the same for the next thirty years, and the Indians became one of the biggest attractions within the exhibition.

Early in his theatrical career Cody had realized the potential popularity of authentic "actors." He recognized that the "public embraced characters who, if not actors, were nevertheless frontiersmen." To give the performances added authenticity, he hired a few Indians to perform with his group.[41] As L. G. Moses pointed out in his book *Wild West Shows and the Images of American Indians, 1883–1933*, "there was nothing extraordinary in the employment of Indians to lend an air of authenticity. . . . Indeed, Indians had been appearing regularly in circuses, carnivals, medicine shows, and plays since the 1840s. . . . Buffalo Bill, however, changed the nature of Indian employment and ushered in the heyday of the Show Indians."[42]

Initially Cody employed Pawnee Indians; this choice was most likely influenced by Cody's acquaintance with Maj. Frank North, who had previously commanded four companies of Pawnee scouts.[43] Then in 1885 Cody hired the notorious Lakota medicine man Sitting Bull, and his focus shifted to the Lakota.[44] Over the years Cody employed a multitude of Indian performers, and it has even been claimed that Buffalo Bill's Wild West "was their largest employer outside of reservation areas."[45]

Yet there were many critics of the shows, and Indian reformers deplored the way they used and depicted American Indians.[46] To placate the concerns of the Office of Indian Affairs, Cody's first contract in 1886 had stated that the company resolved to protect the Indians from "all immoral influences and surroundings." It went on to state that as far as possible the company would select only married men, who would be accompanied on the tour by their wives, and promised to hire a religious representative to look after the Indians' moral welfare.[47]

Nevertheless, criticism of the use of Indian employees continued, and in February 1889 the government introduced a new form of contract.[48] The document stipulated that the Indian performers should receive a fair and reasonable wage, and that they be properly fed and comfortably clothed, be cared for in case of sickness or disability, and be returned home at the end of the tour. A separate agreement needed to be made with each Indian engaged in the show clearly stating the terms of employment, and this had to be approved by the local Indian agent before departure. Agents then forwarded the individual contracts to the commissioner of Indian affairs. If the commissioner authorized the contract, he would then set a bond for the show to deposit, which could range from $2,000 to $20,000 depending on the number of Indians employed.[49]

Such regulation was dismissed as woefully inadequate by reformers who wanted to put an end to this type of Indian employment. But as Commissioner John H. Oberly commented in April 1889, he was in no position "to restrain the liberty of the law abiding person or citizen because in [my] opinion or the opinion of someone else that person or citizen will make an injudicious use of his liberty."[50] Instead, Oberly felt he could only outline the government's opposition to Indians appearing in Wild West shows.[51] Thomas Morgan, a Baptist minister and educator, succeeded Oberly as commissioner of Indian affairs in June 1889. Unlike Oberly, Morgan did not hesitate to "use the coercive powers of his office. . . . Although he had no statutory authority to prohibit Indians from joining the shows, he could threaten aspiring showmen with the loss of their allotments, annuities, and tribal status."[52]

In November 1889, Morgan decided to investigate what effect traveling with Wild West exhibitions had upon the Indians. He forwarded a memorandum to all Indian agents, asking them to provide a list of Indians who had been connected with any show during the previous five years, and the names of those who were still absent from their reservations.[53] He wanted to know "what manner of life" the returned showmen were living, what influence they were having on their associates, and what the general health of the returnees was, including what diseases they may have brought back to the reservations. Morgan ended with a question: "What in your judgement should the Government do about such shows?"[54] In collating such information, Morgan hoped ultimately "to win legislation from Congress that would expand the powers of his office."[55]

The investigation confirmed the commissioner's belief "that the influence of 'Wild West' . . . shows has been harmful both to the Indians individually participating in the 'shows' and also to the Indians generally." He asserted that it was "in the interest of Indian civilization and advancement" and "the duty of this Office to use all its influence to prevent Indians from joining such exhibitions." Indian agents were requested to inform all Indians that the Office of Indian Affairs was convinced that "the practice of leaving reservations to join exhibitions is evil in its tendency and results."[56] Morgan further instructed the agents to "impress upon the Indians the importance of remaining at home and devoting their time and energies to establishing comfortable homes, cultivating farms, building houses, and acquiring thrifty, industrious habits and surrounding themselves with the comforts of a worthy type of civilization." He ended by cautioning any Indian who chose to ignore this advice and join such exhibitions: "they must not look to this Office for favor or assistance."[57]

In the summer of 1890 the stage was set not just for a showdown between the Lakota Ghost Dancers and the U.S. government, but also between the reformers of Indian policy and Wild West shows. Significantly, at the bottom of both conflicts lay the programs of assimilation, which the government believed to be the only option for American Indians at that time. With the absorption of Indians as individuals into mainstream American society, the "Indian problem" would be solved, "for there would be no more persons identified as Indians. The Indian Office would wither away, and government paternalism toward the Indians would be at an end."[58]

The Ghost Dance threatened assimilation on several fronts. First, in a practical way, it diverted the Indians' attention away from the assimilationists' agricultural and educational programs; second, in an ideological way, it maintained a Lakota perspective on religious matters and reinforced the very communal ideas reformers were attempting to break down. The Wild West shows were also perceived to jeopardize the assimilation programs in a variety of ways. They were also seen to be a diversion from the preferred routes to independence of working an allotment, since performers were absent from home for months or years at a time. Furthermore, the financial compensation from appearing in such shows was far greater than any income Indians could expect to earn from agriculture. The shows' greatest threat was their perceived confusing message to the Indians about what was required of them. They offered employment and wages that could indeed encourage independence, but the way they celebrated the performers' Indianness was anathema to reformers, who wished to remold American Indian identity based on a sanitized self-image of white society.

Accordingly, both the Lakota Ghost Dancers and the Wild West's Indian performers rejected total assimilation and instead favored the more acceptable methods of accommodation or adaptation. That these Indians were successful in the long run is illustrated by the survival of their peoples as a distinct part of the larger American society, despite the rigorous and sometimes brutal applications of the assimilationist programs.

CHAPTER TWO

THE LAKOTA AND THE
GHOST DANCE RELIGION

On 28 December 1890 a band of Lakota Indians led by Chief Big Foot were traveling down through South Dakota, from their home on the Cheyenne River Reservation to the Pine Ridge Agency. Perceived by the military as being "hostile," they were intercepted by the Seventh U.S. Cavalry, arrested, and then taken to camp at Wounded Knee Creek. During the night, soldiers encircled the encampment, and four rapid-fire cannon were positioned on surrounding hills. The commanding officer, Col. James W. Forsyth, had orders to disarm the band before escorting them to the agency at Pine Ridge, and so the next morning the Lakota men were called to council. As a white flag flew above their tents, the women and children went about the business of dismantling the camp. When Forsyth's request for the Indians' guns and a search of the camp yielded only a small quantity of arms, he ordered that the men in the council circle should be searched. The warriors resisted, fearful of the soldiers' motives, and while they were being searched, a shot was discharged. The response was indiscriminate firing and the massacre of as many as 300 people.

The U.S. government and army had categorized Big Foot's band as hostile because of their adherence to the new Ghost Dance religion. This religion played a crucial role in the stand the Lakota took against the engulfing culture of the whites, which was being forced upon them in the name of progress. The U.S. government responded to the religion in South Dakota by sending in the army to

stop the dancing. The arrival of the army on the South Dakota reservations caused panic among the Ghost Dancers, who then fled to
the relative safety of the Badlands. Farther north, on the Standing
Rock Reservation, a detail of Indian police were sent to arrest the
Hunkpapa medicine man Sitting Bull on 15 December. In the ensuing scuffle Sitting Bull was shot dead by policeman Red Tomahawk.
Within fourteen days of Sitting Bull's death, the last of the Ghost
Dancers in the Badlands were heading back to Pine Ridge to surrender. But the sound of gunfire emanating from Wounded Knee Creek
stopped them in their tracks and caused a general stampede back to
the Badlands stronghold. After a tense impasse, which lasted a couple of weeks, the Lakota Ghost Dancers finally surrendered on 15
January 1891.

For the Lakota in the years following the massacre, the significance
of the event grew in importance and symbolic meaning. Speaking
over a century later, Bronco LeBeau, the Lakota tribal historic preservation officer for the Cheyenne River Reservation, declared that
"Wounded Knee is that central defining event in our past that
changed us forever. Now we have a real strong sense of identity
loss."[1] The massacre fundamentally and permanently altered how
the Lakota people would integrate themselves into a world domi-
nated by white, Western European culture and spirituality.

The first known interview with the 1890 Ghost Dance prophet was
reported by the white scout Arthur Chapman on 6 December 1890.
Chapman had been sent by Brig. Gen. John Gibbon, the commanding general of the Division of the Pacific, to find and interview the
"Indian who impersonated Christ."[2] The scout had spent a week
questioning people, both whites and Paiutes, learning all he could
about Wovoka and his new religion, eventually interviewing the
man himself. Chapman relayed what Wovoka had told him in his
report of 6 December:

> He . . . told me about going to heaven and seeing all the people who had
> died here on this earth, and what a nice place it was, the dancing and
> other sports, etc.; that God had visited him many times since and told
> him what to do; that he must send out word to all the Indians to come
> and hear him, and he would convince them that he was preaching the

truth; that he must tell the Indians that they must work all the time and not lie down in idleness; that they must not fight the white people or one another; that we were all brothers and must remain in peace; that God gave him the power to cause it to rain or snow at his will; that God told him or gave him the power to destroy this world and all the people in it and to have it made over again; and the people who had been good heretofore were to be made over again and remain young; that God told him that they must have their dances more often, and dance five nights in succession and then stop.[3]

The substance of the religion, as reported by Chapman, was later corroborated by the ethnographer James Mooney, following his interview with Wovoka in 1892. Both interviewers concluded that Wovoka's religion was one of universal peace.

James Mooney and Robert Utley wrote the two most frequently cited secondary sources on the Ghost Dance and the Lakota interpretation of it. Although somewhat dated, Mooney's anthropological classic, *The Ghost Dance Religion and the Sioux Outbreak of 1890*, remains the authoritative text on the doctrine of the Ghost Dance. Utley's *Last Days of the Sioux Nation* has been described as the "definitive modern historical study" of the Lakota Ghost Dance, and it features the "best presentation of the military perspective."[4] Yet, as Omer Stewart noted in 1977, Mooney's "great monograph . . . covered the Ghost Dance phenomenon so completely [that] scholars have been tempted to cite Mooney and look no further for additional data regarding that religious movement."[5] Although there has perhaps been a general overreliance on Mooney, scholars have questioned some of his interpretations.[6]

The doctrine of the Ghost Dance as related by Mooney is based on his interview with Wovoka in 1892, and on letters detailing Wovoka's message, acquired on a visit by Arapaho and Cheyenne delegates in August 1891. All of Mooney's sources for this subject date from a time when the Ghost Dance had already been suppressed by the military on the Dakota reservations.[7] And although Mooney "verified Wovoka's statements by interviewing Ghost Dancers throughout the West," he was unable to interview many Lakota.[8] There are two reasons why Mooney's evidence is limited with regard to the Lakota

Ghost Dance. First, Mooney himself acknowledged that the Lakota were unwilling to talk to him when he visited Pine Ridge in 1891: "I found the Sioux very difficult to approach on the subject of the Ghost Dance. . . . To my questions the answer almost invariably was, 'The dance was our religion, but the government sent soldiers to kill us on account of it. We will not talk any more about it.'"[9]

Second, Short Bull, Kicking Bear, and twenty-one other Lakota Ghost Dancers who might have aided his interpretation were not in South Dakota when Mooney visited. Instead, following an initial period of confinement in Fort Sheridan, Illinois, they had been released into the custody of William F. Cody, and were in Britain performing in his Wild West show. Mooney did go on to interview Short Bull and Kicking Bear after their return from Europe, while the two were still incarcerated at Fort Sheridan, but made no reference in his publication to this interview, or any information they may have divulged.[10]

Mooney instead relied on secondhand accounts of the Lakota Ghost Dance, many of which were biased against the religion. The four primary documents he cited all appear to have originated from Indian police testimony. That is to say, all of his named informants came from the "progressive camp" of the Lakota, men who worked with and for the government and who had little if any sympathy with the Ghost Dance religion.

When the Lakota had been moved onto reservations in the late 1870s, the Indian police had been set up to enforce the government agent's rule. Initially, the government attempted to recruit Lakota from the different factions, and showed particular interest in employing traditionalists, in order to gain influence in their camps. However, these experiments proved to be unsuccessful, especially when the Indian police were called upon to interfere with traditional religions and practices. By definition, the Indian police were assimilationist, and they were perceived by many, both Indians and whites, to be a divisive force introduced to undermine the influence of traditional leaders. The majority of Ghost Dancers came from the camps of those leaders.[11]

Mooney included one source on the Lakota Ghost Dance, which supposedly came from Short Bull, commenting that "valuable light in regard to the Sioux version of the doctrine is obtained from the sermon delivered at Red Leaf camp, on Pine Ridge reservation, October 31, 1890, by Short Bull." This "sermon" has been quoted in numerous secondary sources, which attribute it to two primary sources. It is most commonly cited as appearing in the secretary of war's annual report for 1891, but John McDermott noted that "a copy appeared in a Chicago Newspaper on 22 November 1890."[12]

Capt. C. A. Earnest of the Eighth Infantry had forwarded a report of the speech to the assistant adjutant general, Department of the Platte, in a telegram dated 19 November 1890, and it is Earnest's telegram that appears in the annual report of the secretary of war.[13] What remains unclear is who recorded and interpreted this speech by Short Bull. There is nothing to suggest that Earnest witnessed the "sermon" himself, and he quite explicitly stated that Short Bull "has not been seen by a white man since the dances commenced." It seems most likely that Earnest's informants were members of the Indian police who had visited the camp to arrest those who had killed cattle without authority.[14] Both Earnest and Short Bull refer to a confrontation between the police and the Ghost Dancers that would correspond to the suggested dates.[15]

While contemporaries and historians have used Short Bull's "sermon" to illustrate his hostility and desire for a "general uprising," Earnest's formal report noted that the Lakota "have not declared aggressions but determination to resist arrest or control."[16] This conclusion is borne out by Short Bull's speech, which was not a call for hostilities but rather a reassurance that the Ghost Dancers could depend upon supernatural protection if the dance was interfered with.[17]

The second of Mooney's sources was originally written in Lakota by George Sword, captain of the Indian police at Pine Ridge, and was translated into English by an unnamed Indian for Emma C. Sickels. This account reportedly gives the Lakota doctrine of the Ghost Dance. Some historians have used it to illustrate "the decidedly militant overtones" of the Lakota Ghost Dance, by comparing it to the account of Porcupine, a Cheyenne who also journeyed west to visit Wovoka at the same time as Short Bull and Kicking Bear.[18] The validity of such a comparison is called into question, however, because the Sword statement does not make clear from whom, or how, he heard of this version of the Ghost Dance. One possible source mentioned several times in the text is Good Thunder, although it remains a possibility that Sword's statement is based largely on hearsay and rumors. Sword arrested Good Thunder and two colleagues on the orders of Agent Gallagher, after Postmaster William Selwyn informed the agent that Good Thunder and his colleagues had called a council to inaugurate the Ghost Dance. Sword then questioned the Ghost Dancers, but the prisoners refused to talk and were locked in jail until they promised not to hold councils. It remains unclear whether Good Thunder changed his stance and discussed the Lakota Ghost Dance with Sword at a later date.[19]

Sword was previously known by his Lakota name, Hunts the Enemy. He was the son of Brave Bear of the Oglala Bad Faces and a nephew of Red Cloud. Born in the mid-1800s, he participated fully in traditional Lakota life during his early years as a noted warrior, a Sun Dancer, a medicine man of the Bear Society, and a Pipe Owner. However, later in life his traditional outlook underwent a dramatic change.[20] "I took a new name, the name Sword, because the leaders of the white soldiers wore swords. I determined to adopt the customs of the white people, and to persuade my people to do so. I became the first leader of the U.S. Indian Police among the Oglalas, and was their captain until the Oglalas ceased to think of fighting the white people."[21]

As captain of the Indian police on the Pine Ridge Reservation, George Sword supported the suppression of traditional Lakota religious practices, including the Ghost Dance, which he interpreted as harmful to the interests of his people. In November 1890 the Pine Ridge agent sought Sword's opinion with regard to calling in the troops, a move supported by Sword. Thomas Overholt has commented that as a progressive, Sword "must have . . . viewed [the Ghost Dance] as an embarrassment and impediment to the normalization of relations between the government and the Indians."[22]

(3) The third source Mooney drew upon for Lakota interpretations of the Ghost Dance was an interview with Kuwapi [One They Chased After], a Rosebud Indian who was arrested for teaching the Ghost

Dance on the Yankton Reservation. While Kuwapi was in custody, he was interviewed by William Selwyn, who had been placed in charge of the force sent to arrest the Ghost Dancer. Selwyn then forwarded a copy of the interview to Agent E. W. Foster on 22 November 1890.[23]

A Yankton Lakota who had received "a fair education under the patronage of a gentleman in Philadelphia," Selwyn "had for several years been employed in various capacities at different Sioux Agencies." He had recently arrived at the Yankton Agency from Pine Ridge, where he had been employed as postmaster. It was Selwyn who informed the Pine Ridge agent about Good Thunder's plans to inaugurate the new religion at a council.[24] Once again, Mooney's source was derived from an informant engaged with the Indian police who had been actively working with the government in the suppression of the Ghost Dance.[25]

4. The last of Mooney's sources for the Lakota Ghost Dance, which he describes as "perhaps the best statement of the Sioux version," also originated with the Indian police. It was forwarded as a report by the agent at Standing Rock, James McLaughlin, to the commissioner of Indian affairs on 17 October 1890, and was reproduced in the commissioner's annual report for 1891.[26] McLaughlin's information was based on a speech given by Kicking Bear on 9 October 1890, at a council to inaugurate the Ghost Dance among Sitting Bull's Hunkpapa Lakota. When the agent learned of Kicking Bear's arrival, he dispatched thirteen policemen to arrest Kicking Bear and escort him from the reservation, but the police returned without carrying out the agent's orders. In his book *My Friend the Indian*, McLaughlin reproduced Kicking Bear's speech verbatim. Utley noted, "It was repeated to him word for word . . . by One Bull, an Indian policeman who was also Sitting Bull's nephew."[27] Once again, as with all the other sources on the Lakota Ghost Dance employed by Mooney, this document originated in accounts given by the Indian police.

In this case, however, it is equally important to note McLaughlin's motivation. It would be too simplistic to believe that the Indian police simply distorted their evidence, and the fact that these sources all originated with the police should be viewed in the context of how they were used. What in many cases perhaps started out as a report of events to keep the Indian agent informed was then utilized by the agent to suit his own needs, perhaps to call for military support to reestablish control, or to get rid of troublesome leaders.

McLaughlin sought the removal of Sitting Bull and the lessening of any potential influence he might have had over his followers at Standing Rock. As DeMallie noted, "Agent McLaughlin had been clamoring for the old chief's arrest and removal from the reservation for some time, ever since Sitting Bull had refused to take up farming and be a model 'progressive' Indian."[28] McLaughlin did not hesitate to use the report of 17 October to pin the blame for the Ghost Dance on Sitting Bull, thereby strengthening his calls for the medicine man's arrest: "Sitting Bull is high priest and leading apostle of this latest Indian absurdity; in a word he is the chief mischief-maker at this agency, and if he were not here, this craze, so general among the Sioux, would never have gotten a foothold at this agency. . . . I would respectfully recommend the removal . . . and confinement . . . some distance from the Sioux country, of Sitting Bull and the parties named in my letter of June 18 last . . . some time during the coming winter before next spring."[29]

The agent's assertions that Sitting Bull was "high priest and leading apostle" of the new religion appear questionable. Stanley Vestal, the Hunkpapa's biographer, contended that Sitting Bull was "too entirely Sioux" to embrace a faith based on the teachings of Christianity.[30] Furthermore, in a "Note on Kicking Bear," published in Vestal's *New Sources of Indian History, 1850–1891*, One Bull gave a rather different account "as to what happened when Crazy Walking ordered Kicking Bear away in October, 1890." "Sitting Bull answered him as follows: 'The education of my children is uppermost. I have a school in my locality. This dance is not the most important undertaking. They will, eventually stop.' This is what we reported to McLaughlin upon our return."[31]

Thus, a careful review of the sources cited by Mooney in his highly influential account of the Ghost Dance reveals that with regard to the Lakota interpretation of the religion, Mooney's and almost all later accounts are based upon the highly subjective reports of men who opposed the religion. The authors of the accounts used by Mooney were not active participants or believers in the Ghost Dance, so their evidence on the doctrine is not as reliable as testimony from those who did participate. The uses that were made of their accounts had multiple motivations, such as settling old disputes, whether between two different factions of Lakota, or between an agent and an influential tribal leader opposed to government policies.

Mooney perhaps used what was available to him at the time, but subsequent historians have had a much broader spectrum of sources available to them. Although Mooney's interpretation of the Lakota Ghost Dance can be criticized as being too narrow, this does not invalidate his monumental work on the Ghost Dance as a whole. Mooney's extensive research remains significantly valuable, as long as it is read in conjunction with the various other Indian sources that have since come to light.

The Lakota medicine man Short Bull, who traveled to Nevada to see Wovoka in the winter of 1889–90 and later became one of the most prominent leaders of the Ghost Dance religion, was responsible for perhaps the most significant sources available on the Lakota interpretation of the Ghost Dance. There are five texts dictated by Short Bull that cover his experiences of the Ghost Dance between late 1889 and the summer of 1891, all of which have been reproduced in the appendix.

At the turn of the century Short Bull gave an account of his visit to Wovoka and a brief description of the dance to James R. Walker, the agency physician at Pine Ridge. Both these accounts were published in Walker's *Lakota Belief and Ritual* (see documents 2A and 2B in the appendix).[32] In 1907 Natalie Curtis published another account, "Short Bull's Narrative," along with three Ghost Dance songs dictated to her by Short Bull around 1906 (see document 3 in the appendix).[33] The German painter and ethnographer Frederick Weygold, interviewed Short Bull in 1909. This statement, which was recorded in English but survives only in German translation, has been published by a German scholar, Wolfgang Haberland (see document 4 in the appendix).[34] Another narrative, "Wanagi Wacipi," was dictated to Ivan Stars in 1915 and was published in Lakota in Eugene Buechel's *Lakota Tales and Texts* (see document 5 in the appendix).[35]

The earliest and most detailed of Short Bull's narratives is a twenty-page, handwritten text entitled "As Narrated by Short Bull" (see document 1 in the appendix).[36] Short Bull dictated the text in 1891 to the Lakota interpreter George C. Crager, while they were both touring in Britain with Buffalo Bill's Wild West. Crager was well qualified for the task, for he was fluent in Lakota, having had an intimate relationship with the Brule for a number of years, especially with the old chief Two Strike who had reportedly adopted him in 1878.[37]

Basing his interpretation on the Walker and Curtis accounts, DeMallie noted that "the messianic and strongly Christian nature of the Ghost Dance is very clear in Short Bull's teachings," and "it is possible to proliferate evidence to demonstrate the peaceful intentions of the leaders of the ghost dance."[38] However, both of these accounts are brief and rather undetailed in comparison with the 1891 text, which was recorded within nine months of Short Bull's arrest and imprisonment. This document sheds new light on Short Bull's experiences and gives evidence that challenges the long-accepted version of the Lakota interpretation of the Ghost Dance. It furnishes further evidence that rather than being fanatical or warlike, the doctrine as given to and practiced by Short Bull was one of peace, and that what he advocated was not hostility but passive resistance to white control.

The document is unsigned and undated, simply bearing the title "As Narrated by Short Bull," but it can be roughly dated by context and content. The narrative relates Short Bull's experiences up to and including his hiring by Cody for Buffalo Bill's Wild West, his trip across the Atlantic, and the exhibition's tour in England, ending in the present tense.[39] Buffalo Bill's Wild West left America on 1 April 1891, initially touring in Germany, Holland, and Belgium, before opening the first leg of a provincial tour of England and Wales at Leeds on 20 June. In October the show traveled north to Glasgow for a five-month winter stand in Scotland. This suggests that the most likely date for the document is the summer of 1891.

The handwriting is clearly that of George Crager, the Lakota interpreter for this tour of Buffalo Bill's Wild West.[40] During the exhibition's visit to Cardiff in September 1891, two newspaper articles in the *Evening Express* recorded that Crager was engaged in writing a manuscript on the Lakota Sioux, and one referred specifically to a piece about Short Bull. "This very intelligent interpreter is preparing a work on Sioux Legends, about fifty pages of which are devoted to the chief Short Bull and his craze about the Wakan Nuka [Tanka]."[41]

It is clear that the document has been translated and written verbatim in longhand, with little punctuation except dashes between sentences, a skill Crager would have acquired as a clerk and a journalist.[42] Therefore, there is no Lakota version to compare with Crager's translation, but his association with the Brule should have enabled him to accurately translate and record what he heard. Moreover, it is obvious that he questioned Short Bull for clarification where perhaps he felt the narrative made no sense, placing his understanding of what Short Bull meant in brackets: "2 days from now all nations will talk one tongue (Short Bull thinks he meant 200 or 2 years) the sign talk will be no more."

The sequence of events jumps back at times to add detail, as would an unscripted narrative. Evidence of this is given by Crager's bracketed comment that "at this stage of the story 'Short Bull' went into a trance remaining so for quite a while and then continued." The unedited text has had no alterations to make it more dramatic, as might a published text or newspaper article. Furthermore, Short Bull does not shy away from detailing the depredations of the Ghost Dancers, such as the theft of horses, which further suggests that this narrative is an impartial account of his experiences.

The date, the detail, and the demonstrable authenticity of this document make it the most significant contemporary firsthand account of the Lakota Ghost Dance. Of the five Short Bull narratives, which date from the summer of 1891 to September 1915, covering a twenty-four-year period, four were told to white interviewers who employed a variety of translation methods. The first account, narrated in 1891, appears to have gone through the fewest translations, for it was interpreted and transcribed by the same person. Although the interpreters of the other documents often remain anonymous, their voices or perceptions are occasionally made clear. For example, the Walker text opens with the unknown interpreter's comment that Short Bull "wants to prove that he was not the cause of the trouble of 1890–91."[43]

This is a relevant point, and one wonders what Short Bull might have kept to himself, and whether speaking to white interviewers could have influenced what he did divulge. Yet throughout the twenty-four-year period there is a consistency in what Short Bull said. His testimony with regard to his experiences in Nevada and his interpretation of the pacifist doctrine are corroborated by both Indian and white sources that were recorded before the Wounded Knee massacre, and therefore were not colored by the tragic event. Weygold noted further that Short Bull assured him "that he might have been errant sometimes in the past . . . but he (and this remark is reliable) had always been of honest and best intention. The white officers declared him in unison as a 'perfect gentlemen.'"[44]

Although the identity of the "white officers" Weygold refers to remains unclear, the statement suggests that Weygold considered Short Bull to be a dependable informant. Ultimately, the strongest argument that the Short Bull texts are a true reflection of his experiences is that he stayed true to the Ghost Dance throughout his life, continuing to believe in and practice the religion, and maintaining a pacifist stance. If he had adapted and transformed it into a millennial, violent, antiwhite religion, then it would have failed and died in 1890–91, but as a peaceful religion of accommodation as Wovoka had preached it, it both continued and evolved.[45] Short Bull's religion did not fail him, nor did he lose faith in that religion.

Crager's document details how the Lakota delegation that traveled west to Nevada to meet Wovoka journeyed through the winter and arrived in Mason Valley in March 1890. The journey was a major undertaking, for they had to cross the Rocky Mountains and travel approximately 1,500 miles to reach Wovoka's camp. As they progressed, delegates from other tribes, including Cheyenne, Arapaho, Shoshone, and Bannocks, joined them. Porcupine, one of the Cheyenne delegates, was later interviewed about his experience of these events by Maj. Henry Carroll on 15 June 1890, and his account complements Short Bull's 1891 narrative.[46]

As they traveled west, the delegates began to learn more about the new religion. Both Short Bull and Porcupine note that they saw and participated in the dance before their arrival at Wovoka's camp, and that the chief of the Bannocks, "brother of 'old Washakie,'" suggested they make a peace treaty. The two also made similar comments about the Paiute's lodges, the attire of the Indian women, and the many different peoples, including whites, represented at the gathering.[47]

The white scout Arthur Chapman, who visited Wovoka in December 1890 to gather information for the War Department, stated that "in regard to the Cheyenne Indian, Porcupine, who gave an account of his visit to the Piute camp at Walker Lake, I will say that it is wonderfully correct, as far as I am able to learn."[48] Chapman also noted that J. O. Gregory, the farmer-in-charge of the Walker River Reservation, remembered very distinctly "the big dance which occurred near the agency, when Cheyennes, Sioux, Bannocks and other strange Indians were present, [and] that this meeting took place some time last March [1890]." Two other informants who were both with the Indian police force at Walker Lake, Josephus and Ben Ab-he-gan, told Chapman that this gathering had "numbered about 1,600."[49]

After their long journey, the delegates awaited the arrival of Wovoka with eager anticipation. Both Short Bull and Porcupine carefully noted their first impressions of the man, and while Short Bull's statement is perhaps more descriptive, noting Wovoka's dress, it is still imbued with a strong sense of how deeply the prophet inspired him.[50] Porcupine's description echoes the sense of awe that Wovoka inspired in the visiting delegates. "I looked around to find him, and finally saw him sitting on one side of the ring. . . . I . . . went forward, and when I saw him I bent my head. I had always thought the Great Father was a white man, but this man looked like an Indian."[51]

It is evident that both Short Bull and Porcupine were initially unsure whether Wovoka was an Indian or not. Short Bull related, "I got a good look at him, he was dark-skinned, talked in a language similar to Indian and I believe he was an Indian."[52] Porcupine remarked: "In the night when I first saw him I thought he was an Indian, but the next day when I could see better he looked different. He was not so dark as an Indian, nor so light as a white man. He had no beard or whiskers, but very heavy eyebrows. He was a good-looking man."[53]

Wovoka could only speak Paiute and a little English, and therefore Short Bull was reliant upon others to translate his words through the medium of sign language.[54] Despite this, the first speech made by Wovoka is clearly recognizable in Short Bull's and Porcupine's accounts, both in recording the shortness and the content of the speech, and the fact that it was immediately followed by the dance.[55]

The second speeches reported by Short Bull and Porcupine seem to have been given on different days, but there are numerous common themes, most notably, the idea that the religion was inclusive of whites and that there should be no fighting. In the 1891 narrative, Short Bull gives his most detailed statement of what Wovoka said to him.

"I have sent for you to tell you certain things that you must do. There are Two Chiefs at your Agencies and I want you to help them all you can. Have your people work the ground so they do not get idle, help your Agents and get farms this is one chief—The other Chief is the Church—I want you to help him for he tells you of me; when you get back go to Church. All these churches are mine, if you go to church when you get back others will do the same. I have raised two bodies of men on this earth and have dropped one of them that is the Army, I want no more fighting. [T]ake pity on one another, and whenever you do anything that is bad something will happen to you—I mean fights between the Indians and whites—all over the world one should be like the other and no distinction made, always sing and pray about me, for it is right, 2 days from now all nations will talk one tongue (Short Bull thinks he meant 200 [days] or 2 years) the sign talk will be no more. Educate your children send them to schools"—He prayed again and stopped. These are all the words I got from him— . . . I saw the Messiah daily for five days. . . . On the fifth day I shook hands with him and all he said was that "soon there would be no world, after the end of the world those who went to church would see all their relatives that had died (Resurrection). This will be the same all over the world even across the big waters."[56]

Porcupine's rendition, while differing somewhat from Short Bull's, includes similar underlying themes. "He told us not to quarrel, or fight, nor strike each other, nor shoot one another; that the whites and Indians were to be all one people."[57]

The inclusiveness of Wovoka's doctrine was echoed in the majority of the Short Bull narratives, specifically the Curtis and Weygold texts, which both noted that Indians and whites should dance and pray together.[58] The Walker text embodied the idea of one church and one belief.[59] The Buechel text does not make reference to whites in this way, but includes the ideas of nonviolence and cooperation with whites. "My beloved sons, do not murder one another! Whoever commits murder does evil. And love one another! And take pity on one another! If you act in this manner I will give you more concerning the ceremony. . . . And whatever the whites with whom you will live want, do it accordingly!"[60]

All these accounts stand in stark contrast to the statement of George Sword, the chief of Indian police at Pine Ridge, which reported Wovoka as proclaiming: "When the soldiers of the white people chief want to arrest me, I shall stretch out my arms, which will knock them to nothingness, or if not that, the earth will open and swallow them in. . . . Any one Indian does not obey me and tries to be on white's side will be covered over by a new land that is to come over this old one."[61]

This last statement may hold the clue to the origin of the idea that the religion was antiwhite. Sword's statement refers explicitly to the destruction of the whites through supernatural means, a well-documented and common interpretation of the Ghost Dance, though with multiple variations as to how this might come about. None of the Short Bull texts makes reference to this, and neither does the Porcupine account. But within the Porcupine text there is a somewhat similar statement, which may indicate where the idea originated. Porcupine recorded that Wovoka had suggested that "if any man disobeyed what he ordered, his tribe would be wiped from the face of the earth."[62] One might interpret this as suggesting that if whites were nonbelievers, this would be their fate. This concept appears to be confirmed in Luther Standing Bear's *My People, the Sioux*, in which he quoted Short Bull as saying, "This man told us that all the white people would be covered up, because they did not believe; even the Indians who did not believe would also be covered."[63]

This suggests that rather than being antiwhite, Wovoka's religion was intolerant of nonbelievers, regardless of their race. It was those who did not believe or practice the Ghost Dance who were threatened with annihilation. As with some forms of Christianity, only believers could be saved.

The return of the dead is a recurrent theme within the Short Bull texts, and its centrality to the Lakota understanding of the religion is indicated by the name the Lakota gave the dance, Wanagi Wacapi, which translates as "Spirit Dance" or "Ghost Dance." Mooney stated that "the Ghost-dance songs are of the utmost importance in connection with the study of the messiah religion, as we find embodied in them much of the doctrine itself." While resurrection features in many of the Lakota Ghost Dance songs, none contains any reference to the destruction of the whites.[64]

Within the texts, there are further references to the peaceful nature of the relationship between the Indians and whites proposed by Wovoka. Not only were the Ghost Dancers cautioned not to fight with the whites, they were positively encouraged to work with them. Short Bull tells that Wovoka wanted them to farm, to go to church, and to send their children to school. Similarly, Sword quoted Wovoka as saying "My Grandchildren, when you get home, go to farming and send all your children to school."[65]

Clearly, Wovoka was advocating a form of accommodation. Nancy Shoemaker contends that this "implies an acceptance of some aspects of the dominant culture but not the complete transformation and disappearance that is inherent in the term 'assimilation.'"[66] Thus, within the context of the doctrine that encouraged the Lakota to live in peace and work with the whites, two of the Short Bull texts also allude to an acknowledgment of the cultural differences between the races. In the Buechel narrative Short Bull quoted Wovoka as saying: "Well, it is not possible for you Indians and the white to become the same as long as your generations continue."[67]

This is echoed in the Weygold narrative, in which Short Bull declared: "The Indians were made by the Great Mystery and only for living in a certain way and they should (therefore) not accept the ways of another people. I thought, that this was misunderstood a lot."[68]

Wovoka was not arguing in support of assimilation, but instead that the Ghost Dancers should take the benefits of white society that are offered, with the knowledge and reassurance that doing so would not make them any less Indian.

Short Bull's frustration at the misinterpretation of the religion is evident in the Curtis text, in which he recounted the difficulties he had experienced in his relationship with the whites. "It is true, all men should love one another. It is true, all men should live as brothers. Is it we who do not thus? What others demand of us, should they not themselves give? Is it just to expect one friend to give all the friendship? We are glad to live with the white men as brothers. But we ask that they expect not the brotherhood and the love to come from the Indian alone."[69]

The racism endemic to nineteenth-century America meant that whites did not perceive the Indians as being equal to themselves. White society regarded the Indians not as "brothers" but rather as children, wards of the state who needed to be civilized by a patriarchal government. Moreover, the rights of U.S. citizenship were not extended to the American Indians: they were not protected by the Bill of Rights, which might have safeguarded their religious freedom.

Ironically, Lt. Hugh L. Scott, who was detailed to investigate the religion in December 1890, commented "that this dance is intended as a worship of the white man's God there can be no doubt in the mind of any intelligent person who hears what they have to say on the subject." Scott concluded that the Ghost Dance was "a better religion than they ever had before, [for it] taught them precepts which, if faithfully carried out, will bring them into better accord with their white neighbors, and has prepared the way for their final Christianization." Vestal concurred when he stated that "the Ghost Dance was entirely Christian—except for the difference in rituals."[70]

The evidence shows that the doctrine of the Lakota Ghost Dance was no different from that which Wovoka had originally preached. Short Bull's testimony is corroborated by both white and Indian sources recorded before the Wounded Knee Massacre. Furthermore, the documents maintain that the religion's message remained all-inclusive and peaceful when it was transferred to the South Dakota reservations. There is never any hint of hostility toward whites. Instead, it appears that the religion encouraged the Lakota toward accommodation. This can be seen in the words of the Oglala Ghost Dancer Big Road:

We danced and prayed that we might live forever; that everything we planted might grow up to give us plenty and happiness. There was no harm in the dance. The Messiah told us to send our children to school, to work our farms all the time, and to do the best we could. He also told us not to drop our church. . . . I never heard that the Messiah had promised that the Indians should be supreme or that the white man should be destroyed. We never prayed for anything but happiness. We did not pray that the white people should be all killed. The shirts we wore made us go to Heaven. The dance was not a war dance, for none that went to it were allowed to have one scrap of metal on his body.[71]

The dominant interpretation that the Lakota Ghost Dance leaders "perverted" Wovoka's doctrine of peace into one of war is based on primary source material derived from the testimony of those who had actively worked to suppress the religion. As with so much of history, the events were chronicled by the victors, thus rendering a very narrow interpretation.

CHAPTER THREE

FROM ACCOMMODATION
TO RESISTANCE

Who would have thought that dancing could make such trouble? We had no wish to make trouble, nor did we cause it of ourselves. There was trouble, but it was not of my making. We had no thought of fighting; if we had meant to fight, would we not have carried arms? We went unarmed to the dance. How could we have held weapons? For thus we danced, in a circle, hand in hand, each man's fingers linked in those of his neighbor.

Short Bull, in Curtis, *Indians' Book*

It is paradoxical that a religion with strong Christian elements that preached peace and cooperation with the whites came to be perceived as a hostile movement in South Dakota. Unfortunately for the Lakota, the general perception outside the dance camps was that the dances constituted preparation for an armed uprising rather than the rites of a peaceful religious movement. There are many reasons why this was the general view, and other people were to some extent responsible for distorting the perception of the Lakota Ghost Dance into a hostile movement, to suit their needs.

By the late nineteenth century, white Americans "assumed that Indian culture was stagnant." They believed that only the imposition of Western civilization could transform and indeed save the Indians. The government's policy toward the Lakota became one of hastening their assimilation by destroying their culture and the structures of Lakota society. To achieve this aim, the Indian agents did everything in their power to undermine Lakota tribal organization and weaken the influence of the traditional chiefs and medicine men. The agents appointed Indian police forces that competed with the chiefs for authority, and with the support of the agent, the police soon acquired much power. At the same time, the agents asserted their control by such punishments as imprisonment and withholding of food.[1]

While acknowledging that change was inevitable, both progressive and traditionalist Lakota sought to control this process themselves. The traditionalists' acceptance of the Ghost Dance was in itself an attempt to regain control of their lives within a framework that was both familiar and accessible. The Lakota turned away from Indian agents and police, and looked to traditional chiefs and medicine men for leadership. Commenting on the Ghost Dance religion, George Hyde noted that "the one thing that shocked the whites most was the collapse of all authority. The agents whose word had been law among the Sioux were now flouted and the armed Indian police were in general unable to execute their orders." Disregard for government authority was bad enough, but the disruption of assimilationist programs was worse still. All of the government's planning and work that had been carried out since 1878 with the object of ending Lakota tribal organization was being "destroyed by this messiah craze."[2]

As the Ghost Dance became more popular among the Lakota, it was not only the agents who were losing influence but also the Indian police and those Lakota who had allied themselves to the government. Overholt recognized that "for the more 'progressive' Indians the movement must have meant primarily a setback in the advance of 'civilization' and a potential threat to new-found positions of status."[3] The progressives, who had supported the Sioux Act of 1889, had already lost face as a result of the government's reduction of rations and its failure to carry out its promises. Accordingly, these Lakota, like the agents, found it in their interests to justify the suppression of the Ghost Dance. They did so by portraying it as a hostile movement and a threat to peace in South Dakota. An old Oglala man known as Issowonie told Short Bull that "our own people have caused the soldiers to come here by telling lies." Crow Dog, too, recounted that "his troubles began when interpreters lied to his agent, telling the agent that the Ghost Dance was really a war dance."[4]

If we accept that progressive Indians were losing status and influence, and if we recall that all of Mooney's cited sources are derived from the testimony of the Indian police, it is not hard to see how and why the "perversion myth" could have originated. While some progressives might have been motivated by old personal feuds, it is clear that others believed they were working in the best interests of their people. Luther Standing Bear was a progressive Lakota who worked as a teacher at the Rosebud Agency school. He told fellow Brule that "it would not be right for them to join the ghost dancers, as the Government was going to stop it, and it would not be best for them to be found there. I told them the Government would use soldiers to enforce the order if it became necessary."[5]

Why were the white authorities so willing to accept that the Lakota Ghost Dance was hostile? Their readiness to believe in the danger can to some extent be explained by misunderstanding and bigotry, but it also suited their needs. With the opening up of South Dakota to settlers, the government needed the Lakota to be subservient and easily controlled. In the aftermath of the Wounded Knee Massacre, the perception of the Ghost Dancers as hostile and out of control was used as justification for the actions of the military in responding to the threat and suppressing the "uprising."[6]

The U.S. government and progressive Indians opposed to the Ghost Dance were not alone in portraying the Lakota Ghost Dancers as hostile. The popular media also played a significant role in shaping public perceptions of the Ghost Dance religion. Initially, the ceremony had been seen as "an item of curiosity and entertainment for the local white population."[7] By mid-November 1890, stories of the dance and of rumors about the coming of a messiah filled the nation's press, but as Moses remarked "Dancing, peaceful Indians awaiting their divine redemption did not sell newspapers." Soon journalists were flooding the country with stories about an impending Indian uprising.[8] By the beginning of December, "the newspapers and bureaucrats had created a chain of events from which there was no avenue of retreat." The local white population, who had been suffering from the country's financial depression, exacerbated the situation; they welcomed the influx of hard cash and "wanted the troops, reporters, and other hangers-on with money to stay."[9]

The government's suppression of the Lakota Ghost Dance began as soon as Short Bull and the other delegates had returned from Nevada. At first, they were cautioned not to speak about the new religion, while some enthusiasts were actually imprisoned. Kicking Bear was arrested on the orders of Perain Palmer, the Cheyenne River agent, but when he was tried by an Indian court, the Lakota judges released him.[10]

The acting commissioner of Indian affairs, Robert V. Belt, repeatedly sent circulars to agents directing them to do all in their power to stop the Ghost Dance.[11] Agent Wright of the Rosebud Reservation used the tried and tested strategy of withholding rations, informing Ghost Dancers "that rations would be withheld until they had returned to their homes and ceased dancing."[12] The appeal of the new religion was too great, however, and a substantial number of Lakota refused to relinquish it. With the civilian authorities unable to reassert their control over the dancers, it was left to the military to suppress the Lakota Ghost Dance. Their arrival on the South Dakota reservations caused panic and initially swelled the camps of the Ghost Dancers. Within two months, however, the Lakota were brought under control. In the process the two renowned leaders Sitting Bull and Big Foot, together with many more Lakota men, women, and children, were slain.

For the Lakota Ghost Dancers, noncooperation with government policy did not in itself constitute a perversion of Wovoka's doctrine, as government policy included the prohibition of the religion. The Ghost Dancers therefore faced a dilemma: should they abandon the religion as the government ordered them to, or should they practice it as taught by Wovoka? For those deeply religious Lakota, the answer was simple: ultimately, the Great Spirit, Wakan Tanka, took precedence over the commissioner of Indian affairs. Furthermore, the narratives of Short Bull clearly demonstrate that the Lakota version of the religion differed little in practice from the religion as originally preached, and maintained the key concepts of peace and inclusiveness. Short Bull informed Weygold of what he had said to the dancers at the beginning of the ceremony, and it is evident from this that what Short Bull conveyed to the Lakota dancers was the message given to him by Wovoka:

I said to them (that is: before the Ghost Dance he said to his followers) . . .
"Your children should go to school and learn. The old people should
attend some religious worship and say prayers." I said to them they
should draw something (from) the earth, too (that is: do some farming)
and they should build houses to live in, and take good advice from
respectable white men, too. Then do not kill each other! . . . Then I said
that they should listen to my words, and that I would say a prayer. Take
down all your finger-rings, earrings and all iron before you start dancing. If they would carry iron (with them) they would be tempted to do
something bad.[13]

The only thing in this that is perhaps not ascribable to Wovoka is
the concluding reference to iron. Sword's statement appears to cor-
roborate this idea: "In the ghost dance no person is allow[ed] to wear
anything made of metal." Mooney sees this as being in "accordance
with the general idea of a return to aboriginal habits" and the aban-
donment of "white man's dress and utensils."[14] In a letter dated 7
March 1910 Short Bull makes a similar reference to iron when he
describes how he used a tent for prayers before the dance: "All folks
pray to the great mystery, and no body brings iron into the tent. And
nobody in the tent says something evil, indeed. Yes, so it is tradition,
indeed." Short Bull's letter appears to suggest that this concept came
from ongoing traditional Lakota culture. The Christian elements of
the Ghost Dance undermine Mooney's assertion that the religion
was no more than "a return to aboriginal habits." Weygold commented that the religious views of Short Bull "are an odd mixture of
old Indian and Christian elements, but the outward forms of his religion, the ritual side, are very old Indian practice."[15]

The ritual of the Ghost Dance combined both innovative and traditional elements for the Lakota. Short Bull's brief description of the
dance itself was published in Walker's *Lakota Belief and Ritual:*

First: purification by sweat bath. Clasp hands and circle to the left. Hold
hands and sing until a trance is induced, looking up all the time. Brought
to a pitch of excitement by singing songs prescribed by the Messiah.
Dressed as prescribed. Froth at mouth when in trance. They must keep
step with the cadence of the song. The(y) go into trance in from ten

10 minutes to three quarters of an hour. Each one described his vision. Each vision is different from others. Men, women, children have visions.[16]

The use of the sweat bath in preparation for the Ghost Dance was particular to the Lakota, who had traditionally used this as a religious rite of purification: as such, it was one of many cultural variations of the dance introduced by each tribe in turn. In contrast, the style of the dance was an innovation for the Lakota, and for the first time Lakota men and women danced together, alternating to form a huge circle. It was also a novelty for the Lakota to dance holding hands—"knuckle to knuckle"—and to move round in a sideways motion.[17] The dancers would continue for many hours until a good number of them had fainted from exhaustion.

In the Beuchel narrative Short Bull gave a graphic description of his experience of the trance and two of his subsequent visions. "When I was first about to be overcome, suddenly something flashed in my face a bright light that turned blue. And then I really felt that I was going to vomit and so I was frightened and lost consciousness. And it seemed that I was brought down in a land of green grass and I set out walking and I went up a big hill and stood on the top."[18]

When he came to, Short Bull was sitting in the middle of the dance ground and initially had an overwhelming feeling of sadness. He noted that "[a]nyone who was overcome and fainted told about what he learned, and did not lie." Accordingly, after each vision he shared his experiences with the other dancers. "I stood up at the sacred tree and the people sat around me. And so I told them what I had seen and what had been told to me and I instructed them to do things properly."[19]

Short Bull did not elaborate on the meaning of his visions, but simply stated that "[t]welve times I fainted and each time an eagle carried me and took me to where my relatives lived and with great joy I saw all my fathers, mothers, sisters, and brothers."[20]

As an important part of the ceremony, the Lakota dancers wore special shirts and dresses, many of them bearing unique decoration inspired by the dancer's vision. The Ghost Dance costumes were believed by their wearers to render them invulnerable, having been invested with protective qualities by means of decoration and ceremony. The use of these garments by the Lakota Ghost Dancers has been repeatedly used to illustrate their hostile intentions. For example, Hyde commented, "This Sioux prophet [Kicking Bear] had abandoned the peaceful teaching of the messiah and was telling the maddened Sioux that ghost shirts were bullet proof and that they now had the power to destroy the whites whose troops could not harm the Indians."[21]

Mooney asserted that "Wovoka himself expressly disclaimed any responsibility for the ghost shirt."[22] Yet contemporaries recorded that not only did Wovoka claim invulnerability, but also he utilized shirts when he demonstrated this strength to the Indians. When Chapman interviewed Wovoka in December 1890, he asked, "Did you tell them that you were bullet-proof, and to prove it you spread a blanket on the ground and stood upon it, with nothing on you except a calico shirt, and had your brother shoot at you a distance of 10 feet, and the ball struck your breast and dropped to the blanket?" To which Wovoka replied, "That was a joke."[23]

Hittman also recorded that "Wovoka purchased from [Ed] Dyer's General store and sold to his followers . . . 'calico (ghost) shirts.' The sale of these items joined the sale of eagle and magpie tail feathers and red paint as part of the income he derived from thaumaturgies."[24]

The interrelated ideas of invulnerability and shirts can thus be traced back to Wovoka himself. But while Wovoka's use of the shirt was intended as a demonstration of his power to reinforce his status in the eyes of the onlookers, for the Lakota the idea of protection was applicable to all. This seems to indicate a mindset on the part of the Lakota of feeling vulnerable and open to attack, and there is plenty of evidence to suggest that the Lakotas' use of the shirts was defensive rather than hostile.[25]

Vestal concluded, "Had they intended war, the warriors would have relied upon their war charms. . . . And, had war been their plan, why [would they have] put Ghost shirts on women and children?"[26] The Lakota did not expect women and children to become involved in fighting. That women and children wore the shirts suggests either that these garments were simply part of the religion, or that the Lakota viewed attacks against these "civilians" as a real possibility. In choosing to practice the Ghost Dance, the Lakota were assuming a pacifist stance of noncooperation, but in doing so, they exposed themselves to retribution from the government.

Clark Wissler has likened the protective qualities imbued in the Ghost Shirts by means of decoration and ceremony to the Lakotas' use of protective shield-designs, which were believed to give the owner supernatural protection.[27] Thus, the idea of everyday objects assuming supernatural power was a familiar one. The Lakotas' use of Ghost Dance garments fitted in with their traditional beliefs and practice, and soon developed into an emblem of their belief in the religion. At the same time, the shirts and dresses were perceived to give the dancers spiritual protection, not because the Lakota Ghost Dancers sought armed conflict with the government or their white neighbors, but because they themselves felt vulnerable to attack from such parties.

White Americans, however, were predisposed to view these activities differently. In their eyes, both the adoption of Ghost Shirts by the Lakota and the movement of Short Bull's band from the Rosebud to the Pine Ridge Reservation appeared to be acts of aggression. Yet there is evidence that the initial motivation for Short Bull's movement was the boundary dispute brought about by the Sioux Act of 1889. The act had drastically reduced the size of the Lakota lands, and had brought about the formation of six separate reservations. In line with these changes, it also established a new boundary line between the Pine Ridge and Rosebud Reservations. The new boundary ran due south from the mouth of Black Pipe Creek, and its placement greatly "upset Chief Lips' Wazhazhas, who lived along this creek and Pass Creek," to the west.[28] Utley noted: "Technically Brules, these people had joined the Oglalas in 1854, and lived with them until 1876, when they rejoined Spotted Tail's Brules. . . . Although they had drawn their rations at Rosebud Agency, their ties with the Oglalas were still strong, and, when the new boundary threw them into Pine Ridge Reservation, they insisted upon being counted on the Pine Ridge rolls."[29]

American Horse recalled that "[t]he commissioners promised the Indians living on Black Pipe and Pass Creeks that if they signed the bill they could remain where they were and draw their rations at this agency [Pine Ridge], showing them on the map the [boundary] line."[30] To the Wažáže the solution was simple and logical, and in July they asked Red Cloud's people in council to allow them to be transferred to the Pine Ridge Agency. Red Cloud stated, "We told them we would confer with our agent (Col. Gallagher) about it, this we did and the agent called for our vote when we all raised our right hands in agreement to the transfer. We then requested him to notify the Commissioner of Indian Affairs of our wishes."[31] However, Thomas Morgan, the commissioner of Indian affairs, believed the Wažáže should maintain their ties with the Rosebud Agency and insisted that the families must relocate in the new Rosebud Reservation. At this, the Wažáže took matters into their own hands and instead moved toward the agency at Pine Ridge.[32]

Short Bull details this movement in the 1891 interview, "As Narrated by Short Bull." Once it had been agreed between the various Lakota bands that the transfer should take place, the Wažáže prepared to move. However, during the night, word came to Short Bull that his people were already moving toward Pine Ridge and that soldiers were coming to Rosebud to arrest him. Short Bull urged all the rest to hurry on, while he would remain behind with a few young men. When he heard from his brother that the rumors were "all lies," he followed the trail of the main camp, reaching Medicine Creek two days later.[33]

Suggestions of Short Bull's impending arrest might easily have been dismissed as rumors. However, the arrival of the military and the movement of troops onto the Rosebud Reservation were certainly true and caused a general stampede of Brule Ghost Dancers.[34] Two Strike later stated: "One day a white man employed at the trader's store at the agency came to my camp and told me that the soldiers were coming to stop the dance. This scared us so we put our women and children into wagons and got on our ponies and left our homes. We went to Pine Ridge and asked Red Cloud and his people to let us have a home on their reservation."[35]

Resistance to forced relocation because of the new reservation boundaries thus became intertwined with resistance to government interference with the Ghost Dance itself.

Short Bull and his followers were soon advised by an Oglala to move their camp to the crossing adjacent to American Horse's village. Once they had set up their camp, they went in a body to the home of Little Wound. The Pine Ridge agent had sent for Little Wound to bring Short Bull and his people to the agency. The two leaders started out for the agency with ten other Brule. Short Bull recounted that Little Wound went on ahead to the agency, while he and his men only reached the lodge of Twist Back at sundown. However, when news came that "Indian Soldiers were about to surround" them, they remounted their horses and rode back to their camp.[36] The hasty return of Short Bull's group surprised the camp, and the people there "feared something was wrong." On the advice of an old Oglala crier, they then moved their camp into the South Dakota Badlands.[37]

Short Bull and his followers were joined once again by other Brule Ghost Dancers, "and some of the Ogallallas, who had joined our dance."[38] Two Strike commented, "We went there to keep away from the soldiers. We did not want to fight, we only wanted to be let alone, and be allowed to worship the Great Spirit in our own way."[39] An Oglala, Turning Hawk, later stated: "while the soldiers were there [Pine Ridge Agency], there was constantly a great deal of false rumor flying back and forth. The special rumor I have in mind is the threat that the soldiers had come there to disarm the Indians entirely and to take away all their horses from them. . . . So constantly repeated was this story that our friends from Rosebud, instead of going to Pine Ridge, the place of their destination, veered off and went to some other direction toward the 'Bad Lands.'"[40]

It was this movement away from the agency and toward the Badlands that led many whites to categorize the Lakota Ghost Dancers as hostile. Brig. Gen. John R. Brooke, who commanded the Department of the Platte and exercised field command of the troops at Pine Ridge, was instructed to "separate the loyal from the 'turbulent' Indians." To this end, he dispatched Indian policemen to inform the Lakota that they must abandon their homes and gather at the agency. Soon hundreds of families "who wished to be counted as 'friendlies' had come in."[41] By definition, then, Brooke considered all the Lakotas who had not complied with his order to be "hostiles."

In the 1891 text Short Bull gives a very detailed description of events in South Dakota, from his return up to his arrest and imprisonment by General Miles in January 1891. His narrative includes what is quite possibly the only surviving eyewitness account of life in the Ghost Dance camp in the Badlands. Moreover, Short Bull gives numerous examples of potential conflicts where he had followed the advice of Wovoka, and encouraged others not to fight. Several such instances occurred while the Ghost Dancers were in the Badlands:

> I called them together and bid them to stop, saying "I wanted no trouble"—"You must stop, you should do right, have no fighting. You have taken and butchered other peoples cattle and stolen horses, we will move back to the Agency, sell our ponies, pay for these cattle and have no more trouble, the Ogallalas must listen to what I say as well as the Brules, you have plenty of dried meat now, but do as I ask you"—they would not listen but moved toward White River—I again asked them to listen, they had no ears, telling them to go to the Agency and that as soon as I got over being mad I would come in too—At this the young men surrounded me, I covered my head with my blanket so I could not see who would kill me for I heard their guns cock, one of them spoke up bidding me to uncover my face so I done it—I told them the reason I covered my face was that I did not care to see who would kill me, and wanted no trouble.[42]

Short Bull also detailed the troubles the Ghost Dancers had when they ventured out of the safety of their camp to purchase provisions. He comments on the extent of the local white paranoia about the Badlands camp, and the contagious effect of such uneasiness upon the Ghost Dancers. On all the occasions he mentions, they appear to have been fired upon by locals; in one such instance Short Bull's nephew, Circle Elk, was shot and killed. The young boy, who had been to school at Carlisle and could speak English, had been sent out with the party to purchase provisions.[43] Short Bull's 1891 narrative also makes clear how tense the atmosphere was within the camp in the Badlands. The government constantly sent intermediaries into the camp to try to coax the Ghost Dancers back to the agency at Pine Ridge. This tactic helped to expose rifts and drive wedges between the leaders, and heightened the growing sense of fear within the camp.

On the morning of 29 December 1890 the last of the Ghost Dancers were heading in to Pine Ridge to surrender. Short Bull and his uncle, Come Away from the Crowd, had been the last to leave the Badlands stronghold. They reached the main body of Ghost Dancers shortly after the arrival of some Indians who had been with Big Foot's band at Wounded Knee. "I went into the villiage and was there told that 'Big Foot' (or Spotted Elk's) Band had been all killed—I saw my cousin 'Many Wounds' who . . . confirmed this report . . . he himself [had] been wounded in the shoulder; [and] . . . told me that 'all his relatives . . . had been killed, all of their guns were taken from them and then they were fired on.'"[44]

It was only after hearing of the massacre of Big Foot's band, and the killing of women and children, that Short Bull was tempted to take up weapons and fight in defense of his people.

> I am not to blame the whites fired on us first, Twenty-three of my own relations were killed in this fight, men, women & children, this is like butchery—Why do they kill helpless women and children? This shows the soldiers want us all to die off—When our Indians fought against an enemy of their own color you know what kind of a man I was, I laughed and feared nothing, but now I do not want you to fight, take care of the women and children, I am not looking for trouble, but if I am angered I am the worst among you—I have put all badness from me and want to be a good man—I will go over to where the battle was fought in the morning and see the bodies of my relatives—When I return if the soldiers fire on you, I will remember my old feelings, stand up and be a soldier once more.[45]

The next morning, with four others, Short Bull started for the battlefield. While looking over the dead bodies, he found one of his uncles who had been badly injured. This rescue party then "hitched up" four wagons and picked up all the survivors they could find (some forty-odd), and took them to a deserted house nearby on

Wounded Knee Creek. Those whom they thought were fatally wounded were left there, while the rest were taken back to camp. During the night it began to snow. By morning a heavy snow had fallen, but Short Bull's party started for Wounded Knee about noon. When the group reached the house, they found that those who had been left were now gone. "[A]fterwards [they] ascertained that they had been taken to the Agency by friendlies in charge of 'No Neck.'"[46]

The gunfire of the Seventh Cavalry was heard clearly at the agency, and caused some of the Indians encamped there to flee. Leaving the agency, they joined the Ghost Dancers who had set up camp near No Water's village, creating a temporary settlement of 4,000 people. After a tense standoff, the Ghost Dancers eventually complied with the wishes of General Miles. They moved their camp to the agency at Pine Ridge, and on 15 January 1891 they began to surrender their arms.

Despite very trying circumstances, Short Bull avoided conflict and endeavored to follow what he had been taught in Mason Valley. "[D]uring all this time my heart was bad, yet I did not want my people to fight the Government—I might have done much harm but always kept my people from it. I wanted no fighting, I wanted to do as the Messiah bid me."[47]

As noted by DeMallie, the suppression of the Lakota Ghost Dance "was only another step in the systematic suppression of native religious practices that formed an integral part of the U.S. government's program of Indian civilization," but to the Lakota it was the epitome of white suppression.[48] The Lakota Ghost Dancers had not corrupted Wovoka's doctrine of peace, turning it into a warlike antiwhite movement. Rather, other parties, in their reporting and recording of the religion, had distorted the Lakotas' beliefs to serve their own ends. The majority of historians have too long ignored the words and actions of the Lakota Ghost Dancers, basing their interpretation of the religion on the words of those who opposed it. In the end, we are left with Short Bull's lament: "Who would have thought that dancing could make such trouble? For the message that I brought was peace. And the message was given by the Father to all the tribes."[49]

At the close of the military suppression of the religion in South Dakota, some of the Ghost Dancers were removed by Gen. Nelson A.

Miles to Fort Sheridan, Illinois. Short Bull recalled, "Some ten days afterwards—General Miles asked me to go to Fort Sheridan, with "Kicking Bear" and some twenty-five others."[50] In all, twenty-seven Lakota men and women were removed to Fort Sheridan. Maj. John Vance Lauderdale wrote to his wife Josephine on 26 January, detailing their departure: "Crowds of women and children, the families of the Indians, stood about and kept up a kind of low singing or warbling as they always do when they are taking leave of their friends."[51]

Miles informed the adjutant general that he was leaving for Chicago, "taking with me 30 Indians that I intend to keep for several months at Fort Sheridan under my personal observation." He concluded, "[T]his is the strongest assurance of success and guarantee of permanent peace. In my judgement nothing is necessary now to secure that other than good government in the future."[52] Miles believed that with Kicking Bear and Short Bull out of the way, "an uprising is entirely improbable now that Sitting Bull and Big Foot are dead."[53] This would suggest that Miles viewed these individuals as influential leaders, and soon they alone came to represent the "Hostile Indians."[54]

Yet this perception was at odds with the opinions of other officials. J. George Wright, the Rosebud agent, wrote to the commissioner of Indian affairs stating: "The records of Crow Dog, White Horse, Lance, Two Strike, Eagle Pipe and Turning Bear were fully represented and made known so that no imposition might be practiced, but who are treated as blameless, while Short Bull, at this time a disturber, is merely a Medicine Man, no leader, but used by others, is the only one taken as prisoner, from here, to my knowledge."[55] This sentiment was echoed in a letter to Herbert Welsh, secretary of the Indian Rights Association, from James G. Wright, a former agent at Rosebud:

> Short Bull . . . [is] a man of little influence and no leader, a medicine man of the Sitting Bull persuasion, with little or no following, and as I am told was glad to get away fearing should he return the Indians would kill him as they threatened to do, owing to the non fulfillment of his prophesies, (I know by experience he was not a difficult man to control). The rest of

those sent to Fort Sheridan were young men of neither position, influence, or following. Gen. Miles' interpreter said "he asked Short Bull and others if they were afraid to go East with him, they answering No, he told them to select certain numbers and he would take them."[56]

That the Lakota themselves selected which Indians were to go to Fort Sheridan appears to be corroborated by Miles himself in his autobiography *Serving the Republic*. There he states that "the Indians . . . were advised to give a guarantee of their good faith that such threatening of hostilities or actual war would not occur again in the near future; and, as an earnest of this, they were told that they should send a body of representative men to the East as hostages and as a pledge that in the future they would keep the peace. This they consented to do."[57]

Since those who were perceived as the greatest threat to peace on the reservations were not removed, Miles's motivation for imprisoning those he did remained unclear to many. Commissioner Morgan stated in a newspaper interview that neither the Interior Department nor the Indian Bureau knew anything "of those Indians taken to Fort Sheridan." He went on to state, "Their coming to Fort Sheridan is the sole work of Gen. Miles. . . . This office was not consulted nor was the Secretary of the Interior."[58] A letter written by an Indian named Laurence Industrious from the Pine Ridge Agency suggests that from the Indian perspective, there was quite a different reason for the removal of the Ghost Dancers:

> Kicking Bear and Short Bull each accompanied by 10 followers were taken east by Miles to remain there 6 years [? months], the object of taking them east is to show the Ghost Dance and its effect if any. I understand they have danced and the general opinion of the whites is that the dance was harmless and would not have any bad effect and that a great many lives had been lost for nothing, and these people will be returned to their agencies early next spring. . . . It is possible that they will give Kicking Bear his dance back to him again.[59]

Even the Fort Sheridan prisoners themselves appear to have been unclear as to why they were being held. Mary Collins, a visiting missionary, recalled that the prisoners "asked me to find out" why they had been imprisoned.[60] The ambiguous reasons for the removal of these specific Ghost Dancers give little indication as to why three Lakota women were also taken. If, as Utley states, Miles had removed the "Ghost Dance leaders . . . until passions had subsided enough for them to return to their people," then this would indicate that Calls the Name, Medicine Horse, and Crow Cane were women of influence, who posed as great a threat to white society as Short Bull and Kicking Bear.[61] But if they were selected by the Lakota themselves, it might have been for very different reasons.[62]

Initially, Miles intended that the Fort Sheridan prisoners were to be "instructed in the school of the soldier and inducted into the habits of civilized life."[63] The *Chicago Daily Tribune* commented, "The purpose of the War Department in the matter is not fully understood. It is said it is the intention of Gen. Miles to enlist the Indians in the regular army, subject them to the same discipline as other recruits so as to have them ready for service against hostile Indians in Indian wars which may break out in the future."[64]

Upon their arrival at Fort Sheridan, the commandant, Major McKibben, told reporters that a guard would be thrown around the Indians, but that the detail would not be large enough "to make them believe that they were in durance." They would be allowed every liberty consistent with the circumstances. McKibben went on to state that if Short Bull or Kicking Bear gave any intimation that they were restive, "the guard might be doubled," but he felt that "on the whole the mere fact that their surroundings were strange would keep . . . [them] in a contented condition for some time to come."[65]

On 28 January a reporter visited the fort to see for himself the circumstances under which the Indians were being held. His article, entitled "Are Not Prisoners of War," illustrated the somewhat limited freedom granted to the Ghost Dancers and indicated that the main object of the guards was to keep inquisitive members of the public at bay.[66] Clearly, the so-called "hostile" Indians had become an item of curiosity to the populace of Chicago. "Society ladies" and children were allowed to visit them, and this underlines that the Indians did not pose a threat. More than anything, the Ghost Dance prisoners were a spectacle. The *Omaha Morning World-Herald* reported that when Miles paid a visit to Fort Sheridan, he had been accompanied by "two car loads of young ladies," and that the "Indians had been appraised of the onslaught and were in full glory of war paint and feathers."[67]

The Indians, now living under guard in an alien, cold, and "swampy place," soon found themselves an object of concern to the Indian Rights Association.[68] It was reported that members of the association were "talking of applying a writ of habeas Corpus for the purpose of discovering what rights, if any, the Indians now held at Fort Sheridan have. . . . The idea of the association, it is said, is to use the case to thoroughly test in the courts the power of the government in the matter, and if necessary appeal to Congress for a change."[69] There are no indications that the association took the matter any further, and a possible reason for this might have been the Indians' ambiguous status. After all, Miles could claim that they were not prisoners as such: he had asked them if they would accompany him, and they were granted the freedom to come and go, though with some limitations.[70]

Short Bull's only reference to his confinement at Fort Sheridan occurs in the 1891 text "As Narrated by Short Bull," in which he recalled that "[w]hile there we were often visited by General Miles who, with all the officers there made us as comfortable as could be, doing all in their power for us."[71] By mid-March it was reported that the Indians were to be released, but not to return to their homes in South Dakota. William F. Cody proposed to engage the Ghost Dancers in Buffalo Bill's Wild West show, which would shortly be departing to conclude its monumental tour of Europe. All but four of the Fort Sheridan Ghost Dancers agreed to go.[72]

It is apparent from the evidence that Short Bull had embraced Wovoka's pacifism. The religion remained essentially peaceful, combining elements of white religion and culture with traditional Indian concepts and practices. The Ghost Dance "became a part of the Lakotas' own evolving religion rather than a brief experiment with an exotic belief."[73] Yet within the context of a peaceful religion that preached accommodation, the Lakota Ghost Dance can also be viewed as a rejection of dependency. The Ghost Dancers were encouraged to take from white culture what was of benefit, but to remain independent. This was a bold stance at a time when, as Francis Paul Prucha noted, "the Indians on the reservations became almost completely dependent, a dependency that paradoxically was intensified by the very programs and policies that the paternalistic government of the United States instituted to assist the dependent Indians."[74]

Through the religion, the Ghost Dancers were attempting to assert their autonomy from government control. In the government's view, this made the Ghost Dance a challenge to its authority. When the Office of Indian Affairs banned the religion, the Ghost Dance became a form of passive resistance. It was an essentially peaceful movement that advocated noncooperation.

When Short Bull and Kicking Bear consented to accompany Miles to Fort Sheridan, they accepted the label of "hostile" for the good of the Lakota people as a whole. Their continued belief in the religion gives further evidence that the Lakota Ghost Dance had not been transformed into an aggressive antiwhite movement, which most likely would have failed and died with the massacre. Rather, it was a religious form of accommodation that could and did endure.

CHAPTER FOUR

INDIAN PERFORMERS
IN BUFFALO BILL'S WILD WEST

At the same time that the Ghost Dance was spreading across the Lakota reservations, about sixty-five Lakota men and women were touring in continental Europe with Buffalo Bill's Wild West. However, while William F. Cody and his Wild West exhibition were thrilling European audiences, back in the United States the press was criticizing the show, reporting that the health and morals of Indian performers were being neglected. The contrast could not have been greater: in Europe Cody was fêted as an American hero, while in his home country, in the words of the *New York World*, the "hatchets [were out] for Buffalo Bill."[1]

Six Indian performers had died in Europe, and Americans read the descriptions of ill health and improper care from dissatisfied Indians who had left the show, along with accounts of Indians being allowed to drink, gamble, and womanize. Reformers fanned the flames of discontent, suggesting that rather than helping to reform and "civilize" the Indian performers, the show demeaned and demoralized them.[2] Thomas Jefferson Morgan, the commissioner of Indian affairs, shared this view and stated in his annual report for 1890: "I have endeavored through the various agents to impress upon the minds of the Indians the evil resulting from connecting themselves with such shows and the importance of their remaining at home and devoting their time and energies to building houses, establishing permanent homes, cultivating farms, and acquiring thrifty, industrious habits, thus placing themselves in [a] fit position for absorption into our political and civil life."[3]

The dispute between Wild West exhibitions and the reformers of Indian policy was primarily a conflict over "whose image of the Indians would prevail."[4] Francis Paul Prucha noted that "it soon became clear to humanitarians interested in the education of the Indians as American citizens . . . that the Wild West shows were retrogressive, that for both the Indians who performed and the whites who were entertained the image presented of the Indians was the wrong one."[5] As reformers attempted to foster "an alternate image of the Indian as a sober, God-fearing, industrious, independent farmer or herder," Wild West shows were continuing to depict the Indians as "savage" warriors.[6] Christian reformers also believed that the shows were antagonistic to creating a healthy approach among the Indians toward "work and productive citizenship."[7]

The criticisms of Buffalo Bill's Wild West grew from anecdotal evidence to something more tangible when one of the Indian performers returning from Europe died in New York City. When the Bremen steamship *Saale* landed at the port of New York on 14 June 1890, James R. O'Beirne, the assistant superintendent of immigration, insisted on detaining five passengers who had boarded the steamer in Leipzig, Germany. The five were all Lakota Indians who had been in Europe performing in Buffalo Bill's Wild West, and who were now on their way home to the Pine Ridge Agency in South Dakota. It was reported that "they were tired of Buffalo Bill and wanted to get back to Dakota."[8] They gave their names as Eagle Horn, Blue Rainbow, Little Lamb, Running Creek, and Kills Plenty. O'Beirne detained the men because they were all in a poor physical state, but eventually all but Kills Plenty (Otakta) were allowed to land. As Kills Plenty was suffering from a severely injured wrist, and was unable to travel, O'Beirne had him transferred to Bellevue Hospital for treatment. The following day his comrades started for home.[9]

The injury to Kills Plenty had occurred during a performance of Buffalo Bill's Wild West in Germany, when the Indian's horse had fallen on him and crushed his right arm.[10] The wound had not been properly treated, and upon further examination at Bellevue, it was found that blood poisoning had set in. Moreover, tuberculosis had already weakened the patient, further hampering his recovery.[11] Kills Plenty was visited in hospital by Rev. Father Craft, a Lakota-speaking Indian missionary who was acquainted with him and who happened to be in New York on a lecture tour, and by George C. Crager, a Lakota interpreter who had previously been employed by the Wild West show.[12] The two had several meetings with the sick man, who expressed the hope that he might live until he reached his home. Those attending the patient conferred with O'Beirne and then cabled Cody to ask if he would defray the expenses of an attendant to accompany him home. Cody agreed, so tickets were procured and arrangements set, but on the night of 18 June Kills Plenty died.[13] The death of Kills Plenty was briefly covered by the New York City newspapers, which detailed the circumstances of his death and funeral preparations.[14] O'Beirne once again cabled Cody, informing him of the Indian's death, and requested that Cody immediately forward $200 to cover the cost of the undertaker's bill and transportation of the body back to the agency.

After repeated attempts to contact Cody had failed, the matter was placed before the secretary of the interior, in the hope that he would take action to compel Cody to "fulfil his contract and pay the expenses incurred for caring for this body or forfeit said Cody's Bonds."[15] In order to hire Indians to travel and perform with the exhibition, the management of Buffalo Bill's Wild West had to make individual contracts with each Indian. In addition, as the Indians were "wards" of the government, they were not permitted to leave their reservation until a bond had been lodged with the Office of Indian Affairs to cover any expenses incurred from circumstances such as bankruptcy. For the European tour, Buffalo Bill's Wild West had lodged a $20,000 bond with the federal government in order to hire between 85 and 100 Lakota Indians for a period of two years.[16] The commissioner of Indian affairs ordered that Kills Plenty's body be transported to the Pine Ridge Agency, after which he would contact the management of Buffalo Bill's Wild West with a view to securing "repayment . . . of the expense incurred."[17]

George Crager, who had brought the matter to the attention of the secretary of the interior, supervised the arrangements in New York City. Six pallbearers escorted the body "in a fine hearse through the

Ferry to the [baggage] car."[18] Hank Clifford accompanied the remains home, where Kills Plenty was interred at the Catholic cemetery at the Holy Rosary Mission, four miles northeast of the agency on White Clay Creek.[19] The death of Kills Plenty and the Wild West's apparent disregard for his welfare fueled the mounting opposition to Indians performing in Wild West shows. It also sparked a controversy that would cause Cody to cancel a proposed winter stand in the French Riviera and return to America with his show Indians to refute the claims of his critics.

The case against Cody had been steadily building from the beginning of the year. On 27 January 1890 U.S. Consul Charles B. Trail wrote from Marseilles informing the assistant secretary of state, William F. Wharton, of the deaths of Chief Hawick and Featherman. When Buffalo Bill's Wild West left Marseilles the previous December, the two Indians, who were sick with typhoid fever and smallpox respectively, were left at the Conception Hospital and entrusted to Trail's care. John Burke, the Wild West's manager, paid in advance for a private room, a doctor, and an attending nurse. Chief Hawick died of the fever on 1 January, and Featherman of "small pox of the most virulent type" on 6 January. A Catholic priest officiated at the funerals, and their property was forwarded to Cody to be delivered to their heirs.[20]

In February 1890 U.S. Consul Edward Camphausen wrote from Naples reporting the death of Goes Flying at the Hospidale Cotugoro, Naples. Goes Flying had died of smallpox on 15 February at the age of forty-five, and the Italian authorities had burned all of his possessions.[21] This was followed by another letter in March from Augustus O'Bourn, U.S. Consul in Rome, reporting the death at midnight on 2 March of Little Ring at the age of thirty-three. He was found dead in his bed; a postmortem examination showed heart disease as the cause of death. His body was interred at the main cemetery in Rome, known as Campo Verano. He left only his clothing, which was taken by his brothers, Piece of Iron and Yellow Horse, who were also with Cody's show.[22]

With the demise of Kills Plenty in New York City, the total of Indian deaths for the 1889–90 tour had risen to five. Unlike the other four, who had died from disease or illness, Kills Plenty had been a young man whose death had been caused by the inadequate treatment of an injury incurred during a performance of the Wild West. Of greatest significance was the fact that he died not in a far-off country but in New York City, and therefore in the American public eye. O'Beirne wrote to Hugh Gallagher, the Pine Ridge agent, that he was "very much annoyed at the manner these Indians have been treated and will lay the matter before the government at Washington."[23] O'Beirne recalled that in 1877, while he had been employed at the Red Cloud Agency, Cody had applied to the commissioner of Indian affairs to hire some Indians for his theatrical show. O'Beirne had "contended for favorable consideration towards Mr. Cody with the understanding . . . that the contract should stipulate that they [the Indians] should be kept free from demoralizing influences, liquor and other temptations, and should be safely returned to their Reservation."[24] O'Beirne concluded that this had not been the case for Kills Plenty and his four companions, who "came here without an interpreter, or anyone to conduct them, or to supply their wants, excepting a boy sent from an imigrant boarding house who fortunately came to me."[25] When three more Indians from Cody's employ returned from Europe, O'Beirne's "agitation of the issue caused the controversy to explode in the newspapers."[26]

On 19 July 1890 White Horse, Bear Pipe, and White Weasel disembarked from the *Augusta Victoria,* having traveled in steerage from Hamburg. During the voyage the Indians had suffered from seasickness, and upon arrival they repeated that they had been unable to get proper food. This time Cody had sent Richard Matthews along as chaperone (Matthews was the driver of the Deadwood Stagecoach in the show). Matthews, however, had traveled as a saloon passenger and "did not go near them during the trip."[27] The next morning, before the showmen left for Pine Ridge, O'Beirne organized a press conference, with George Crager acting as interpreter. Bear Pipe stated that Rocky Bear, their acting chief in the show, and the interpreter Bronco Bill had treated them very cruelly. He complained that although the food they received was not fit for dogs, they were completely reliant upon whatever the cook supplied. Bear Pipe also contended that Buffalo Bill insisted that the Indian men should strip to the waist and come out in war paint and feathers at every show, refusing to allow them to wear shirts even in the coldest weather.[28] White Horse stated that "all the Indians in Buffalo Bill's show are discontented, ill-treated and anxious to come back home."[29] Agent Gallagher reported to the commissioner of Indian affairs in a letter dated 28 July, "these Indians like the ones preceding them have nothing to show for their services except shattered constitutions, which may or may not be built up again." He went on to quote O'Beirne, who had stated in a previous letter that "the treatment of these returned Indians is inhuman and shows plainly how little concern is felt for them after they have been broken down in the service and are no longer profitable to their employers."[30]

The return of White Horse, Bear Pipe, and White Weasel attracted a great deal more newspaper coverage than the return of the previous group and the subsequent death of Kills Plenty. The newspaper articles were longer and the tone much less complimentary about Cody and his Wild West. The *New York Herald* reported: "For months past the warriors have been straggling back in groups of three or five, sick and disgusted with their treatment while abroad. Fully one third of the original band have returned to this country."[31] Bad press was not a new phenomenon for Buffalo Bill's Wild West. Cody had ended a personal letter dated 15 February 1890 with the observation: "I see the New York press is giving me thunder every once in a while. What for I don't know, I only wish they would stick to the truth."[32] The claims of Bear Pipe and White Horse as published in the *New York Herald* prompted John Burke, the Wild West's press agent, to take action to refute the claims, but with only limited success. Burke's first initiative was to invite the Berlin consul general and the secretary of legation, as well as the consul in Hamburg, to inspect the Indians and the Wild West's encampment. All three officials were favorably impressed. Burke forwarded their report to the European edition of the *New York Herald*, which subsequently printed a retraction of the allegations.[33]

The second tack taken by Burke was an attempt to counter the claims of the returning Indians with the testimony of another Indian performer. The showman in question, No Neck, sailed from Germany on 19 July aboard the Bremen steamer *Kaiser Wilhelm*. Burke cabled the Lakota interpreter George Crager, asking that he meet No

Neck, and that he also contact John Hamilton of the *Illustrated News.* Hamilton felt confident that No Neck would "speak of the management as he found it" and would "refute the allegations made by the others."[34]

No Neck arrived in New York on 29 July 1890. He had traveled as a "second [class] cabin passenger," but contrary to the usual custom of permitting cabin passengers to land at the steamship dock, No Neck had to travel with the steerage passengers to the Barge Office before he was permitted to "re-enter the land of his fathers."[35] Crager and Father Craft met him at the pier and escorted him to the Barge Office, where he was registered. He then went to O'Beirne's office, where the immigration official was waiting to receive him. William O. Snyder, the American ticket agent for the Wild West show, was also on hand to represent Cody.[36]

No Neck's appearance and demeanor was in stark contrast to that of Bear Pipe, White Horse, and White Weasel, whose shoes and clothing had been described as "poor and worn out."[37] The *New York World* reported: "His handsome silk umbrella—imported duty free—was deposited in a corner, his heavy winter overcoat was pulled off and his raven locks were arranged with the aid of a nice pocket-brush and sweetly scented with Parisian musk. . . . No Neck's appearance was that of an extra good liver, and to prove that he had not been starved by Buffalo Bill he was weighed on the baggage scales of Barney Biglin. Two hundred and six and one half pounds was his weight."[38]

Speaking through interpreters Crager and Craft, No Neck proceeded to give an account of the treatment received by the Indians in Europe. He agreed with Bear Pipe in saying that Rocky Bear, who was in charge of the Indians, treated them cruelly, gave them inadequate and insufficient food, and swore at them in Lakota, but in general his report on the treatment of the Indians was quite favorable to Buffalo Bill.[39]

No Neck reported that the Indians were fed on a diet of "bread, meat, coffee, tea, milk in cans, butter, rice, barley, prunes and bacon." The men were each paid $25 a month, although he himself received $30 as the chief of police at the Wild West show. He observed that "the Indians thought that good pay when they first went to Europe, but after they got into civilized fashionable life and stayed out at night they did not think it was sufficient." While a few had saved their earnings and others had bought clothing, many had spent their money on gambling and whiskey.[40]

The gathered pressmen were then informed that Buffalo Bill employed a doctor in all of the cities that the show visited, and that one of the Indian lodges was set aside as a hospital. No Neck recounted that Indians taken sick were sent home, while those who had died were buried in nearby graveyards with their names painted on slabs. Doctors and medicine had been supplied for the sick Indians, but they feared both the medicine and the hospitals.[41]

No Neck went on to acknowledge that Red Shirt, who had left the show in Barcelona and returned to America, had been in charge of the Indians until December 1889, when he had quarreled with Rocky Bear at Marseilles. Agent Snyder interrupted at this point to suggest that Rocky Bear had replaced Red Shirt because the latter had not restrained the Indians as Buffalo Bill wished, but No Neck replied that Rocky Bear had done little better.[42] He elaborated that Rocky Bear and Red Shirt had had trouble after the show left Paris, "Bruin [Rocky Bear] being jealous of favors shown by the Parisianne belles to the other gentleman [Red Shirt]." In consequence, Red Shirt came home.[43] The *New York Journal* went on to report:

> Buffalo Bill evidently knowing the reputations of the wicked continental cities told his Indians that they must not go out at night or go with the gay frivolous young women who see Paris by gaslight and told No Neck to enforce that order. "When I tried to do so," said No Neck, "the braves had no ears and paid no attention." In consequence of their dissipations they were attacked by various forms of debility which are the inevitable results of fashionable life as lived by our own gilded youths. "Rocky Bear," the chief said, "did not try to enforce Buffalo Bill's orders and was a sad rake himself doing considerable mashing among the continental belles. . . ." [No Neck] admitted to Father Craft, amid loud laughter, that, as he found he could not keep the Indians in the way they should go, he thought he might as well take a hand himself and sallied forth and saw the elephant on his own account.[44]

No Neck would not say whether he had any complaints against William Cody or his partner Nate Salsbury, and evaded the questions by smiling in a "bland manner" and saying that he was glad to get home. In describing his parting with Buffalo Bill, he said: "Colonel Cody gave me a suit of clothes, paid my wages, and gave me $100 besides, telling me at the time that I should meet the newspapermen, and I was to give a good report of the treatment of the Indians."[45]

Then, rising from his chair in a dignified manner, he said in solemn tones, "All I have spoken is truth. What I said they did not teach me."[46]

This attempt by the show's management to refute the charges of ill-treatment worked to some extent; No Neck was clearly well fed and handsomely clothed. Nevertheless, at the same time the interview also illustrated the management's failings—principally, that it was unable to ensure that the Indians were being kept free from "demoralizing influences, liquor and other temptations." Also, the extra payment of $100 that No Neck had received to give a good account of the show's treatment of the Indians aroused suspicions among the New York reporters. The subsequent coverage only heightened the controversy, which Burke had hoped to quash with No Neck's return and interview.

Upon his return to Pine Ridge, No Neck informed Agent Gallagher that a month previously an Indian named Wounds One Another, who was with Buffalo Bill's Wild West, had been killed when he had fallen from a train while traveling through Germany. The agent informed Commissioner Morgan that Wounds One Another had $108 due him at the time of his death, and that he also "possessed a number of trinkets and a quantity of clothing," which his father wished to have returned. The agent was disturbed that he had received no official notice of the death, and thought it "hardly possible that No Neck would make such a statement if it was not true."[47]

Meanwhile, O'Beirne penned a letter to Commissioner Morgan on 3 August, stating, "The question is asked now, why are not the Indians protected by the Government in their rights under the bonds which the contractors who have taken them away have given to the Indian Office?"[48] The next day John Noble, the secretary of the interior, directed "that no permits be granted for Indians to go with these shows, under any circumstances," and Commissioner Morgan was instructed to investigate the facts in regard to the treatment of the Indian performers.[49]

The changing attitudes at the Interior Department encouraged the commissioner of Indian affairs in his mission to end Indian employment in Wild West exhibitions. Morgan had been the corresponding secretary of the Providence branch of the Indian Rights Association before his appointment as commissioner, and his philosophy mirrored that of prominent Indian reformers of the day, who saw Indian participation in Wild West shows as anathema.[50] Where previously the secretary of the interior had appeared favorably disposed toward Wild West shows, checking Morgan's enthusiasm on numerous occasions, now even Secretary Noble had reason to be disturbed. The evidence seemed to suggest that such shows did more than just foster negative perceptions of Indians in the public mind. They risked "not only the health of Indians, but also their very lives."[51]

Commissioner Morgan's patience had paid off, and on 22 August he swung into action. He wrote to Cody and Salsbury, outlining the complaints that had been received by the bureau. He requested that they refund O'Beirne in full for all expenses incurred in transporting Kills Plenty's body back to his agency. Morgan also required an account of the circumstances under which the injury to Kills Plenty had occurred, and a report on the nature and cause, so far as known to them, of the diseases the returned Indians were suffering from when they left the show.[52]

Morgan also wrote to Gallagher instructing him to question all the returned Indians about their treatment while abroad, obtaining affidavits from the Indians showing all the facts. The agent was advised to establish if the employers had failed to comply with their contracts to properly care for them, or if the Indians had been grossly maltreated in other respects.[53] Finally, he wrote to O'Beirne, asking that if any more Indians arrived from Europe in a similar condition, he would "ascertain from them the full particulars relative . . . [to] their treatment while abroad and advise this office as to the facts." Morgan reassured O'Beirne that if it should appear from all the facts presented that the employers of the Indians had violated their contracts, proper steps would be taken to obtain adequate redress. He ended, "It is against the policy of this department to again permit Indians to be taken from their Reservations for exhibition purposes."[54]

In his report to Morgan on the treatment and health of the returned show Indians, Gallagher responded that seventy-two healthy young Indian men had left his agency in the spring of 1889 to join the Wild West show's tour. Five had died among strangers in foreign lands, while the ill health of seven others had rendered them unfit for work, and these had been sent home. He continued, "I find it very difficult to get any information from these young men in regard to their treatment while away but their condition upon arrival here speaks more forcibly than words and is sufficient proof that their lot was a hard one while in the service of the Wild West show."[55]

Two more Indians from Cody's Wild West arrived back in New York on 26 August. Armed with the official support of the commissioner of Indian affairs, O'Beirne decided to investigate, and George Crager escorted the returning Indians, Little Chief and Short Horn, to O'Beirne's office. Short Horn wore his badge of office—a tin plate with the word "Police" printed on it, indicating that he was employed as such by Buffalo Bill's Wild West. He condemned No Neck, alleging that he often incited the Indians to go out and get drunk.

Little Chief stated that Buffalo Bill always treated the Indians well, but they did not like him because he was too much of a ladies' man. Far from being destitute, the Indians had $500 between them, although this represented not their accumulated salaries but winnings from their fellow performers after a poker game played on their last payday. O'Beirne condemned the management of the Wild West for allowing the Indians to gamble, noting that while a few might profit, most would lose everything.[56]

Commissioner Morgan's letter of 22 August, which outlined the complaints against the Wild West show, was delivered to the show's management by the consul general in Berlin. Nate Salsbury acknowledged receipt of the communication in a letter dated 18 September, in which he noted that a "suitable reply shall be made to the demands."[57] However, at the beginning of October news reached Washington that while the show was in Bremen, another of Buffalo Bill's Indians had died. Uses the Sword had died during a performance on 9 September after falling from his horse and being trampled by a buffalo.[58] His body was buried at the Rhiensbury Cemetery, and the "little Estate left by him" was delivered to his sister, Spotted Elk, who was also with Cody's show.[59] This bought the total of Indian deaths during this tour to seven, and American press interest in the returned Indians showed no signs of abating. Burke's attempts to smother the controversy had served only to fuel the debate.

The show faced an investigation by the commissioner of Indian affairs, a man who disapproved of Indians being employed in such ventures. If he found that the management had been negligent, Buffalo Bill's Wild West would lose its $20,000 bond. The secretary of the interior had banned the issue of further permits, and since the Indian performers were essential to the success of the show, the consequences for Cody's Wild West were serious. It became apparent that decisive action was needed to halt the accusations of mistreatment. So on 26 October Burke cabled Morgan to inform him that Buffalo Bill had decided to bring the Indians to Washington, where they would be glad to explain matters personally. He signed off with "don't believe all you hear, justice to all is [the] foundation [of] good government [and] Christianity."[60]

The majority of complaints made by the returning Indian performers had not been aimed at Cody himself, but instead primarily at other Indians with the show, most notably Rocky Bear. Their comments about Cody seem rather trivial and perhaps signify that while on tour the Indians had little contact their employer outside of the arena. The only white man openly criticized was the interpreter Bronco Bill, the principal intermediary between the management and the Indians. It is possible that Cody was initially unaware of the Indian performers' disquiet, as Bronco Bill was unlikely to relay complaints about his own behavior. Yet ultimately Cody and the management of the Wild West remained responsible, and they hoped to comprehensively refute the charges made against them with their return to the United States.

On 13 November the *Belgenland* docked at the Delaware Wharves in Philadelphia. On board were thirty-eight returning Lakota performers and the Wild West's general manager, John Burke. Among those waiting on the dock were James O'Beirne, assistant commissioner of immigration at New York, and Herbert Welsh, the secretary of the Indian Rights Association, who was there to investigate the charges of ill treatment, improper care, and drunkenness. O'Beirne, Father Craft, and George Crager had traveled down from New York the previous day in order to meet the Red Star steamship.[61]

Once the steamship had moored, Burke held a reception for the press in the forward saloon. Rocky Bear answered questions regarding the treatment of the Indians, with William Irving (Bronco Bill) acting as interpreter. He told the reporters that the food the Indian performers had been supplied was excellent, and that he had been "fed so well that the bucks in the Pine Ridge Agency would have to stand out of his way when he got back." Burke informed the gathered reporters that "all American Consular representatives dined with us and have signed a paper declaring that the food of the Indians was of the best." In Hamburg they had met imitators of their show, and Burke claimed that it was these competitors who had "caused these reports to be made against us through malice." He concluded his speech by announcing, "We are going back next year in April."[62]

Following the press conference, Welsh and O'Beirne met with Major Burke in the first-class saloon. Welsh stated that as the representative of the Indian Rights Association, he was present to make an investigation into the charges. Father Craft would act as interpreter, and he proposed that the Indians should be questioned with Burke absent.[63] After a heated exchange, Burke announced that he would be taking the Indians to Washington, and after questioning Welsh's authority, he rejected his proposal to question the Indians.[64]

George Chandler, the acting secretary of the interior, and Robert V. Belt, acting commissioner of Indian affairs, had enjoined Welsh "to make a full and impartial examination of the Indians upon their arrival in the city." Welsh wrote to Chandler detailing his unsuccessful attempts to get Burke to comply.[65] Later in the day Welsh received a telegram from Chandler, which clearly confirmed that he had authority to conduct the investigation in Philadelphia. He again attempted to persuade Burke to release the Indians for interviews, but Burke refused, complaining that the affair was none of Welsh's business.[66] Rebuffed and slighted, Welsh cabled Chandler and informed him that Burke declined to permit the examination, and that they had instead started out for Washington. His telegram closed with the cautionary remark, "Interpreter suggested by him should not be employed nor should he be present at examination."[67]

Commissioner Morgan had left Washington in early September for a tour of agency schools, and was not present when Burke and the Indians arrived back in November. Acting Commissioner Robert Belt took charge of the matter in his absence.[68] Nate Salsbury and John Burke called at the Office of Indian Affairs on Friday, 14 November, expressing the wish that their Indians be seen and examined. Belt reprimanded them for not allowing Welsh to conduct the examination in Philadelphia, but Salsbury and Burke explained that they feared "the examination would not be impartial."[69] Belt responded that if the Indians in their employ had been well treated, Salsbury and Burke ought to have had sufficient confidence in the fairness and integrity of Welsh. Salsbury and Burke then "expressed a perfect willingness that the Department should make the examination in whatever manner it deemed proper," and Belt agreed to receive the Indians at 10 A.M. the next day.[70]

Upon arrival Salsbury and Burke were informed that the examination would be conducted privately, with only Belt, his stenographer, the Indians, and the interpreter Chauncey Yellow Robe (a Lakota student from Carlisle School who had been brought down for the purpose) present. Salsbury and Burke protested, "urgently requesting that their interpreter be allowed to remain in the room," but their request was denied.[71]

The acting commissioner began by welcoming the Indians to Washington before explaining the reasons for the meeting. "[Salsbury and Burke] have brought you here . . . to afford the Department . . . an opportunity to see and hear itself your condition, and for that purpose I have arranged to meet you today . . . [to ascertain] whether the contract made with you . . . has been carried out."[72]

Belt urged all who wished to talk "to feel free to speak to me your own minds as to your treatment." In reply to his question, "who will speak first," Rocky Bear began. His opening statement indicated that he was a "progressive" Indian who had always worked with the government, despite incurring the wrath of his own people. He concluded, "I have been in the show four years, but I think it comes out all right. If it did not suit me, I would not remain longer."[73]

Belt then went on to question the Indians, covering all the charges made in the preceding months. He asked how many Indians had died abroad; if they slept in houses; if they ate at tables, "with chairs, knives, forks, plates, etc."; and what they had to eat. The acting commissioner's questions were all answered by Rocky Bear, who gave a report of exemplary treatment and care.[74] "I tell you they treated us well. If these things do not suit the great father, I would stop. If the great father do not want me to go on and show, I would go without it. . . . That is the way I get money. If a man goes to work in some other place and goes back with money, he has some for his children."[75]

The acting commissioner asked if they had been paid regularly, and what Rocky Bear had done with his money. He responded, "I have bought some clothes and sent some money to my children; sent it to the Agent." Rocky Bear then opened his "pocket-book," which the acting commissioner calculated held about $300 worth of gold coin, stating, "I saved this money . . . to buy some clothes for my children." This prompted Belt to inquire if all the Indians had such well-filled pocket books. "At the reservation," Rocky Bear explained, "the children sometimes have nothing to eat, and they ask [for] money, so they send money to their children."[76]

Belt now turned his attention to questions concerning the alleged demoralizing influences. He asked if the Indians had been "allowed any whiskey, or fire water"; if visitors were allowed to enter their quarters "at all times"; if they went as they "pleased in the cities and towns . . . without escort, among bad people"; or if they were allowed to visit "houses where bad women lived." While Rocky Bear admitted that they were permitted to leave the camp by themselves, he asserted that they were not allowed to visit brothels or consume whiskey.[77] However, in his study of Wild West shows, Paul Reddin noted that while the Buffalo Bill show was in Europe, just before their return, Indians were regular visitors to local inns and taverns. The Indians "drank along with the others, and offered 'colorful toasts,' even though show policy forbade Indians from drinking alcohol."[78] Rocky Bear may not have been lying to the acting commissioner, for Belt had not asked if the Indians actually drank "whiskey, or fire water," but rather if they were allowed to do so, and Rocky Bear had answered this question quite honestly.

The focus of Belt's questioning then turned to what happened within the exhibition arena. He wanted to know if there was any physical danger in appearing in such shows, and what kind of clothes the Indians wore while performing. When Rocky Bear responded that they wore different kinds of clothes, Belt pushed him further, asking, "Did you appear on exhibition without any clothes on?" Rocky Bear explained, "There is none needed when not cold, but when cold, we wear clothes." To clarify the point the acting commissioner asked again, "I mean when you were exhibiting before the people did you go without clothes?" To which Rocky Bear repeated, "When it was not cold, we did, when it was cold, we did not."[79] Moses speculated that "wearing breechcloth, as far as Belt was concerned, constituted nakedness."[80]

The acting commissioner continued the interview, asking if performing was hard work; if Rocky Bear had asked to be brought home; if they had been attended by a doctor when they were sick; if they were well cared for on the crossing home; if they had exhibited on Sundays; and if they had attended church. Throughout the interview Rocky Bear had answered the acting commissioner's questions. He may have been nominated to speak for the group, or he may have done so because of his supervisory role. In any case, his answers appeared to suggest that Cody and Salsbury had fulfilled their contracts. Belt then stated, "If there is any one here who has any complaint or grievance to make about his treatment, I would like to hear from him." After a pause, with no one making a complaint, Black Heart spoke up saying, "I want to say a few words.... What O'Beirne [assistant superintendent of immigration] has said, that is not to be listened to. What the great father says, that is to be listened to."[81] He then went on to explain to Belt the appeal of exhibition work:

These men have got us in hand. We were raised on horseback; that is the way we had to work. These men furnished us the same work we were raised to; that is the reason we want to work for these kind of men. At the end of every month we drew our salary. What we eat was just the same as the whites eat, and we sit in the camp with them just the same, exactly. When one of our people got sick, we went for doctor; doctor looks at him. If he thinks fit to send him home, send him home right away. If he is able to stay, doctor says keep him there. The company have spent lots of money on us, certainly; that is what we with them for.[82]

Black Heart went on to maintain that the Indians should be allowed to work wherever they chose, as whites did. "If Indian wants to work at any place and earn money, he wants to do so; white man got privilege to do same—any kind of work that he wants. . . . When this show is ready to go again, I want to go with it."[83]

Concluding that the examination was not developing any complaints or grievances, Belt then decided the door should be opened, allowing entry to Salsbury, Burke, and the awaiting reporters. Whether the acting commissioner was persuaded that the charges against Cody and Salsbury were inaccurate, or whether he instead believed that "the Indians had been well prepared," is impossible to say.[84] It is evident that the Indian performers were aware of the accusations made in the press, and both Black Heart and Rocky Bear expressed the desire to continue their work with Cody. They were surely well aware that complaints or accusations against their employers would have had detrimental effects on their future employment. Moreover, the majority of prior complaints of cruelty had been made not against Buffalo Bill, but against Rocky Bear. It seems unlikely that any Indian would have spoken out against him in his presence, or would have risked incurring the wrath of colleagues, if such complaints resulted in the loss of a prized job.

After being granted permission to speak, Salsbury expressed his appreciation to the Indians for their cooperation. Then, perhaps with the ongoing investigation in mind, he counseled them to be on their best behavior when they returned home.[85] Belt concluded the interview by stating that "full opportunity has been given to you to make any complaints of breach of contract, and I have heard no complaints from you, and therefore must assume that these people are filling the contract." Belt also added a note of caution: "You have traveled a great deal and you have learned a great deal. Now you are going back to your reservation, where you will find some little excitement growing out of the religion of your people, who believe in the coming of a new Messiah. They are laboring, we believe and feel that we know, under a great delusion, and as you have learned a great many things we want to ask that you will use your influence and your exertions on the side of the Government . . . to restrain your people from any undue excitement."[86]

The acting commissioner then informed the assembled group that the time had arrived for them to leave, and the Indian performers responded by giving Belt three cheers before departing.[87]

O'Beirne was greatly displeased when he read the newspaper accounts stating that there "was no truth in the charges" and that the Indians insisted that they were well treated. He wrote to the acting commissioner to ascertain whether the investigation had actually taken place and to request a copy of the report.[88] The *New York Press* reported that O'Beirne was dissatisfied with Belt's decision, and that he intended to ask for another examination to be held at Pine Ridge.[89] Belt also doubted that he had managed to get the full facts, and on 24 November he wrote to Daniel F. Royer, the new agent at Pine Ridge. The acting commissioner informed the agent of the details of the case, and went on to say that he desired a further investigation to be made with a view to "eliciting all facts bearing on the subject which it is possible to obtain." To determine whether contracts had been violated, whether the management was liable under its bonds, and the amount of such liability, he instructed the agent to secure affidavits of the returned Indians showing all the facts. This was to be accompanied by a report of the names and whereabouts of all Indians who had left their agency with such shows and had not returned, "with cause of their absence."[90]

Cody himself returned to America on 18 November, aboard the French liner *Normandie*. As soon as Cody stepped ashore, he was met by members of the press who were eager to interview him about the controversy. The *New York World* reported that "Mr. Cody was not at all backward in pronouncing the charges not only false but prompted by malicious motives." Nate Salsbury stated that "the vindication which we received in Washington, when Secretary Noble . . . was convinced that all the charges were unfounded, is perfectly satisfying to us, and I think if Gen. O'Beirne has any sense of manhood he will now come out and openly and publicly admit the injustice of the charges made against us."[91]

Cody felt confident that he had the support of the government, and that his interests coincided with those of the government. "The theory of the government's management of the Indian," he said, "is that he should be made self-supporting. Therefore when I employ Indians and comply with the agreement with Mr. Noble to feed, clothe and pay them for their services, we are advancing in a practical way the ideas of the government." Undaunted, Cody announced that he would procure seventy-five more Indians from Pine Ridge the following spring.[92] However, in an extract from his report printed in the press on 30 November, Secretary Noble gave a rather different impression. He stated that "it has been ordered that no more . . . licenses or contracts shall be made or approved, and that the Indian agents shall exert themselves to prevent and defeat any attempts in the future to take Indians from the reservations or elsewhere for [exhibition] purposes."[93]

On 1 December 1890 Belt wrote to the secretary of the interior informing him of the action taken. He reported that the Indians had made no complaints whatever as to their treatment by their employers and had insisted that they had been well treated. He commented that they "all looked exceedingly well, and manifested attachment for Messrs. Cody, Salsbury and Burke, which I had no reason to suspect was simulated." Yet he felt constrained to pursue the matter further and had instructed agent Royer to make a further examination. Belt wrote that he had no objection to Herbert Welsh or any other representative of the Indian Rights Association attending Royer's investigation, or to Welsh conducting a separate investigation. He concluded, "I must confess that I do not consider that any further action is required." He noted that no reply had yet been received from Royer, presuming the delay to be due to the "prevailing excitement of the ghost dance among the Sioux."[94]

While the management of the Wild West show could perhaps be accused of neglecting its responsibilities toward the Indian employees, the allegations of mistreatment are harder to ascertain. The death rate among the Lakota who traveled with Cody to Europe mirrored that of the majority of Lakota living on the Dakota reservations in the care of the U.S. government, and more precisely the Office of Indian Affairs. The deaths abroad represented roughly 10 percent of the Indian contingent, while the death rate at the Pine Ridge Reservation for the winter of 1889–90 was reportedly "25 to 45 a month in a population of some 5,500" (between 5 percent and 10 percent).[95] Similar accusations of mistreatment and neglect could just as easily have been laid against the government itself. Bishop Hare, a veteran Episcopal missionary among the Lakota, later stated:

> In the year 1890, drought, the worst known for many years, afflicted the western part of South Dakota, and the Indian crops were a total failure. There is ample evidence that, during this period, the rations issued lasted, even when carefully used, for only two-thirds the time for which they were intended. Added to their distress, this period, 1889 and 1890, was marked by extraordinary misfortune. The measles prevailed with great virulence in 1889, the grippe in 1890. Whooping cough also attacked the children. The sick died from want. . . . The people were often hungry, and, the physicians in many cases said, died when taken sick, not so much from disease as for want of food.[96]

Moses noted that "the number of Indians who had died on tour, five from disease and two in accidents, was for Morgan and his friends (indeed, for anyone reading accounts in the newspapers) a shocking statistic that they hoped to turn to their advantage." However, such statistics soon paled into insignificance, for "the death toll—from starvation, exposure, and gunfire—at Pine Ridge reservation within a month of their return would shock the nation."[97]

Nellie Snyder Yost, in her book *Buffalo Bill: His Family, Friends, Fame, Failures, and Fortunes,* commented, "There is an expanded version of Cody's return and his motives." She related that "Tim McCoy remembers the 'autumn evening in 1913' when three or four fellows were grouped around the Colonel at the Irma Hotel listening to him tell stories. In the fall of 1890, Cody said, he had been reading and hearing from visitors about 'Indian troubles' back in his West—about the Ghost Dance popularity, about rumblings among the Sioux. Portents. In the Colonel's estimation things were going to be happening, so he returned to be in on them; it would be good publicity."[98]

Yost cites Tim and Ronald McCoy's *Tim McCoy Remembers the West*, but goes on to note that she asked McCoy "specifically about his understanding of what Cody [had] said that day." McCoy responded "that he had no doubt in his mind that desire for publicity was a major reason for Cody's returning then to the U.S. 'It would,' Cody said, 'give the show a goosing.'" Yost also records that John Burke had written a line in 1911 for the Wichita *Eagle* that could "be interpreted to support this notion."[99]

A similar version appeared in the *New York Herald* in July 1894, when Burke made no mention of any trouble for Buffalo Bill's Wild West, instead suggesting that they returned to Pine Ridge on a peace mission:

> When the news came to us in Europe of the last Sioux outbreak Colonel Cody took the fastest available steamer for America and hastened at once to report at Pine Ridge Agency, and to offer his services as mediator. I was at that time in Strasburg with Black Heart and sixty-five other Indians. We were instructed to return to the reservation with all possible despatch in order that the Indians who were with me might use their influence toward quieting their people and restoring friendly relations with the government. We stopped at Washington, where Commissioner Belt, in the absence of General Morgan told us of the threatening state of affairs on the reservation and asked us to hasten with all speed to the seat of the trouble.[100]

It is apparent that the "story" of the return in 1890 was rewritten over time. It was preferable to claim that the Ghost Dance was disturbing both Cody and the Indian performers, rather than admit that the show was having a crisis over its use of Indians.

It is hard to imagine how Buffalo Bill's Wild West could have continued without Indian performers, for they were crucial to Cody's narrative of the conquest of America. The Indians were used to reinforce

Cody's status as a heroic frontiersman, for the show presented them as formidable barriers to civilization, over whom white America had triumphed in the winning of the West.[101] To give his exhibition an edge that would raise it above ordinary shows, Cody needed the authentic characters his audiences had come to expect. Without the Indians, Buffalo Bill's Wild West would have lost its core component.

Cody's exhibition was not theater in which actors represented individuals by playing characters; such a performance would have been too polished and tame for the Wild West extravaganza. Instead, Cody's show was about excitement and danger, and "the 'realism' of the Wild West helped to intensify the drama . . . [and] heighten the excitement." The Wild West tapped into "the hunger of a broad audience for amusements that set their pulses racing and also reassured them that the rapidly modernizing world was a safe and stable place."[102] These contradictions were, in Joy Kasson's words, "a crucial sign of the Wild West's modernity. Audiences understood that its spectacle was fiction but approved its claims to authenticity. They realized it represented an exaggerated and idealized view of frontier life but thought they were seeing 'the real thing.'"[103]

However, "realism" was also key to the show's educational claims. "The object of the show was not to present a circus performance, but to give a true picture of American frontier life with real characters who had played their part in the history of a portion of the American continent which would soon be a thing of the past."[104]

Not unlike the salvage anthropologists of the day, Cody purported to offer the last glimpses of the "real" or "authentic" to his audiences before they vanished. Furthermore, as Kasson maintained, "the Wild West's great achievement . . . was made possible largely through the contribution of the American Indian performers," who not only brought a perceived element of authenticity to the exhibition, but also played the crucial role of "a counter-force against which the hero displayed his virtues."[105]

Cody's use of Indian performers, and more specifically the image he presented of them, clashed with the idealized image of the Indian championed by reformers. Cody presented, and indeed celebrated, the Indians as wild mounted warriors and hunters of a bygone age. The reformers "wished to foster the ideal of Indians as tamed humans in a tamed land, who were embracing civilization through land allotment, education and industry."[106] Consequently, government officials became concerned about the negative effects on their assimilation programs of Indian participation in Wild West shows.

The Indian performers, who welcomed the chance of employment with Cody's Wild West, did not share the concern of the reformers. On the Indian reservations in the late nineteenth century, even those Indians who had been educated and given a new set of goals and expectations had very few employment opportunities. The government invested little in Indians after educating them, and often it was all but impossible to survive on land not suitable for agriculture. Cody offered the Indian performers a job that appealed to them because it came from the Indians' own experiences, while also guaranteeing them wages, travel, and status—and, perhaps more important, independence from government control.

When the Lakota performers returned to South Dakota, the ban on issuing any more permits to Indians for employment in Wild West shows remained in place. Although they had convinced Acting Commissioner Belt that the management had kept good faith with regard to their contracts, the Indians still faced the possibility of losing a prized job. This must surely have affected their behavior upon their return home. Both the management and the performers were very much aware that the press, then present in significant numbers at Pine Ridge, would be watching their every move and that the journalists' reports would be read throughout the nation. The involvement of the Wild West's personnel in the suppression of the Ghost Dance needs to be viewed against the backdrop of the secretary of the interior's ban and the need to overturn it.

CHAPTER FIVE

SUPPRESSING THE GHOST DANCE AND SAVING BUFFALO BILL'S WILD WEST

Having, in their opinion, successfully refuted the charges made against the management of Buffalo Bill's Wild West, Burke and the forty-five Lakota performers left Washington and headed home to Pine Ridge. Their arrival was eagerly awaited, but upon their return they entered the "charged atmosphere" of the Lakota Ghost Dance. Moses recorded that "one of the ironies is that the Indian Bureau, frequently hostile toward the Show Indians, now expected them to act as harbingers of Euroamerican civilization. . . . The Indian Bureau asked the Show Indians, reviled as symbols of a way of life on the verge of extinction, to explain to their people the nature of things to come . . . [and] persuade their families and friends to awake from their fevered dreams."[1]

Their return coincided with the arrival of the military on the South Dakota reservations, and the trains pulling out of Omaha carried not only the troops but also a group of newspaper reporters from around the country. One such correspondent was C. H. Cressey of the *Omaha Bee*. He commented: "They seem to a certain extent to realize the gravity of the situation, and it is believed they will do much toward restoring quiet. Several of the party had received letters from their friends at Pine Ridge speaking of the Christ and Messiah craze just before they had sailed from Europe."[2]

Bizarrely, in the same article, Cressey also speculated that the returning Indians were plotting an ambush of the train.[3] However, contrary to that imaginative story line, all reports suggest that the returning showmen worked tirelessly in support of the government. According to Carl Smith, the *Omaha World-Herald* correspondent at Pine Ridge, "All Bill Cody's Indians, past and present, are on the right side."[4] Daniel Royer, the Pine Ridge agent, appears to have concurred, as he recruited several of them for the Pine Ridge Indian police force.[5] Others were hired as army scouts at $13 a month plus rations, and "simultaneously the army used [some of] the Wild West show Indians to coax others who had fled the agency to return."[6] Charles W. Allen, the editor of the *Chadron Democrat*, recalled that "the company placed Major Burke at Pine Ridge and he remained through the entire duration of the trouble, looking after the welfare of former employees of the show. His influence in behalf of peace and loyalty to the government was effective. He organized a score of intelligent, upstanding young braves, under the leadership of Black Heart, who were constantly on the alert among the various factions, counseling not only their fellow showmen but others, and reporting everything to him."[7]

Not everyone was so favorable toward Burke and his presence at Pine Ridge. In a confidential letter to Herbert Welsh of the Indian Rights Association, Rev. Charles Cook confided, "It has come to me through the Indians that in this confusion . . . [Burke] is quietly trying to run off Indians to the 'show.' I know the Government *orders,* but these men have managed before to evade all such. I had a real fight of words with him yesterday. I believe he is laying some scheme."[8]

Burke and the Wild West's Indians were not the only ones who became embroiled in the military suppression of the Lakota Ghost Dance, for Cody himself almost stole the show. In the "Report of the Major General Commanding the Army," which appeared in the secretary of war's annual report for 1891, Nelson A. Miles detailed Cody's mission to arrest Sitting Bull: "He was authorized to take a few trusty men with him for that purpose. He proceeded to Fort Yates on the Standing Rock Reservation and received from Lieut. Col. Drum, commanding, the necessary assistance, but his mission was either suspected or made known to the friends of Sitting Bull, who deceived him as to his whereabouts. This had the effect of delaying the arrest for a time."[9]

The official version of events is somewhat misleading, as it was the Standing Rock agent, James McLaughlin, who thwarted Miles's plan, rather than the "friends of Sitting Bull."

Sitting Bull, the Hunkpapa medicine man, was a leading traditionalist with influence among the Lakota. The majority of white Americans held him responsible for the annihilation of George Armstrong Custer and his Seventh Cavalry at the Battle of the Little Bighorn in 1876. In 1890 Sitting Bull lived on the Standing Rock Reservation, where he was a persistent thorn in the side of agent McLaughlin. There is some debate as to whether Sitting Bull was himself an adherent of the Ghost Dance. However, it is clear that he had invited Kicking Bear to come to Standing Rock, after which members of his band became Ghost Dancers. To government personnel, both in Washington and in the West itself, Sitting Bull was a dangerous troublemaker. Some historians have argued that officials seized upon the Ghost Dance religion as an excuse to remove influential traditionalists who opposed the onslaught of white civilization.[10] The medicine man had toured with Buffalo Bill's Wild West for a short season in 1885, and Cody considered himself to be "an old friend of the chief."[11]

In *A Sioux Chronicle*, George Hyde posed the question of "why Cody was chosen for this extremely delicate piece of work."[12] Utley has suggested that "Miles let himself be convinced that, if anyone could capture the Hunkpapa leader, Cody was the man."[13] Cody himself later stated, "I received a telegram to meet General Miles at Chicago to discuss the situation. I had only set foot on American soil a week before, and the upshot of our talk was that I set out . . . to bring in Sitting Bull."[14] Don Russell maintained that "Miles, convinced that he was faced with a widespread Indian war, wanted information about the Bad Lands country, with which Cody was familiar. Whether the mission to Sitting Bull was the purpose of Miles' telegram to Cody or was an afterthought is not clear."[15]

It appears that the two men spent several days discussing the situation, so Cody's decision to go was hardly made impulsively. A Chicago reporter commented: "For two days he has been frequently consulting General Miles about this uprising at Pine Ridge, but as yet has reached no definite decision. . . . 'I don't know yet whether I shall fight them or not. It might not look exactly right for me to do so, for I have made a fortune out of them, but if they get to shedding innocent blood I may, if I can be of any service, go up there.'"[16]

On 24 November 1890 Miles authorized Cody "to secure the person of Sitting Bull and . . . deliver him to the nearest com'g officer of U.S. Troops, taking a receipt and reporting your action." On the back of a visiting card Miles wrote: "Com'd'g officers will please give Col. Cody transportation for himself and party and any protection he may need for a small party."[17] The next day the papers reported that "Buffalo Bill has been ordered to the seat of the trouble." Intriguingly, in the interview Cody stated, "I shall arrive at Omaha on Monday. Thence I shall probably proceed directly to Rushville, thirty-one miles from Pine Ridge." Perhaps this was just a ruse to throw people off the scent of his real mission at Standing Rock, but his ending statements indicate that it was Sitting Bull who was on his mind: "Of all bad Indians, Sitting Bull is the worst. Rock[y] Bear and Red Shirt, who are fighting chiefs, will do whatever is necessary to defeat Sitting Bull. These were with me. Sitting Bull will always be found with the disturbing element. If there is no disturbing element, he will foment one. He is a dangerous Indian and his conduct now portents trouble."[18]

Four days later the press reported that Cody had arrived in "Bismarck on his way to Standing Rock Agency, whence he will go directly to Sitting Bull's camp." The true purpose of his mission had still not been disclosed to the press, which reported that Cody had "been sent to investigate the 'Messiah craze' among the Indians, with almost unlimited authority."[19]

The historian Stanley Vestal maintained that as "the Ghost Dance and the Sioux were front-page news, Buffalo Bill saw a chance to make a grand *coup* and acquire huge publicity for his show."[20] Coming immediately after a summer of bad press for Buffalo Bill's Wild West, this suggestion is perhaps understandable. Cody was joined on his mission by three old friends: Dr. Frank Powell (White Beaver), Robert Haslam (Pony Bob), and John Keith.[21] They arrived by train at Mandan, Dakota, on Thanksgiving, from whence they sent a telegram to Fort Yates "announcing that they would arrive at the fort that night."[22]

James McLaughlin, the Standing Rock agent, was greatly dismayed at this news. He had planned to have the Indian police arrest Sitting Bull on ration day "when all Indians except Sitting Bull came to the agency."[23] He later commented in his autobiography, *My Friend, the Indian*, "The threat came on us like a bolt from the blue. . . . [and] The threat took form in Colonel William F. Cody (Buffalo Bill)."[24] McLaughlin sent a courier to Jack Carignan, a schoolteacher who lived about three miles from Sitting Bull's camp, informing Carignan that he had received the telegram from Cody, and expected the party to arrive later that night.[25] Carignan replied: "I am positive that no trouble need be apprehended from Sitting Bull and his followers, unless they are forced to defend themselves and think it would be advisable to keep all strangers, other than employees, who have business amongst the Indians away from here, as Sitting Bull has lost all confidence in the whites."[26]

Meanwhile, Cody and his party were delayed at Mandan and did not arrive at Fort Yates until 28 November.[27] Upon arrival, Cody presented his authorization to the post commander, Lt. Col. William F. Drum. Drum reported that a "discussion was commenced in regard to the situation, but it was noticed that Col. Cody who asked for whiskey was somewhat intoxicated." The meeting was adjourned to allow Cody a few hours' rest. However, as Drum recorded, "the Colonel continued to drink and was in no condition to attend to business that afternoon and evening."[28] In a letter to Herbert Welsh, Bishop W. H. Hare corroborated this description of Cody's condition, recalling that "Buffalo Bill reached Fort Yates drunk, bearing an autograph letter from Miles authorizing him to capture Sitting Bull. He was kept drunk on his arrival at Yates (justifiably?) and did not get off as soon as he otherwise would have done."[29] The Bishop's comment that "He was kept drunk" perhaps more correctly describes the situation than Drum's official version.

Upon Cody's arrival, McLaughlin had wired the commissioner of Indian affairs, Thomas Morgan. He requested that Miles's order to Cody be rescinded, as "such a step at present is unnecessary and unwise, as it will precipitate a fight." McLaughlin asserted that he had the matter in hand and would have the Indian police arrest Sitting Bull in due course.[30] The commissioner forwarded the telegram to John Noble, the secretary of the interior. Noble then met with President Harrison and the secretary of war. At the same time, Drum wired General Miles, but Miles insisted that Cody should proceed with his mission.[31] Meanwhile officers at Fort Yates conspired to delay Cody until McLaughlin had received an answer. They invited Cody to the Officer's Club with the intention of drinking "him under the table," but as Russell noted, "Cody's *capacity* was such that it took practically all the officers in details of two or three at a time to keep him interested and busy through the day."[32]

Despite their best efforts, Cody was none the worse for wear the next morning, and as no new orders had been received, Drum and McLaughlin made one last effort to dissuade Cody from his plan.[33] Undeterred, Cody set out for Grand River and Sitting Bull's camp at 11 A.M.[34] The press now knew that Cody had been authorized to arrest "the disaffected chief Sitting Bull, and convey him to the nearest military post." Reuters also noted that "trouble is anticipated should an attempt be made to arrest that chief. The troops are quietly preparing for a campaign. Ammunition and rations have been issued, and everything is ready for a move at a moment's notice."[35]

On the night of 29 November Cody and his party camped where the Sitting Bull Road crossed Oak Creek. Only four hours after their departure, McLaughlin had received a telegram from the president repealing Cody's orders. As Cody and his friends made leisurely progress toward Sitting Bull's camp the next morning, they were overtaken by a messenger sent by the agent.[36] The next day the group returned to Fort Yates and a little later started for the railroad. Cody returned to Chicago, where he submitted a claim for $505.60 to cover the transportation costs of himself and his three friends, before heading home to North Platte.

As Louis Pfaller noted, "We can only speculate what might have happened if Buffalo Bill had reached Sitting Bull's camp."[37] Furthermore, it remains unclear how Cody hoped to achieve his aim. Sitting Bull would have accompanied Cody willingly only if it had also suited his purpose—that is, if it was in the best interests of his people. Being unarmed and unsupported by troops or the Indian police, it is very doubtful that Cody would have been able to compel Sitting Bull to leave his home against his wishes.

Cody later stated to European journalists that "jealousy and diplomacy had intervened, and the order for Sitting Bull's arrest was countermanded."[38] In sending his telegram McLaughlin asserted that he had "saved to the world that day a royal good fellow and most excellent showman."[39] Russell remarked that "Cody was apparently unaware of McLaughlin's part in his recall."[40] Instead, Cody believed that it was "some well-meaning philanthropists, who divined a sinister motive in my action . . . [and] impressed President Harrison that it would create a war, ending in the death of Sitting Bull."[41] General Miles was reportedly "furious over the interference of the upstart agent," and was also aware that somehow Colonel Drum had conspired to thwart his plan. His adjutant general wrote confidentially, "If reports are correct, the Division Commander is not entirely satisfied with the action of the military at Fort Yates."[42] This would suggest that when Miles came to write his official version of the event for the secretary of war, he was well aware that it had been McLaughlin and Drum who had thwarted his plan, not "friends of Sitting Bull," as he had implied.

Historians have dismissed this episode as a "comic opera" that was "straight out of vaudeville."[43] Russell commented that "most of those who have written about the incident have considered it the height of absurdity."[44] But he goes on to assert, "It has been popular to ridicule his mission as a publicity stunt, which ignores the point of view of General Miles, who at the moment was far from being interested in promoting Buffalo Bill's Wild West."[45] Leaving aside Miles's motivations for the moment, and taking into account Cody's approach to the whole assignment, which included heavy drinking and hiring old show friends to accompany him, it might appear that he perceived the mission as a none-too-serious jaunt. Coupled with the bad press his Wild West exhibition had been receiving, Cody may have been understandably anxious to secure some good publicity. What better way to get the American public and even possibly the Office of Indian Affairs back on his side, than to capture the old adversary of the U.S. government and help quell the present crisis? Yet, as Russell pointed out, this does not explain Miles's role. Perhaps Miles himself was seeking publicity "to promote his own presidential candidacy" as suggested by Bishop Hare.[46] To be the man responsible for the mission that captured Sitting Bull and ended the perceived rebellion would certainly have raised Miles's national profile.[47] Whatever the motives behind Cody's failed mission, and despite a vigorous campaign waged against them, within a few months Miles and Cody would triumph.

McLaughlin also failed to arrest Sitting Bull "without bloodshed," as he expressly desired. Within two weeks, Miles had issued an official arrest warrant, and on 15 December a squad of Indian police was sent out by McLaughlin to "secure the person of Sitting Bull, using any practical means." The Hunkpapa medicine man was seized from his bed in the early morning. As he was brought out of the cabin, his followers crowded around and tried to rescue him, but in the fight that ensued, he was shot dead, along with eight other members of his band and six Indian policemen.[48]

With the death of Sitting Bull, several of his followers fled south and were taken in by the Minneconjou traditionalist chief Big Foot. But Big Foot's name also appeared on the military's list of influential leaders to be arrested, and on 23 December his band quietly slipped away from the Cheyenne River Reservation and headed south, seeking safety with Red Cloud at Pine Ridge. The Seventh Cavalry intercepted the band five days later, arrested them, and took them to camp at Wounded Knee Creek.

John Shangrau, who had been employed by Buffalo Bill's Wild West as an interpreter on many occasions, was chief of Brig. Gen. John R. Brooke's headquarter scouts.[49] He was present at Big Foot's arrest on 28 December, and on the following morning Colonel Forsyth ordered him to bring the Indians to council in front of the chief's tent. Shangrau translated the demands of Forsyth for the Indians' arms to be surrendered, and tried to persuade Big Foot to comply. Later, Philip Wells replaced Shangrau as Forsyth's interpreter, while Shangrau accompanied Capt. George D. Wallace. They had just completed their search of the village when the fight broke out, Shangrau was chatting with another scout, when they were forced to flee along with the women and children to avoid the crossfire of the soldiers.[50]

sus now biography

Not all Lakota who had been previously employed by Buffalo Bill's Wild West worked to suppress the Ghost Dance. Black Elk, who had been with Cody in England in 1887–88, embraced the new religion, despite having been approached by two policemen urging him to work as a scout. On the morning of 29 December 1890 Black Elk, who was encamped at the agency, heard the shooting at Wounded Knee. He left Pine Ridge with about twenty other young men, and in his own words "started out to defend my people." Black Elk maintained that he led a charge against the soldiers and succeeded in driving them back, engaging the soldiers for most of the day. When it was dark, they headed back to the agency, but were fired upon, so they turned away and took the trail to the main camp of Ghost Dancers on White Clay Creek.[51]

Cody was at home on his ranch in North Platte when news of the massacre spread across the nation. Previously, on 23 November 1889, he had been commissioned a brigadier general as aide-de-camp on the staff of Gov. John M. Thayer of Nebraska, and on 6 January 1891 the governor activated this commission. Thayer requested that Cody "proceed to the scene of the Indian troubles and communicate with General Miles." He was also asked to visit the towns along the Elkhorn Railroad, using his "influence to quiet excitement and remove apprehensions on the part of the people," and to meet with Brig. Gen. L. W. Colby, who was the commanding general of the Nebraska National Guard.[52] Six days after Cody had received his orders from Governor Thayer, Miles informed him that "the entire body of Indians are now camped near here," and that "[n]othing but an accident can prevent peace being re-established. . . . I feel that the State troops can now be withdrawn with safety."[53]

While in Pine Ridge, Cody had met up with John Burke and some of his former Indian employees, and it was from here that Cody began a concerted effort to overturn Secretary Noble's ban and hire more Indian performers for his exhibition. Cody needed real Indians to authenticate his Wild West show and give credence to its educational claims, and fortunately "the Sioux crisis [had] come along and upset the new policy."[54] For the present the military was in control of the reservations from which he would normally recruit his Indian performers, and while he may have had enemies in the Office of

Indian Affairs, Cody had many friends in the War Department, significantly Maj. Gen. Nelson A. Miles.

On 10 January agent Royer completed his report on Cody's Indian performers and sent it on to Acting Commissioner Belt who had requested it two months earlier. Royer reported that the Indians had made no complaints against Buffalo Bill's Wild West, and furthermore since their return "they have all used their influence and shown by their actions that they . . . stood by their government to a man in the late excitement among their people. The great number of them belong[ing] to the Police and scout force."[55] Commissioner Morgan himself was forced to concur that they had learned much in their travels, and praised them for remaining loyal.[56]

The newspapers also praised Cody's Indian performers for their efforts in helping to suppress the Lakota Ghost Dance. On 15 January T. H. Tibbles wrote in the Omaha *Morning World-Herald*:

> A good deal has been said about the Indians who were with Buffalo Bill and I took a good deal of pains to inquire about them, for many of them were the most prominent men among the Indians and they were all on the right side. . . . Their foreign travels have done them good and given them enlarged views. It would be a good thing if the government would employ Colonel Cody to take the whole Sioux nation on a European tour. Bill may not keep a Sunday school . . . but it is a better place than an Indian agency on half rations and nothing to do.[57]

In addition to such public praise, John Burke endeavored to elicit favorable recommendations from other sources. On 15 January Red Cloud signed an open letter of support for Buffalo Bill's Wild West.[58] The following day two more letters arrived that endorsed the Wild West's employment of Indians. The first came from Valentine McGillycuddy, a former Pine Ridge agent. He reported that the Wild West Indians had "sustained the authorities not only incurring the ill will of the hostile element, but risking their lives as policemen and enlisted scouts in defense of the Agency and in endeavor to preserve the peace." He concluded that "their association with you has certainly had a practical civilizing result as their general deportment and costume indicates the addition to the above."[59]

The second letter, written on the day of the Ghost Dancers' surrender, was General Miles's reply to Cody's inquiry as to whether Miles had any objection to him "employing a body of Indians" to accompany the exhibition to Europe in the coming spring. Miles remarked that he knew of no objection, and said that "such a measure would meet with my approval" for the following reasons:

> First: It would give them occupation, and enable them to support themselves and their families.
>
> Second: It would lessen the expense of the Government and lesson the danger of any trouble with these Indians as between them and the Government or the white race.
>
> Third: It would be an educational measure, as it would teach them as no other lesson could do, the power and numerical strength of the white race, and the benefits and advantages of civilization.[60]

Miles's last two points appear to indicate that Cody had proposed to employ the Indians who had recently opposed the government. In the light of his later acquisition of the Fort Sheridan prisoners, it seems that even before the formal surrender, let alone the removal of twenty-seven Ghost Dancers to Fort Sheridan, Cody might have discussed such a proposal with Miles.

On 23 January Burke added another letter to his collection. H. D. Gallagher, the former Pine Ridge agent who had been so dismayed at the poor condition of the returning showman, wrote: "I am glad to learn . . . that the . . . Indians who returned in ill health from Europe have recovered and are working for the Government and enjoying good health. And that it was really a relapse of the influenza they were suffering from and no permanent constitutional ailment, as I at the time feared."[61]

While in Washington to present Lakota grievances to the president, a delegation of Lakota men all signed a document that proclaimed they had "no objection to our young men going with Buffalo Bill's Wild West, as they are well paid and well taken care of in every respect. We believe an Indian should have the right to follow any agreeable employment offered him."[62]

These letters were forwarded to the commissioner of Indian affairs on 26 February 1891, in support of Cody's request for permission to hire seventy-five Indians to accompany him to Europe. Cody laid out the facts as he saw them, starting with a brief résumé of Buffalo Bill's Wild West. He pointed out that the rest of the exhibition's entourage was currently wintering in Germany under the care of Nate Salsbury; the Indians had been returned "at very great expense" in order to satisfy the Office of Indian Affairs. "I think you will find upon inquiry that these Indians, and also those who were with us upon former occasions, have been important factors in producing peace and quiet upon the Sioux reservation during this winter."[63]

Cody specified that he would require sixty adult males, and fifteen women and children. The men would be paid $25 a month, with "Chiefs" receiving between $30 and $60, while the women would earn $10 per month. He asserted that they would be accompanied at all times by an interpreter, and that they would be "shown a disposition to save their money."[64]

Cody stated that it was "highly important that we should be able to procure these Indians as soon as possible," as the company planned to resume its tour in Germany "not later than the 15th of April." Moses noted that Cody "enticed the commissioner with a promise to make his selection from among those Oglalas and Brules who 'might be mischievous in the Spring if allowed to remain upon the reservation.'"[65] He also requested Morgan to "please note that we have an existing unexpired contract (and bond) for two years or longer," claiming that "our immediate return to Europe was only delayed by the late serious trouble in the Sioux country where duty and humanity demanded our presence, personal acquaintanceship and influence in the cause of order and peaceful solution of a dangerous situation, to the extent of our humble ability."[66]

Cody's letter had been written on the letterhead of the U.S. Senate, and was accompanied by one from Senators Charles F. Manderson and A. S. Paddock, with the endorsement of Representatives G. I. Laws and George W. E. Dorsey.[67] The senators' letter began by highlighting Cody's achievements, before going on to support his application. Manderson suggested that "an important factor in the prevention of

further outbreak would be the absence and the profitable employment of some of the Indians who have hostile tendencies." He also
endorsed the Indians' right to work.[68]

The management of Buffalo Bill's Wild West based their argument
on four main points. To begin with, they stood by their past record,
which two investigations had endorsed. Second, they highlighted the
fundamental right and freedom of Indians to contract for employment. Third, the recent military suppression of the Ghost Dance
enabled Cody to illustrate the positive effects upon Indians of participation in his show, and he concluded by suggesting that further hostilities could be avoided by his hiring of potential troublemakers.

Thomas Morgan, the commissioner of Indian affairs, replied to
Senator Manderson on 2 March 1891. Obviously unswayed by the
arguments laid before him, Morgan stated that he could see no reason for changing his views and that the granting of further permits
was "expressly prohibited by the Secretary of the Interior." For Morgan, how Cody and Salsbury had treated the Indians was beside the
point; the key problem lay in the practice of Indians traveling with
Wild West shows. He believed that such practices were "very
demoralizing to them from nearly every point of view."[69]

In contrast to his predecessor, Commissioner Morgan "did not
share Oberly's concern about the freedom of decision of the Indians."[70] He aggressively laid out the facts as he saw them:

> As to the *right of the Indians to enter into employment* (for exhibition
> purposes) in the face of the opposition of this Department thereto. I have
> to say, that the Indians are under the care and pupilage of the Govern-
> ment, which disburses large amounts annually for their support and
> whose strong arm protects their homes and property against the lawless
> element of the dominant whites. . . . The relations thus existing should
> certainly be reciprocal, and should the Indians in defiance of the regula-
> tions of this Department adopted for their protection and welfare, leave
> their reservations for exhibition purposes, they would thereby strike the
> arm which protects and the hand which feeds them, and morally loosen
> the bond upon which they must mainly rely for protection, and they
> would thereby be liable to all proper repressive measures which the
> Government should see fit to adopt.[71]

Morgan concluded his letter with a thinly veiled threat aimed at Cody and Burke. He informed Manderson, in order "that there may be no mistake," that the Pine Ridge agent had been instructed to arrest anyone who was found on the reservation attempting to hire Indian performers for exhibition purposes.[72]

Morgan's victory was short-lived, for on 6 March the acting secretary of the interior informed the commissioner that "[p]ermission is hereby granted Messrs. Cody and Salsbury to engage Seventy-five Indians."[73] The *New York Times* commented that "no amount of evidence that Col. Cody could produce . . . could affect Commissioner Morgan, nor would he listen to the recommendations of Indian agents and Gen. Miles . . . that it would be the best way to prevent a renewal of troubles in the Spring." The *Times* went on to state that "Cody has been here [Washington] a week working hard to prevent the destruction of his show by Morgan's arbitrary act. The matter was finally laid before Secretary Noble, and to-day the Secretary overruled the Commissioner."[74] Three days later Morgan informed the Indian agents on the Dakota reservations of the reversal of policy.[75]

The military suppression of the Lakota Ghost Dance had given Buffalo Bill's Wild West the perfect platform upon which to base its case against the secretary of the interior's ban on permits. Cody was able to demonstrate that, contrary to the assertions that touring with the exhibition was detrimental to Indian assimilation, the Wild West Indians were prominent in their active support of the government. With the accusations of mistreatment and neglect dismissed, Cody was also now able to make an attractive proposition to the government, by offering to take into custody the perceived troublesome element. Without the timely military suppression of the Ghost Dance, Cody's efforts in this direction would have been decidedly more difficult, and without an Indian contingent, Buffalo Bill's Wild West would have lost one of its most successful and popular elements.

Despite the management's outward optimism, the Wild West had taken very seriously the possibility of an Interior Department ban on the employment of Indians. Salsbury had revised the show in anticipation of such a ban. Until March 1891 there was no assurance that the Indians would be allowed to return to Europe, and as their role had been at the core of the show, management had to be prepared for a drastic reorganization. Salsbury had put into effect his idea of a show that "would embody the whole subject of horsemanship," and had recruited equestrians from around the world, creating what was to become known as the Congress of Rough Riders.[76] Cody's success in obtaining the required Indian performers meant that the new show delayed its debut until Buffalo Bill's Wild West returned to London in May 1892.

Cody was particularly keen on hiring a specific group of Indians, namely, the Ghost Dancers whom Miles had confined at Fort Sheridan. This small group of men and women had come to represent "the Hostiles," and as such would be a great asset to the European tour. Richard Slotkin has argued that Buffalo Bill's Wild West had a "commitment to historical authenticity and . . . [a] mission of historical education" vouched for in part by its "use of figures publicly recognized as actual participants in the making of history." Therefore, "authentic historical celebrities," such as the Fort Sheridan prisoners, would "lend credibility and . . . exploit public curiosity."[77] In light of the recent controversy, being entrusted with the Fort Sheridan prisoners would not only give Cody added status but also publicly symbolize the government's seal of approval for Buffalo Bill's Wild West.

Armed with Secretary Noble's permission to hire more Indian performers for his show, Cody traveled to Chicago to lay the proposition before the prisoners. Under the headline "Braves Go to Europe," a Chicago newspaper reported:

> When the Indians saw the handsome and well known face of Buffalo Bill an expression of joy came into their sullen countenances. Upon the instant they arose, and Kicking Bear, who since his imprisonment has been the most morose and uncommunicative of them all, came forward and taking Buffalo Bill's hand said:
>
> "For six weeks I have been a dead man. Now that I see you I am alive again."[78]

After explaining the reason for his visit, Cody asked, "Will you go with me?" The Indians discussed the proposition among themselves, before Kicking Bear replied that he "advised them to go and they will go. I think I may go too."[79] Cody later told reporters that by the time of his planned return to America "in time for the world's fair" in 1893, he was confident that "[a]ll vestige of hostility in the breasts of the Indians will have disappeared."[80]

Hiring the Fort Sheridan Ghost Dancers was a brilliant coup for Cody. The prisoners were given a choice: they could either remain at Fort Sheridan for six months, and then face the possibility of arrest, trial, and imprisonment upon their return to South Dakota, or they could accompany Cody for one year, receive a wage of up to $50 a month, plus expenses, and then be returned to their agency without further consequence.[81] All but four, who were too sick to travel, agreed to go.[82] That the prisoners should choose to tour with Buffalo Bill's Wild West rather than remain at Fort Sheridan is hardly surprising. Cody offered them not only wages, which could go to support their families back home, but also a degree of independence and stimulation, compared to the restrictions and monotony of life at the fort.

General Miles wholeheartedly supported the plan, and sought permission from the War Department on Cody's behalf.[83] The chance to get the Indians out of the country, and at the same time to relieve the army of the trouble and expense of their support, greatly appealed to Miles.[84] He believed that the "experience would be most valuable to them as they would see the extent, power and numbers of the white race, and when they eventually return, would be entirely different men."[85] Miles also contacted Captain Penny, the acting Indian agent at Pine Ridge, suggesting that he should "advise those restless spirits to go with Cody."[86]

Meanwhile, news of Cody's success did not please the Indian reformers, who had greatly welcomed Morgan's actions against Wild West shows. Herbert Welsh of the Indian Rights Association decided to arm himself "with the facts" and wrote to numerous people requesting their opinion of the matter.[87] He had been disturbed to receive information that the Italian press was reporting that Cody planned to bring to Europe "50 of the worst hostile Indians, and will give a Ghost Dance as given on the Plains."[88]

Using information he had gathered, Welsh reported Cody's failed attempt to arrest Sitting Bull to the Indian commissioner, referring specifically to the showman's drunkenness. Welsh concluded his letter to Morgan by observing that "a man of this type is not fitted for the care of Indians," remarking, "I submit this simply for your private information."[89]

When Miles learned of the moves afoot to oppose Cody's hiring of the Fort Sheridan prisoners, he wrote to the adjutant general, urging that the decision not be reversed. He added to his previous arguments that it "also relieves the settlers who are most interested and who would be glad to be relieved from the terror of their presence."[90] On 18 March Cody and Burke were informed that the War Department had no objection to their hiring the Indians "now at Fort Sheridan," provided that the Interior Department did not object.[91]

Mary C. Collins, an Indian missionary, then took up the cause against Cody, taking her case before the relevant parties in Washington.[92] Collins had been sent by the American Board of Congregational Churches to do missionary work among the Lakota, and she had spent twelve years at the Cheyenne River Agency, and four years at Standing Rock.[93] As a result of interviews Collins had conducted with Sitting Bull about his experiences with Cody, she had become "an inveterate opponent to the employment of Indians in Wild West shows."[94]

Collins had learned about the prisoners at Fort Sheridan while visiting the veteran humanitarian, Gen. Oliver O. Howard, at his home in Glencoe, Illinois. Hearing that the Indians were due to join Cody's European tour, and fearing that they were going unwillingly, she inquired into the arrangements. She reported on her visit with the prisoners: "One man said if they remained there they would not receive any pay, and not be allowed any privileges, but that if they went with Buffalo Bill, he and one other man were to receive fifty dollars ($50.00) a month, and all the others each twenty-five dollars ($25.00) a month, and all expenses paid, and they would be able to travel all over the foreign country. They would only have to be gone a year, they could return to the Agency, and the past would be forgotten, and nothing would be done to them."[95]

She returned to the fort the following Sunday, 15 March, to "hold services with them." At which time several of the Indians reportedly begged her "to interfere in their behalf, [as they] did not want to go with Buffalo Bill, but were willing to stay there for six months and then return to Pine Ridge." The missionary promised to see what she could do.[96] Miles was furious when he learned that Collins had given the Indians "the impression that she was going to Washington with a delegation to urge the President to send them back to their reservations." He asserted that the "meddling of people with Indian affairs, who are in no way responsible, has been very annoying and injurious, and I trust that no attention will be paid to them."[97]

On 16 March Collins attended a meeting of Congregational ministers in Chicago, with the intention of consulting with Commissioner Morgan, who had been invited to address the meeting. Morgan assured Collins that he was opposed to the entire matter of Wild West shows, but that he had been overruled by Secretary Noble and felt that he could do nothing more.[98] Collins then addressed the gathering, which was composed of about three hundred "Ministers and business men." Those assembled drafted a resolution "protesting against any man being allowed to go with Buffalo Bill," and then appointed a committee of three and elected Collins as chairman, after which they sent her "to Washington to carry the resolutions to the President."[99]

Three days later Collins met with President Harrison, who informed her that "he had no sympathy with any kind of exhibition of wild Indians" and that he would far rather see "an Indian at his plough than at his war dance." Furthermore, he felt that to allow the prisoners to accompany Cody would be "too much like rewarding the bad boy." The president directed Collins to take the matter before the secretary of the interior. Secretary Noble informed her that he had based his decision on three main factors: Belt's examination of the returned show Indians, which had shown them to be in good condition; the impressive amount of money they had sent home, perhaps as much as $18,000, which led him to conclude that "they had better be off in a show making money than to be at home fighting or doing nothing"; and a letter from the secretary of state, James G. Blaine, who had seen the show in England and had found "nothing objectionable in it." When Collins quizzed him about the Fort Sheridan prisoners, Noble replied that "they are under the War Department, and I have nothing to do with them."[100]

Collins's next port-of-call was the secretary of war, but finding him absent, she instead met with Acting Secretary Lewis Addison Grant. Grant promised to look into the matter, and he reassured Collins that prisoners who did not want to go could remain. He went on to state: "[The] Department had not been consulted in regard to bringing in the prisoners, they did not know what the Indians had done, why they were prisoners, [nor] for how long they were to be made prisoners."[101]

Grant assumed "that there were about forty of them [who had been the] leading men in the late trouble," and was reportedly astonished to learn that there were instead only "twenty-seven, among them boys and women." He pointed out that it was Secretary Noble who had suggested the Fort Sheridan Indians should go, and that the War Department "had simply allowed it."[102]

Acting Commissioner Belt was the next to receive a visit from Mary Collins. The missionary advised him of what Secretary Noble had said, but Belt informed her that "he was thoroughly opposed to Buffalo Bill taking any Indians." Collins now felt that she had "the sympathy of all except the Secretary of the Interior." She returned to the acting secretary of war. Grant advised her "that he himself would go to the President, and if the President gave him permission he would countermand the order."[103] He added that with regard to the Ghost Dancers now at Fort Sheridan, "perhaps Gen. Miles might now think that he had made a mistake in bringing these men in and that he had them on his hands and did not know what to do with them and so thought this the best method of getting rid of them."[104]

Unfortunately, we have only Collins's version of these events. On 21 March Grant had forwarded to the president a copy of Miles's telegram "protesting against the interference of irresponsible parties who seek to influence the President."[105] However, despite Collins's optimism, the permission granted to Cody was never rescinded. Yet while Collins and her fellow reformers failed, the episode illustrates the high profile and significance of the controversy, and reveals that high-ranking government officials, including the president himself, found time to take part in the debate.

In her report to the members of the Congregational Club, Collins suggested that the "prisoners" should be turned over to the eastern schools. Having visited Gen. Samual Chapman Armstrong at Hampton Institute, she found that he was more than willing to take the Indians as students.[106] She also met with Herbert Welsh in Philadelphia, who "could hardly believe that in the face of so strong a protest and of all the facts, that the President would not interfere." Collins remained confident that her work had "not been in vain and that He who knoweth the end from the beginning will bring our desires to pass."[107]

On 26 March Capt. Charles Penny, the acting Indian agent at Pine Ridge, forwarded to Morgan the complete list of Indians to be employed by Buffalo Bill's Wild West, including those to be taken from Fort Sheridan.[108] On 28 March the Indians recruited at Pine Ridge left for Chicago by "special train."[109] Two days later twenty-three of "the Indian prisoners," accompanied by John Shangrau, who had acted as their interpreter the whole time they had been at Fort Sheridan, were released into the custody of Cody's representative, John Burke.[110] Cody was instructed to inform the War Department when the prisoners terminated their employment with him, as they would not be permitted to return to their reservations without official permission.[111]

Four Indians now remained at Fort Sheridan: Little Horse, Takes the Shield Away, His Horse's Voice, and White Beaver.[112] The post surgeon reported on 6 April that three of the four were sick. In the absence of an interpreter he found it impossible to give them proper medical treatment and therefore recommended that they be returned home at once.[113] Brigadier General Brooke, who remained in charge of the Department of the Platte, did not think it wise to return the four men just yet, and advised against such a course of action.[114] Instead, Louis Shangrau, John Shangrau's brother, was temporarily employed as an interpreter.[115]

Mary Collins attempted to visit the remaining Lakota men at Fort Sheridan, but was stopped by the commandant of the fort. She informed Herbert Welsh that "John Young an Indian at school at Highland Park, reports them in a deplorable condition, and others, white people, who have visited them say they are terribly neglected."[116]

She urged Welsh to "take hold of the case," and in response, Matthew Sniffen, the clerk of the Indian Rights Association, forwarded

Collins's letter to Commissioner Morgan.[117] Morgan was advised by
Secretary Noble to return the letter to Welsh, "with the information
that they will no doubt receive attention if they are sent directly to
the Secretary of War, whose action they criticize and whose attention
the subject needs."[118] On 30 April, the four remaining Ghost Dance
prisoners held at Fort Sheridan were released, and Louis Shangrau
escorted them back to Pine Ridge.[119]

Not only had Cody succeeded in getting his Indian performers, but
also he had managed to hire genuine participants from the latest
episode of Western history. He lost no time in making the most of this
coup when it came to publicizing the show. But even after Buffalo Bill
and the Indians left for Europe, the debate over their employment
continued to rage in America. On 26 March the *Christian Register* had
run an editorial entitled "Stop the Farce," which attacked the government for allowing Cody to acquire more Indian performers for
his exhibition, specifically the Fort Sheridan prisoners. "There are
twenty-seven prisoners now at Fort Sheridan who took part in the
recent fight at Pine Ridge. It will undoubtedly add something to
[Cody's] receipts . . . but if the government . . . sends these Indians off
on such an expedition, it will become party to a shameful and foolish
enterprise. If these Indians are guilty of bringing about the recent disturbance, they may properly be tried and sentenced for the offence. If
they are guiltless, they should be set free."[120]

Collins and Welsh wrote to various people canvassing support
and maintaining their campaign in opposition to Buffalo Bill's Wild
West. Welsh believed that their major obstacle was the secretary of
the interior, "whom we have found highly unsatisfactorily. Hon.
Morgan is anxious to do the right thing, but Noble is more affected
by other considerations than by interest in the welfare of the Indians."[121] Welsh continued to urge friends and associates to petition
the president, believing that he also shared their views.[122]

Welsh wrote to Morgan on 3 April stating that he was preparing a
statement for the public and wished to know "whether the Government has definitely and positively granted Mr. Cody authority to take
the Indians?"[123] Welsh was too late, for Cody and the Indians had left
the country two days before. Undaunted, Welsh wrote a letter to the
editor of the *New York Evening Post* entitled "Demoralizing the Indi-

ans," which was based on information received from Mary Collins. The letter, written on 9 April and published on 27 April, detailed Collins's account of the attempts to have Cody's permission rescinded. Overall, it was a damning indictment of the government.

> And thus the Government put itself into the position of assisting a private speculation, and gave Indians to an exhibition under the inducement that their alleged evil deeds would be forgotten and justice would not reach them. What an admirable object-lesson to the evil-doer on the one side and the loyal Indian on the other! The evil-doer gets $25 a month, a foreign trip, and freedom from punishment as the reward for treason, thieving, and possibly murder, while the peaceable man remains at home in poverty and contemplation as to the true significance of the white man's ways. . . . What are the residents of other countries to think of our methods of dispensing justice, and what shall we ourselves think of them! Since the highest official authorities in the country have in vain been applied to, we now turn to that court of last appeal, the public sentiment of the people of the United States.[124]

On 3 June the Indian Rights Association addressed a letter to the secretary of the interior outlining its opposition to the use of Indian performers in Wild West shows. In the letter the association asked that Noble reconsider the decision to grant permits for Indians to go with Wild West exhibitions, arguing that the practice was the antithesis of the government's policy of assimilation. Although the government could not prevent any Indian who was a citizen or who lived outside of an reservation from joining such exhibitions, the association believed that reservation Indians were different, as the government could prevent them from leaving. Furthermore, the commissioner could also use his powers to remove anyone from the reservations who was there without authority, or whose presence could be deemed detrimental to the peace or welfare of the Indians. The association then went on to consider the case of the Fort Sheridan prisoners, arguing strongly against Cody's use of them. "Such a course must tend to create in the minds of those who have been guilty of disorder or violence the belief that the Government does not disapprove their conduct, and that it will lead the peaceable and law-abiding Indians to the equally unfortunate conclusion that the Government, while indifferent to them, will reward evil doers."[125]

While the Wild West exhibition was in Duisburg, Germany, Salsbury read Welsh's letter "Demoralizing the Indians" in the *New York Evening Post* and wrote to the editor himself on 18 May. Salsbury enclosed a letter to Herbert Welsh and asked the editor "in the interest of truth and justice" to publish his reply. He went on to assert that "Mr. Welsh is malicious and untruthful in his attack and I do not imagine the *Evening Post* desires to be a party to persecution."[126] The editor forwarded Salsbury's reply to Welsh on 2 June.

Salsbury's anger is clearly visible in his letter, and the forcefulness with which he impugns Welsh and Collins is perhaps due to his frustration that the negative stories and attacks of the previous summer were continuing. He began by refuting specific charges made by Collins. With regard to "Sitting Bull's son" acquiring "vile habits and physical disease with Buffalo Bill's Wild West," Salsbury responded that Sitting Bull's son had never traveled with the show. He also challenged Collins and Welsh to provide evidence that Cody had advertised in a London paper that he was bringing with him some of the worst element of hostiles from the late trouble. "As to the prisoners who were at Fort Sheridan, let me give you this information; that they are as well behaved as any Indian Peace Commissioner I ever knew, and abide by all the rules and regulations of the camp with cheerfulness and fidelity to their contracts. For look you, Mr. Welsh, we have rules and regulations, and we enforce obedience to them from all our employees, white or red."[127]

As an illustration of the falseness of the claims made against the exhibition's treatment of its Indian contingent the previous summer, Salsbury informed Welsh that "No Neck is *now* the chief of our Indian Camp police. Otakta [Kills Plenty] died in New York of lingering consumption, from which he had suffered for years, and so much did White Horse resent his treatment by us, that he not only returned to our employ, but brought his father, a man *eighty-one* years old, with him. The old man seems to enjoy a clean bed, a good suit of clothes and three square meals a day."[128]

The tone of Salsbury's letter is scathing. Perhaps the management of Buffalo Bill's Wild West perceived that Herbert Welsh posed more of a threat than O'Beirne had.[129] As secretary of the Indian Rights Association, Welsh certainly had more influence, and therefore Salsbury is likely to have felt that the story had to be quashed.[130] That Collins erred in her testimony would also have given Salsbury both confidence and ammunition to attack her and undermine her allegations.

Undoubtedly stung by Salsbury's caustic reply, Welsh swung into action. He wrote to people who knew Collins, suggesting that he felt honor-bound to respond to the charges made against her, and he inquired into her "reliability as a witness" and "her general character for trustworthiness." At the same time, he maintained that "there is nothing in Mr. Salsbury's letter which affects the validity of our position . . . namely, the propriety of the Government permitting reservation Indians to join wild west shows." In a letter to the Standing Rock Agent, James McLaughlin, he asked, "Will you kindly inform me as to any mis-statements of fact made in my letter," noting that if he were in error he would gladly withdraw his statement.[131]

The following day, 4 June, Welsh wrote to Mary Collins and forwarded her a copy of Salsbury's letter. He requested that at her earliest convenience she answer the charges against her, and he requested an exact copy of the newspaper clippings she had made reference to.[132] Welsh also wrote to the editor of the *New York Evening Post*, inquiring "if the Salsbury letter is to be published and if so on what date," but the editor reassured him that he had no plans to publish the letter.[133]

Welsh heard from Agent McLaughlin on 12 June that Miss Collins "is a lady of high respectability, truthful and conscientious," but that she had erred in stating that Sitting Bull's son had traveled with Cody. None of Sitting Bull's sons had traveled with Buffalo Bill's Wild West. The "depraved individual" Collins referred to was Louie Sitting Bull, a step-son of the medicine man, "raised by the latter until quite a youth." The agent went on to assert that while "Louie Sitting Bull's general character is as Miss Collins stated," Cody was in no way responsible for it as he had "never been on exhibition or in any way connected to a traveling show." While disapproving of the practice of allowing Indians to join exhibitions, McLaughlin felt he had to state that the Indians who traveled with Cody "always spoke in the highest terms of the treatment they received . . . and never mentioned to me of their having gotten whiskey or visited low places."[134] Collins also replied to Welsh, admitting that she no longer had the newspaper clipping, as she had given it to the acting secretary of war who had failed to return it. She also conceded that she had erred in her statement regarding Sitting Bull's son.[135]

Welsh was unperturbed, and perhaps more determined than ever to make a stand against Wild West shows in general and Cody and his company in particular. On 26 June he wrote to Collins reassuring her that her mistake was "comparatively trifling," but again asked about the missing newspaper clipping. His closing words revealed his resolve not to be beaten: "In the meanwhile, please gather for me any further information which you consider thoroughly trustworthy regarding the Buffalo Bill matter. Cannot you get for me some statement from reliable persons at Standing Rock concerning the facts in the case of Buffalo Bill's visit to Ft. Yates last autumn for the purpose of arresting Sitting Bull?"[136]

Buffalo Bill and the Wild West's Indian performers would not have become involved in the suppression of the Ghost Dance had they not been forced to return to America to refute the charges of mistreatment and neglect. Their involvement was motivated by the need to overturn the secretary of the interior's ban and preserve the Lakotas' right to be employed as performers in Wild West shows. While the Wild West Indians would no doubt have been equally concerned with the plight of their people, the ability to gain employment with Cody's Wild West and be guaranteed a good wage and regular food was obviously important to them. There would be no such guarantee if they were forced to remain on the reservations, where work was rare and government annuities were poor and scarcely sufficient. At the close of the military suppression of the Lakota Ghost Dance the management of Buffalo Bill's Wild West was able to illustrate to the government the positive effects on the Indians of touring with the exhibition and to secure the show's position as an Indian employer. By disarming the arguments of the reformers, the Wild West protected the Indians' right to work on their own terms at a job of their choice, not as assimilated Americans, but as American Indians.

To crown the success of overturning the secretary of the interior's ban, Cody employed twenty-three of the Fort Sheridan prisoners. Buffalo Bill's Wild West could now boast of a unique attraction to pique the curiosity of potential audiences. And having the government sanction Cody as the custodian of reputedly dangerous Indians bolstered his status as an Indian employer. The decision of the Ghost Dancers to accompany Cody on his tour of Europe rather than remain at Fort Sheridan is hardly surprising. Cody offered not only wages and status, but also a good deal more stimulation and independence than was available either at the fort or on the reservations. Yet it was Cody's hiring of the prisoners that motivated the Indian Rights Association to renew their efforts to make Indian employment in Wild West shows a thing of the past. Despite its best efforts and influence, the Indian Rights Association failed to end Indian employment in Wild West shows, and instead turned its attention to creating alternate public images of Indians.[137]

The controversy and debate over Indian participation in Wild West shows illustrates that the Indian reformers wanted to do more than make the Indians self-supporting; they wanted to remake the Indians' very identity. The reformers' ethnocentrism led them to view the Indians as inferior and childlike, incapable of knowing how best to help themselves, and therefore in need of the guidance of benevolent humanitarian reformers. This paternalistic perception motivated the reformers' and policymakers' opposition to Indians exhibiting in Wild West shows. It is clear from the debate over Cody's employment of Indian performers that what the Indians wanted was beside the point, as the reformers doubted the Indians' competency to judge for themselves. Reformers hoped to promote a specific reconstructed image of American Indians based on an idealized concept of white Christian Americans, and deplored anything that might jeopardize this notion or their process of "civilization."

"SHORT BULL," CHIEF.

Tous ces Indiens que dont je t'envoie les portraits sont des vrais personnages.

Short Bull, c. 1891. The handwritten message in French affirms, "All these Indians whose portraits I am sending you are real people." Author's collection.

"KICKING BEAR."

Kicking Bear, c. 1891. The handwritten message in French comments, "How handsome he is with his civilized cravat! A little girl who saw the image said, 'I know why he wears a feather in his hair. It is because he is going to get married!'" Author's collection.

Sitting Bull and William F. Cody (Buffalo Bill), photographed by A. William Notman, 1885. Buffalo Bill Historical Center, Cody, Wyoming; P.69.1493.

Black Heart, a veteran performer with Buffalo Bill's Wild West who spoke in defense of an Indian's right to work for such shows. Buffalo Bill Historical Center, Cody, Wyoming; Vincent Mercaldo Collection, P.71.609.

"Indian Chiefs and U.S. Officials." At Pine Ridge Agency, 16 January 1891, Lakota leaders pose for a photograph with Buffalo Bill, John Burke, and journalists. *Standing, left to right:* Dent H. Robert of the *St. Louis Post-Dispatch*, Rocky Bear, Good Voice, Two Lance, Two Strike, William F. Cody, Crow Dog, High Hawk, Short Bull, John Burke. *Sitting, left to right:* Thunder Hawk, American Horse, George Crager, John McDonough of the *New York World*, Young Man Afraid of His Horses, Kicking Bear, J. C. Worth. Library of Congress, Photoduplication Service, LC-USZ62–17608.

"The Fighting Chief, Kicking Bear and Staff, Campaign 1891, Pine Ridge."
Buffalo Bill Historical Center, Cody, Wyoming; Ms6.6.A.1.10.

Nineteen of the twenty-seven Ghost Dancers removed to Fort Sheridan, Illinois, at the close of the military suppression of the Lakota Ghost Dance. *Standing, left to right:* Brave, Take the Shield Away, Brings the White, Knows His Voice, One Star, Close to Home, Standing Bear, Lone Bull, Standing Bear, Scatter, Sorrell Horse, Horn Eagle, High Eagle. *Sitting, left to right:* Crow Cane, Medicine Horse, Call Her Name, Kicking Bear, Short Bull, Coming Grunt. Unidentified photographer; courtesy of Colorado Historical Society, F-2562 10028432.

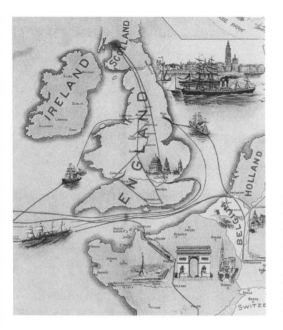

Detail taken from Wild West show poster "From Prairie to Palace, Camping on Two Continents," which shows the route of the 1891–92 tour of Britain by Buffalo Bill's Wild West. Buffalo Bill Historical Center, Cody, Wyoming; Gift of the Coe Foundation; 1.69.167.

Part of the encampment of Buffalo Bill's Wild West exhibition, Chicago, 1893, showing the Indians' living quarters on left. Buffalo Bill Historical Center, Cody, Wyoming; Vincent Mercaldo Collection, P.71.186.

Indians in the encampment at Buffalo Bill's Wild West exhibition, London, Earl's Court, 1892. Buffalo Bill Historical Center, Cody, Wyoming; P.69.987.

Short Bull, from the 1891–92 program of Buffalo Bill's Wild West that was used during the British tour. He is identified as "Brule Sioux,—Leader of the Ghost Dancers, 'High Priest' of the 'Messiah Craze.'" Mitchell Library, Glasgow.

"SHORT BULL"—Brule Sioux,—Leader of the Ghost Dancers, "High Priest" of the "Messiah Craze."

Kicking Bear, illustration from the 1893 program of Buffalo Bill's Wild West. Buffalo Bill Historical Center, Cody, Wyoming; Ms6.6.A.1.10.

Young "Johnny Burke No Neck," from the 1891–92 program for Buffalo Bill's Wild West. The boy is identified as having been "found on the Battle Field of Wounded Knee after the annihilation of Big Foot's Band." Buffalo Bill Historical Center, Cody, Wyoming; Ms6.6.A.1.10.

Show Indians watching the performance, Nottingham, 1891. Buffalo Bill Historical Center, Cody, Wyoming; gift of Jess Frost, P.69.1918.

Kicking Bear, photographed by D. F. Barry. Kicking Bear maintained his belief in the Ghost Dance, returning in 1902 to see Wovoka for a second time. Buffalo Bill Historical Center, Cody, Wyoming; Vincent Mercaldo Collection, P.71.664.

Short Bull dressed in his Ghost Dance shirt, photographed by Frederick Weygold, c. 1909. Museum für Völkerkunde, Hamburg.

CHAPTER SIX

THE WILD WEST SHOW'S 1891–1892 TOUR OF BRITAIN

On 1 April 1891 the SS *Switzerland* sailed from Philadelphia carrying personnel associated with Buffalo Bill's Wild West, including seventy-five Lakota Indians. These men and women were traveling to Europe to resume the Wild West's first tour of the European continent, which had begun in the spring of 1889.[1] The majority of the Indian performers had been hired from the Pine Ridge and Rosebud Reservations in South Dakota.[2] Twenty-three others had traveled down from Fort Sheridan, Illinois, where General Miles had confined them since late January.[3] Shortly after their arrival in Antwerp, the new contingent of Indian performers met up with the rest of the cast, who had been wintering in Alsace-Lorraine, and the show continued where it had left off the previous autumn. After a brief tour through Germany, Holland, and Belgium, the Wild West then sailed from Antwerp to Grimsby, and in the last week of June 1891 the tour of provincial England opened at the Cardigan Fields in Leeds.[4]

The 1891–92 tour of Britain by Buffalo Bill's Wild West was significantly different from the show's previous visit to the country in 1887, when the performers had appeared as part of Queen Victoria's Golden Jubilee celebrations with the American Exhibition at Earls Court in London. Generally regarded as the "chief attraction" of the American Exhibition, the show was an enormous success and Cody became "the hero of the London season."[5] When ticket sales declined, the show moved on to visit Manchester and Birmingham before returning to America in 1888. The 1891–92 sojourn differed in two respects. First, it toured the principal towns of England and made its first visit to Wales and Scotland before finally arriving in London for a summer season, thus bringing to a much larger British audience their "image" of the American West. Second, and perhaps more significant, it featured the presence of twenty-three Lakota Ghost Dancers, who were perceived by the majority of the British public to be "hostages" or "prisoners of war." The presence of the Ghost Dancers made this tour by Buffalo Bill's Wild West unique.

The exhibition was "organized around a series of spectacles which purported to re-enact scenes portraying different 'Epochs' of American History." Following the "Primeval Forest," peopled only by Indians and wild animals, the story of conquest was portrayed.[6] The Indians played the role of the "hostiles," representing "the Other" against whom the progress of white civilization was measured. This message was strengthened by the audiences' awareness—reinforced by publicity for the show—that some of the Indian performers were "prisoners" of the U.S. government. The *North British Daily Mail* concluded that "there could not be better specimens of the untamed courageous sons of the prairie."[7]

The notoriety of the Ghost Dancers was used by Cody to pull in the crowds. Their presence added authenticity to what was purported to be educational entertainment. Cody's own role as custodian enhanced his status among the British public. The Brighton *Argus* suggested that "the privilege accorded to Colonel Cody of taking these famous warriors on tour with him is an unique one, and . . . granted solely in consequence of the great services he has . . . rendered his country."[8]

It is perhaps one of the greatest ironies of American Indian resistance that the last Lakota to have forcibly resisted the government of the United States were released into Cody's care where they proceeded to act the very "roles" ascribed to them a year earlier. Commenting on Short Bull's appearance in the Wild West, one British journalist remarked: "In the spectacle of this leader of a vanquished people exhibited to the gaze of the multitude in the arena we seem to find a modern parallel to that experience of Caractacus, who, exiled from his island home, was exposed to the gaze of the Roman populace."[9]

The Indians removed to Fort Sheridan were the only living Lakota Ghost Dancers to be punished. In the words of historian George Hyde, "their punishment was a queer one"—but perhaps not altogether surprising.[10] In a letter to the editor of the *Daily Graphic* (London) on the subject of the slaughter of Big Foot's band at Wounded Knee, R. B. Cunninghame Graham, the Liberal member of Parliament for North West Lanark had sarcastically, yet prophetically, commented: "It seems a pity . . . to waste so many good Indians who might have been so advantageously used to turn honest pennies for enterprising showmen, if no other method of utilising them occurred to the great American Republic."[11]

The second visit to Britain by Buffalo Bill's Wild West began with a long tour of the populous industrial cities. The show gave two performances daily, "come rain or shine." Starting in the north of England the show progressed down through the Midlands, across to Wales, and then finally along the southern coast. The whole exhibition was transported about the country by three or four specially commissioned trains.[12]

As a preliminary to the daily exhibitions, a parade through the principal thoroughfares took place on Monday morning, to whet the public's appetite.[13] The route of the parade was publicized along with the show's main advertisement, which was usually to be seen on the front page of every newspaper of the towns visited. The spectacle announced the arrival of Buffalo Bill's Wild West to its potential audience, a point not lost on a Brighton newspaper, whose reporter commented, "the sight was certainly worth witnessing and calculated to heighten the interest for what was to follow."[14]

The show always opened on a Monday. The first of the two daily performances took place at 3 P.M., the second at 8 P.M. Members of the public were encouraged to arrive early to view the whole of the encampment.[15] Of greatest interest was the "Indian Camp"; the press and the show management encouraged the public to wander through and view the living quarters and arrangements of the Indians.[16] At 3 P.M., the playing of the cowboy band signaled the start of the entertainment, and the ensuing exhibition closely followed the tried and tested formula that had been so successful in both America and Europe.

The exhibition appealed to both young and old, and was accessible to all sections of the community. Tickets were priced from 1 shilling to 4 shillings, the latter for a seat in the grandstand, and altogether 15,000 seats were available at each performance. By taking Buffalo Bill's Wild West on a tour throughout the country, Cody was able to present his image of the West to potentially well over 4 million people, a much wider British audience than in 1887.[17]

The summer tour of provincial England was plagued by bad weather, which put to the test the show's promise to perform "come rain or shine." Overall, the torrential downpours do not appear to have dampened the public's enthusiasm to see the show.[18] At the same time, there can be no doubt that the inclement conditions to some extent marred the enjoyment of the exhibition. In Nottingham, "the rain was so heavy that it was with difficulty that the performers were seen at times."[19] Despite their own discomfort, the spectators were filled with admiration for the performers who persevered throughout. The *Sheffield and Rotherham Independent* recounted: "the rain descended in one very heavy, open torrent, and occasionally there were claps of thunder. But still the performance went on, and the Indians on parade covered their heads and smiled; they had got used to this common sample of our weather."[20]

By October the bad weather was beginning to take its toll, and in Portsmouth the press suggested that it "constituted a drawback to the entire prosperity of the visit." Cody was reported as commenting, "If our experiences of the weather were all like those at Portsmouth, we should have shut up and gone home."[21] Worse was to come in Brighton when great damage was caused by a gale, which destroyed a large portion of a huge structure that was being erected for Buffalo Bill's Wild West. The continued high winds forced the management to cancel the exhibition for two days, the first performances lost since the Wild West had arrived in England.[22]

Not surprisingly, the Indians found the British climate to be very trying. A reporter for the *Sheffield and Rotherham Independent* commented: "They want to know when are we going to have summer. They can stand intense heat and intense cold, but the moisture in our heavily laden atmosphere is too much for them. . . . I was a privileged visitor on Tuesday to some of their tents. In one was an Indian suffering severely from rheumatism brought on I imagine by exposure to damp and whose spirits were greatly depressed."[23]

The weather became the chief topic of conversation in the Wild West camp, among Indians and whites alike. Cody was quoted as saying, "The most interesting thing I can talk about is the weather. This is the first fine day we have had for eight weeks." Johnnie Baker, one of the show's marksmen, stated that "England he liked, but not England's climate"—a sentiment echoed by Short Bull, who remarked, "I like the English people but not their weather as it rains so much."[24] Luther Standing Bear recalled in his book *My People, the Sioux* the difficulties of performing outdoors during an English summer. "In some places in England I have seen those fogs so thick that one could not see across the arena in which we were giving our performance, and we had to ride very close to our audiences so they could see what we were doing. We suffered very much from wet feet, as we wore moccasins, which are not made for wet weather."[25]

The tour did enjoy some good weather, and in Bristol it was estimated that 100,000 people paid a visit to the show grounds during "a particularly fine week."[26] Unfortunately, pleasant atmospheric conditions also had a downside, as was witnessed in Nottingham on the last day of the show's visit. A tremendous crowd of 20,000 people gathered, owing to the fine weather and special trains bringing in spectators from all parts of the surrounding countryside. At three o'clock the approaches to the exhibition were thronged, every seat was occupied, and the pressure was reportedly "enormous." During Annie Oakley's performance of sharpshooting a portion of a stand collapsed "and 500 or 600 people were precipitated to the ground." The *Nottingham Daily Express* reported that "happily, although there were minor casualties, there was only one spectator seriously injured."[27] When the show moved on to Leicester, the management of the Wild West took measures to reassure the public "as to the absolute safety of the seating arrangements," by inviting the Borough Surveyor to inspect and satisfy himself that "everything possible had been done . . . for the protection of the public."[28]

Despite the forces of nature, which may have seemed to conspire against Buffalo Bill's Wild West, the show did make money. The greatest returns were in Cardiff, where in one week it drew in

170,000 spectators, which brought in £10,000 from ticket sales.[29] Once again the last day of the show attracted huge crowds of over 37,000 people. So great was the desire to see Buffalo Bill's Wild West that when all available space within the enclosure was occupied, "officials had to refuse offers of 20s[hillings] for standing room."[30] In Sheffield Cody's profit for the week was £1,500, and even on one of the wettest afternoons in Nottingham the exhibition took £600 at the door.[31]

There were also economic benefits for the towns that Buffalo Bill's Wild West visited. The *Bristol Evening News* recorded that "excursion trains . . . carried thousands of our country neighbours yesterday morning into the city . . . and tradesmen . . . must surely feel indebted to Buffalo Bill for bringing in trade for them as well as for the Wild West Exhibition."[32] The *Sheffield and Rotherham Independent* also commented that the visit of the Wild West "caused some hundreds of pounds to circulate," further noting that "the cab and carriage proprietors having been among those who have largely benefited by it."[33] In Nottingham so many people came into the town "by excursions, that the theatres have turned money from the doors . . . some of the eating houses have been laid as bare as Mother Hubbard's cupboard; and the bus fares have been put up to twopence."[34] Local publicans were also enabled to cash in, by applying for temporary licenses "to sell intoxicating liquors from 11am to 10pm at the Buffalo Bill's 'Wild West' show."[35]

At the start of every performance thousands of British spectators eagerly awaited Cody's presentation of the conquest of the American West. The part played by the Indians was central to the whole exhibition, their primary role being to attack whites. Richard White has observed that "in Cody's story Indians were vital. The scout, a man distinguished by his 'knowledge of Indians' habits and language, familiar with the hunt, and trustworthy in the hour of extremest danger,' took on meaning only because he overcame Indians. . . . [And] Buffalo Bill made the conquest of savages central."[36] A reporter for the *Leeds Daily News* remarked that the Indians seemed not to "have any other function in life than to be defeated." He went on to suggest "with the utmost diffidence . . . that the Indians should have a chance for once in a way. Too much defeat of the Red Man is apt to become monotonous."[37] Yet Buffalo Bill's Wild West did not always represent the Indians as being the vanquished; occasionally they were presented as powerful and formidable barriers to the march of civilization.

When the exhibition traveled north to Glasgow for the winter season, Nate Salsbury revived Steele MacKaye's indoor pageant "The Drama of Civilization," which was originally written for the Wild West show when it performed at Madison Square Garden in New York.[38] The pageant depicted "notable events in American history" and consisted of six "epochs." One could argue that the fifth epoch cast the Indians as victors, in depicting the defeat of Custer at the Little Bighorn.[39] The *Glasgow Evening News* gave the opinion that this episode was "perhaps the finest of the series"—a thought echoed by the *Glasgow Herald*, whose correspondent remarked, "The fall of General Custer formed one of the most striking series of pictures shown during the evening."[40] Kasson astutely noted that "by presenting an episode from frontier history that did not end happily, the Wild West risked contradicting its promise of triumphant conquest. Yet in the show as in the battle itself, the death of Custer gave advocates of expansionism a martyr whose death could justify their cause. And Custer's death did not end the performance: Buffalo Bill galloped in, too late to rescue Custer but poised to continue the work of conquest."[41]

Unlike many contemporary interpretations of the history of America, Cody's show acknowledged the history of the continent before the arrival of the Europeans.[42] The first epoch of the drama was set in "the primeval forest, before the advent of Cortez and his faithful horse, when the redman had the place all to himself."[43] The *North British Daily Mail* related that following the opening "parade of the celebrities . . . a realistic view of a primeval forest in America is given. Here the spectators, one might say, are startled with a rush of Red Indians, who bear down on the central part with great speed and a whooping cry. They divide and pass out by side exits almost before the spectators have recovered their equilibrium. Then an amusing meeting of two Indian tribes takes place, the sign language causing no end of merriment."[44]

This section of the exhibition was also echoed in the provincial tour of England. The *Birmingham Daily Post* noted that with the Wild West's return visit, the program had been "a little amplified so as to illustrate more comprehensively the Indians' modes of life in peace and war."[45] Other publications took note of the costumes of the Indians, and the London journal *The Queen* recalled how the Indians' attire added to the overall effect.[46] In contrast, *The Morning* ridiculed the Indians' dress, disdainfully noting that "the Indian has a weakness for ornaments, and an objection to wearing apparel, except paint, when on parade."[47]

Unlike Sitting Bull, who had enjoyed a privileged role in the 1885 show, the Ghost Dancers' role in the exhibition was the same as all other Indian members of the cast. Vine Deloria wrote that Cody the showman had understood Sitting Bull's "drawing power and personal dignity, and gave him a positive role to play in the show. Rather than require Sitting Bull to participate in the mock battles and otherwise make a fool of himself, Buffalo Bill treated the old man as a distinct and noble personality. At an opportune time in the show Sitting Bull would ride impassively and nobly into the arena alone on a horse and for several moments be the sole attraction of the show. Rather than the fearful savage of pulp novels, Sitting Bull was seen as the charismatic statesman of an Indian nation."[48]

The notoriety of the Ghost Dancers was used in the exhibition's publicity in order to affirm the integrity of the Indian performers, and thus to pull in the crowds. A poster for the performance in Leeds stated that the exhibition included "some of the most celebrated amongst the 'Friendlies' and 'Hostiles' of last winter's campaign in Dakota, notably 'Kicking Bear,' 'No Neck,' 'Yankton Charley,' 'Long Wolf,' 'Black Heart,' 'Scatter,' 'Revenge,' 'Big Wolf,' and 'Short Bull.'"[49] However, most such promotion occurred in the advance publicity notices, in newspaper interviews with Cody or other Wild West personnel, or in articles inspired by the exhibition's press releases.

More often than not, the British press compared the Ghost Dancers with the other notable Indian performers, and subsequently all of the Indian performers were conveniently categorized as either "Hostiles" or "Friendlies." "Some of them are men who were friendly to the

Government in the late troubles, others are from the ranks of the hostile Indians and are being held as hostages or prisoners of war. . . . Probably the two most interesting Indians in the troupe are 'Kicking Bear' and 'Short Bull,' both of whom were hostiles."[50]

Other newspapers discussed the Ghost Dancers in more detail when they reviewed the opening night, as illustrated by the *Birmingham Daily Post*:

> The processional review with which the entertainment opened served to introduce the most conspicuous members of the troupe not already known. By far the most remarkable of these is Short Bull, the John Baptist of the Sioux Messiah. He is a tall, phlegmatic Indian, whose face betrays the temperament of an ascetic and a visionary. They say that he still cherishes the dear delusion which was first implanted in his mind by a missionary from Utah, whose teaching of a militant Christianity he would seem to have understood with a pathetic literalism. It is easy to conceive how such a man as he, speaking his golden prophecy among a people desperate with famine, gave hope and purpose to their discontent. Kicking Bear, the fighting chief of the ghost-dancers, has a face in which, even when his features are at rest, one reads plainly the bitter resentment and potential cruelty of another Sitting Bull. Then there are Lone Bull, Scatter, and Revenge, younger if not handsomer men, and eighteen other hostages. The friendly chiefs are headed by No Neck, an important Government scout in the campaign, and now the leading chief of the Aston camp. Long Wolf is an "old-time warrior," with a great record, which served him in good stead as a conciliator of the rebels. Bone Necklace, once a mighty man of valour also, has become in his extreme age the legendary historian of the Sioux. Black Heart, when in England last, had hardly won his spurs, but in the critical negotiations with the Bad Lands chiefs he incurred great peril, and did yeoman service.[51]

The Ghost Dancers were not specifically referred to in the advertisements that appeared daily in the local press. A correspondent of the Manchester publication *The Umpire* complained, "I don't think Colonel Cody has made enough in the advertisements of the fact that a great many of his Indians took part in the very natural rising against Yankee fraud which took place last year."[52] Cody may have avoided such direct advertisements, because of Herbert Welsh's accusation that he had advertised in the European press that he was "coming to Europe 'with fifty of the worst Indians who had been engaged in the Wounded Knee fight.'" Welsh's allegation had been strongly denied by Nate Salsbury, who in his reply had defied Welsh's informant Mary Collins to produce her evidence.[53] Nevertheless, under such circumstances the Wild West's management may have felt that it would not do to give the exhibition's critics further ammunition.

Buffalo Bill's Wild West did not reenact the Wounded Knee Massacre on this or any subsequent tours, despite encouragement to do so. The management's decision not to include such scenes suggests a degree of respect and sympathy toward the Lakota performers, for to reenact an event so significant and still raw would surely have been very painful. Practically every single Lakota performer in the show either had lost relatives in the massacre or had been indirectly touched by the tragedy. Therefore, they would have been very unlikely to agree to "perform" a reenactment of it.[54]

Neither did the exhibition give a display of the Ghost Dance in the arena. None of the innumerable press reviews of Buffalo Bill's Wild West refers to any such display, and with the presence of the Lakota Ghost Dancers and the amount of column space given over to them, it would surely have not been overlooked.[55] It is unlikely that the Lakota Ghost Dancers who had maintained their belief in the religion would have "performed" such a sacred religious ritual as entertainment in the Wild West show. Cody himself stated: "I prohibit the 'ghost dance' in my camp, as it stirs up fanaticism." If he really had undertaken the job of reconstructing the hostiles, as he claimed, then performing the Ghost Dance would have been contrary to this objective.[56]

Yet at other functions, demonstrations of the Ghost Dance did occur. At the end of the winter season in Glasgow, a smaller, separate company did a short tour of local towns.[57] The *Glasgow Evening News* commented that the people of Greenock had been "exceedingly entertained," further noting that "it was a unique spectacle . . . to witness the 'Ghost Dance' by the Indians."[58]

Perhaps the management of Buffalo Bill's Wild West was sensitive enough to their Indian performers to avoid reenactments of Wounded

Knee and performances of the Ghost Dance. Just as likely, they may have been motivated by a desire to avoid bad publicity in the United States, and they may also have realized that their Ghost Dancers would want no part of such spectacles. Yet their exploitation of both the Ghost Dancers' notoriety and their association with the recent military suppression went one stage further with one of their child performers.

In her book *Lost Bird of Wounded Knee*, Renee Flood stated that while in Pine Ridge, John Burke "had acquired an infant survivor of the massacre" found beside the body of her dead mother. He had gotten the baby from John Yellow Bird, a local storekeeper. Burke purportedly was representing a childless friend at the time.[59] "The major saw the little waif from Wounded Knee and hit upon the idea of securing the child for a wealthy socialite in Washington, D.C., Mrs. Alison Nailor, whose husband was Buffalo Bill's old hunting partner. Details of the transaction are unknown, but Burke stood godfather as the little girl was baptized Maggie C. Nailor in a Christian ceremony."[60]

Flood speculated that "even though he had ostensibly allowed the Nailors . . . to adopt her," Burke probably had plans to exhibit the child in the Wild West show. Later Burke told the tragic tale of the infant to Cody's friend and commanding officer Brig. Gen. Leonard W. Colby of the Nebraska State Guard. Colby was reportedly "moved by 'the pathos,' and mesmerized by the baby's seemingly immortal spirit." Flood relates that "as soon as Burke sensed Colby wanted the baby girl, the bargaining became heated. Buffalo Bill, Colby and Major Burke sat by the warm woodstove in Yellow Bird's store and bartered for the child. . . . Colby made the winning bid and late that cold night, January 6, 1891, the general took . . . his newly acquired baby to his tent, where they would stay until he arranged for transport to Rushville the next day."[61]

Whatever the truth behind this, the Wild West show did acquire a "Wounded Knee orphan," little "Johnny Burke No Neck," reportedly named after his two adoptive fathers.[62] Whether Burke was legally the boy's adoptive father remains doubtful, as the child was referred to by this name only in Wild West show publicity and press reports. The Pine Ridge census records for 1893 record that No Neck and his wife, Ellen, had an adopted son known as Young Cub, or Cub Bear, who was aged eight at the end of 1893. Short Bull recorded that those survivors whom they could not transport on the day of the massacre, when they visited the site to see the dead and help the injured, were later taken by a party led by No Neck.[63]

That No Neck removed the injured Lakota left by Short Bull's party might also reinforce the idea that it was No Neck and his wife who had adopted the boy, having found him orphaned and injured. This assumption appears to be confirmed by the Cardiff *Evening News*, which stated: "He is the only survivor of the Battle of 'Wounded Knee,' and when found on the battlefield by the chief 'No Neck,' had lost his skin by the combined action of sun and snow."[64]

No Neck received $55 a month for performing in Buffalo Bill's Wild West, the largest wage of all the Indian performers. Yankton Charley, Short Bull, and Kicking Bear were each paid $50 a month; and Blackheart received $35. All the other Lakota men received $25, and the eight Lakota women were each paid $10 a month. The list of Indians who left to travel with Buffalo Bill's Wild West on the 1891–92 tour records that the remuneration of $55 was for both No Neck and his "Adopted son, from the Wounded Knee battlefield."[65]

The program for the second tour of Britain by Buffalo Bill's Wild West included a photograph of the young boy in a section entitled "Ghost Dances in the West." The caption underneath reads: "'Johnny Burke No Neck'—Found on the Battle Field of Wounded Knee after the annihilation of Big Foot's Band."[66]

Most of the British newspaper references to the orphan were taken from this cue.[67] The Brighton *Argus* was one of many British newspapers that erroneously stated the child was "the sole survivor of the decisive battle of Wounded Knee."[68] The idea that he was the "sole survivor" enhanced the perception of the boy as the symbolic embodiment of the prevailing Social Darwinist concept of the "vanishing race."

Cody was not the only white American to exploit and profit from the tragedy in South Dakota. When the burial party went out to bury the dead three days after the massacre, they were joined by photographers who later sold copies of the infamous Wounded Knee pictures, and by "relic hunters" who profited by selling artifacts removed from bodies and the massacre site. "Everything of interest in the late Pine Ridge War are held by us for sale," proclaimed one company.[69]

The market for "historical souvenirs" was by no means restricted to America. As the Wild West toured Europe, enthusiasm for souvenirs and artifacts followed it. Museums around the Continent were acquiring treasures from supposedly inferior, conquered civilizations all over the world, and several seized the opportunity to purchase whatever they could of Sioux culture. Glasgow Museums was typical, and during the Wild West's lengthy visit to the Scottish city it acquired from George Crager a number of items, including four "Wounded Knee" artifacts.[70]

Cody's former business partner, "Doc" William F. Carver, went one stage further than Buffalo Bill's Wild West, when his company Doc Carver's Wild America performed in San Francisco in June 1892. The show advertised in the press that its program "The Scout" included "Splendid Specimens of the Savage of the Plains; a Band of Warriors from the Tribe of Sitting Bull, who took part in the Battle of Wounded Knee." Moreover, when the company performed on the Piedmont Baseball Grounds in July 1892, the program included not only "Scalp and War Dances," but also "the Ghost Dance by the Indians who first performed it."[71]

One of Carver's performers had been a Fort Sheridan prisoner and had toured Britain with Cody. Standing Bear, an elderly Brule leader, had returned home from Britain in August 1891 suffering from "lung problems," which had been exacerbated by exposure during the previous "winter's troubles." Touring with Carver was little better, and he complained to a journalist, "My feet ache here; I cannot breathe."[72]

Carver's exploitation of the Ghost Dance and the Wounded Knee Massacre differed from Cody's in that he had no compunction about having the Lakota perform a Ghost Dance. Moreover, the show was performed before white Americans, a potentially more hostile audience than those in Europe. But as Moses noted, "Standing Bear and the others in the troupe would be the last Indians employed by Carver for some time to come." The commissioner of Indian affairs had successfully banned Carver (and his partner Fred C. Whitney) from employing any more show Indians, when it was found that his agent had illegally coerced the Indians into joining the show.[73]

Cody's use of the twenty-three Lakota Ghost Dancers and "Little Johnny Burke No Neck" as performers in Buffalo Bill's Wild West conformed to the management's desire to employ authentic characters from the "Old West." Cody had learned early in his theatrical career that the paying public delighted in seeing the genuine article— a belief shared by a correspondent in the *Leicester Daily Post* who commented, "The scenes which will be depicted derive a peculiar interest from the fact that many of those taking part in them have been actual participants in such episodes in the ordinary course of existence."[74]

It was not only Buffalo Bill himself who had "been there" in reality, but also many of the other performers in the exhibition, including, of course, the Indian contingent.

That the show contained actual participants from recent American frontier history fascinated the British press. The London *Evening News and Post* went as far as offering the U.S. government "our warmest thanks," for such an "international courtesy."[75] The use of such characters was not merely meant as a novel and entertaining idea, for at the same time such "realism" was also calculated to give the appearance that Buffalo Bill's Wild West was a true and educational representation of life in the American West. "It is not only entertaining because of its novelty, but is paramountly instructive, and no one who has read the history of the Western States for the past quarter of a century can fail to appreciate the object lessons of the Wild West Show."[76]

But not all of the characters represented were genuine. The Lakota Indians were also required to play the role of other Indian nations. In an advertisement that appeared in the *Liverpool Mercury*, the exhibition was listed as including "Arapaho, Brule, Cut-Off, Cheyenne, and Sioux Indians."[77] The Brule and Cut-Off bands were both subdivisions of the Teton Sioux (Lakota), while the Arapaho and Cheyenne were separate Plains Indian nations that shared strong bonds with the Lakota.

Luther Standing Bear, who traveled with the show when it toured Britain in 1903–1904, noted that "while all the Indians belonged to

the Sioux tribe, we were supposed to represent four different tribes."
To reinforce the image of tribal bands, each group rode horses of a
specific color, which Standing Bear gave as being "black, white, bay
and buckskin-colored."[78] Vine Deloria acknowledged that "such fic-
tions were a necessary part of show business and were not seen by
the Indians as anything more than an effort to increase the excitement that the show engendered."[79]

When the exhibition played at Madison Square Garden in New
York during the winter of 1886–87, Buffalo Bill's Wild West
employed both Lakota and Pawnee Indians. Black Elk, at that time a
young Lakota performer who had recently joined the show, recalled
that while the new arrivals were eating "in the center of the Hippo-
drome," they "heard the Pawnee Indians whooping at us. They
couped us in a friendly way and we just had to hurry out of there."[80]
While the incident described by Black Elk appears to have been
nothing more than friendly rivalry, traveling with only one group of
Indians had the obvious advantage of avoiding any potential conflicts between the members of traditionally antagonistic tribes.
Moreover, communication was essential in carrying off such a mam-
moth production; interpreting for and between several different
tribes would only have complicated matters. Finally, employing
members of more than one tribe would have made the hiring of the
Indian performers a longer and more convoluted process. It thus
made sense to employ only the one group of Indians and have them
play the part of others.

Cody's exhibition did not challenge British preconceptions of Indians as exotic savages, but instead relied upon this "image" to give
the performances heightened drama, reinforced by the use of real
characters, especially the Fort Sheridan prisoners. Yet the image presented of the Indians was not consistent with the experiences of the
Lakota of the time. The Lakota were no longer nomadic warriors and
hunters of the plains, but instead lived on reservations supported by
government annuities, and the majority wore "Western"-style clothing day to day rather than the costumes of the Wild West. There was
no representation of reservation life in the Wild West arena; reservation Indians did not convey romantic notions of danger, and therefore
did not fit Cody's meta-narrative of heroic conquest.

Buffalo Bill's Wild West presented a story of conquest based on Indian and white conflict, but as the suppression of the Lakota Ghost Dance had illustrated, reality was rather more complicated. After all, the Indian police had shot Sitting Bull, and Wild West Indians had fought on the side of the government in order to secure future employment. Perhaps a more honest telling of the story of conquest would have been Indians used against Indians for the benefit of the dominant white society. However, Buffalo Bill's Wild West was selling an American myth that told of Anglo-Saxon superiority and the inevitability of the "survival of the fittest." That British audiences bought into it betrays their shared sense of racial and cultural superiority.[81]

CHAPTER SEVEN

PERCEPTIONS OF "THE OTHER" ON THE BRITISH TOUR

The military suppression of the Ghost Dance had been covered on a daily basis by the British press, gleaning information from either the Reuter's or Dalzeil's news agencies. The coverage started on 19 November 1890 and carried through until 20 January 1891, detailing almost every aspect of the events unfolding in South Dakota. The British public learned of Cody's involvement in the suppression and that of the recently returned Wild West Indians; they were also made aware of Short Bull's and Kicking Bear's prominence among the Ghost Dancers.

As the vast majority of the news articles originated in America, there was little difference between American and British reporting of the anticipated "Indian Rising." Thus, the Wounded Knee Massacre was reported as "Indian Treachery" by the *Daily Telegraph,* which went on to state that "the slaughter among the Indians is said to have been terrible, despite the fact that the soldiers had to run them out of their ambuscade. . . . With cheers and cries of 'Remember Custer!' they sent the Indians in disorder in the direction of buttes to the North. . . . The latest reports indicate that Big Foot's band has been almost wiped out."[1]

While the general tone of the reporting appears to have been in support of the action of the U.S. government, some individuals spoke out against the slaughter. A letter entitled "Massacre of Indian Women and Children" was printed in the *Standard* on 2 January 1891. The correspondent, who signed himself as "Humanity," wrote:

"Indians are execrated as monsters of cruelty when they murder the families of white settlers; but it appears that the white soldiers are not one whit less barbarous, their idea being obviously one of extermination. Americans covet the few tracts of land left to the poor Indians, and it is to this covetousness that the whole of the present disturbances are due."[2]

Another dissenter was the Liberal member of Parliament for North West Lanark, Robert Bontine Cunninghame Graham, who at the height of his political career wrote three letters "on the Indian question" to the *Daily Graphic*. The first, entitled "The American Indians: Ghost Dancing," appeared on 29 November 1890, and was a response to the articles that had begun to appear from the United States, further commenting on British indifference. John Walker, who republished the three letters in his book *The North American Sketches of R. B. Cunninghame Graham*, maintained that they were "an anguished cry from the heart against the cruel treatment of the American Indian from a humanitarian who had learned his lessons first-hand on the plains and hills of South-West U.S.A."[3]

Cunninghame Graham portentously speculated that "civilization, perhaps, one day will remember them when civilized Indians, [whom] commercialism is creating, are dancing around the flames of European capitals." Little did he realize that within less than a year it would be not only those "civilized Indians" who would be dancing in Europe, but also the unreconstructed "hostiles," the Ghost Dancers themselves. Cunninghame Graham saw parallels between the oppressed on both sides of the Atlantic, and his socialist leanings were clearly evident.[4]

On 22 December the *Daily Graphic* published Cunninghame Graham's second letter, "Salvation by Starvation: The American-Indian Problem," which was written in response to Sitting Bull's death and was a caustic condemnation of the U.S. government's treatment of the indigenous population. Cunninghame Graham's perception of American Indians was by no means typical of the British people. He wrote: "I speak not as a sentimentalist who takes his Indian (coloured) from the pages of Fenimore Cooper. . . . I am one of those who think that the colour of the skin makes little difference to right and wrong in the abstract." He ended his second letter with a disdainful comment aimed at the American people: "Even in America, where public opinion is, perhaps, more brutal than in any other country of the world, surely a flush of shame must rise to the faces of honest men when they receive the telegrams from Dakota."[5]

The second letter was reported unfavorably in the American press, including a dismissively titled article, "Seems to Know All about It," in the *Denver Rocky Mountain News,* which noted that Cunninghame Graham "condemns the Americans for murdering Sitting Bull."[6]

In his final letter, "The Redskin Problem: 'But 'twas a Famous Victory,'" Cunninghame Graham denounced the massacre of Big Foot's Band at Wounded Knee: "I see that our 'brave troops' remorselessly slaughtered all the women and children, and our special correspondent, in estimating the 'bag,' remarks that by this time probably not more than six children remain alive out of the whole Indian camp. Can anything more miserable be conceived. . . . We are told that the Indians planned an ambuscade, but it would seem a curious kind of ambuscade that 120 men should allow themselves to be surrounded by 500, backed by artillery."[7]

However, despite Cunninghame Graham's letters, the British public generally shared the common perception of the Lakota Ghost Dancers as "Hostiles." The appearance of the twenty-three former Fort Sheridan prisoners, who had accompanied Cody on his tour of Britain, did little to alter and may even have strengthened this perception. The Wild West's program for the 1891–92 tour of Britain included a ten-page article entitled "Ghost-Dances in the West." The feature described the origin and development of the "Messiah Craze and the Ghost-Dance" on the Pine Ridge Reservation, and had been lifted from the publication *Illustrated American.* While the piece contained some factual errors concerning the origin of the Ghost Dance, it did give a generally balanced and detailed description of the religion in South Dakota.[8]

While being sympathetic to the plight of the Lakota, the article nonetheless maintained that under the influence of "the medicine men and politicians in the nation," the Ghost Dance had "changed from a sacred rite to a warlike demonstration." No reference was made to Wounded Knee, and no criticisms were leveled at the military. A short note by John Burke followed the article, in which he contended that while the report was in many respects accurate, "the whole matter has yet to be investigated to get at the bottom of the facts."[9] Buffalo Bill's Wild West was engaged in the business of making a profit through entertainment, and it did not suit the show's needs to portray the Lakota Ghost Dancers as anything else but "Hostiles."

Despite the individual dissenting voices of people like Cunninghame Graham, the British public largely endorsed the Wild West's message, which slipped seamlessly into the popular forms of British entertainment of the day. John MacKenzie maintained that "military subjects had long been popular in spectacular theatrical presentations and in melodrama," and that in the late nineteenth century the army and its personnel had risen in the public's esteem. This interest in warfare and militarism was "wedded to an overseas adventure tradition. . . . War became a remote adventure in which heroism was enhanced by both distance and exotic locales."[10]

As the century progressed, the deeds of imperial expansion were found to fit perfectly the tradition of translating topical events into spectacular display, combining the Victorians' search for realism with an admiring self-regard in their own exploits.[11] Buffalo Bill's Wild West clearly satisfied British audiences' desires and expectations; the one significant difference, which was also no doubt an added attraction, was the presence within the exhibition of the defeated "others." However, audience responses to the Indians on display may have been more complex and "multiple meanings were also possible." As Kasson contended, "Press stories stressed the adventure, exoticism, and sometimes pathos of the American Indian performers. They elicited excitement almost always and admiration often."[12] Yet despite such complexity the Indian performers remained exotic "others" in the eyes of British onlookers. It is scarcely surprising, then, that the Wild West exhibition confirmed the overwhelming British perception of the Lakota people as being "wild" or "savage" and their religions as being naïve and pagan.

The exhibition had a very good and mutually beneficial relationship with the British press. Buffalo Bill and stories of his Wild West sold newspapers, while press coverage of the personalities and the show itself provided extensive free publicity and no doubt boosted ticket sales. Reporters were given access to the whole encampment and were granted interviews with Cody, Nate Salsbury, John Burke, or one of the star performers, such as sharpshooter Annie Oakley. Often the Lakota interpreter George Crager had the responsibility of giving the members of the press a guided tour, which would include introductions to the Indians and a glimpse of camp life.

The Lakota were perceived as being so different from British people that they were seen as item of curiosity wherever they were encountered, and this meant that they were also on display outside of the arena. When a reporter for the Cardiff *Evening Express* was exploring the Indian camp, he was introduced to Lone Bull, one of the Lakota Ghost Dancers. The journalist commented, "I am convinced Lone Bull does not care to be made an exhibition of, but he submitted quietly to an examination of his dress and general appearance."[13]

The Indians were also open to constant scrutiny whenever they left the encampment and ventured out to explore their surroundings. A correspondent for *Land and Water* described it as "the most delightful surprise of the sort I ever experienced," when early one morning he happened to encounter some of Cody's Indians. In August it was considered newsworthy that the Indians had been spotted at London Zoo.[14] Even by doing such mundane things as going to buy new clothes or riding on a tramcar, more often than not the Indians became the focus of attention.[15]

The press also covered the more significant events in the lives of the Wild West's entourage, including the marriage of the Lakota interpreter John Shangrau to Lillie Orr, a young woman from Liverpool. Shangrau's father, Jule, had been a stock raiser of French descent, and his mother, Mary, had come from the Smoke band of the Oglala.[16] Previously, Shangrau had worked irregularly as a scout for the U.S. Army and, in December 1890, as chief of Brooke's headquarter scouts. He was present at Big Foot's arrest on 28 December and was forced to flee to avoid the crossfire of the soldiers during the Wounded Knee Massacre.[17] He later accompanied the Ghost Dancers who had been placed under arrest and transported to Fort Sheridan, acting as their interpreter. When Cody acquired the prisoners for his tour of Europe, Shangrau accompanied them, and the

Wild West show program referred to him as being "in charge of the Military Hostages."[18]

The marriage certificate records that John Shangrau was a thirty-eight-year-old widower.[19] His first wife had died not long after he left Pine Ridge to tour with Cody. In May 1891 he sent $10 in care of Captain Penny, the acting Indian agent, for his wife who had remained home in South Dakota, but she died "before the money came to hand."[20] Within two months of his sending the money, the Wild West show was in Liverpool, where John met Lillie Orr. Lillie was the daughter of a Liverpool ship captain, and at the age of eighteen she "fell in love" with John while the show performed in her hometown.[21] The marriage took place before Sheriff Spens at the County Buildings in Glasgow's East End on 4 January 1892.[22] The "Lady Representative" of the London *Morning* later commented, "It seemed strange to think of this fair-faced, blue-eyed English girl married to a man who, although educated and in every way 'civilised,' is so closely allied to the 'Red-skins.'"[23]

Other romances between Lakota men and British women were also noted in the press. While the show was in Leeds, newspapers reported that "many a dusky fellow could be seen parading the streets with some highly dressed female by his side." It was not uncommon "to discover some redskin who had won fame in the recent Indian rising drinking at one of the numerous public houses in Aston with some fair admirer." The attraction appears to have been mutual, a local Leeds reporter noted that the Lakota performers' "picturesque attire appeared to exercise an infatuation over the majority of the females." Similarly, however "stolid and indifferent . . . the red man appears when seen at a distance, he is not unsusceptible to the charms of the daughters of the whiteface." One performer was so taken with a woman from Aston that he left the show once it had departed and returned to Leeds, only to be escorted back by Wild West representatives a few days later.[24]

A story that appeared in the *Glasgow Evening News* illustrates the difficulties the Indians faced when it came to courting local women. "The red man has conceived a violent passion . . . for a prepossessing young lady in a shop near the show, and he looks in during his leisure hours on the pretence of wanting to buy things, but really to enforce his suit. . . . The awkward thing, however, is that the red man's arrival at the shop is the signal for the neighbours to gather round, and the progress of the courtship is watched by a little crowd which generally extends out to the street."[25]

The idea of an interracial relationship was not such an alien concept to the Lakota, who had been intermarrying with whites since their first contact. These marriages generally involved white men, rather than white women, because it was European men, trappers and traders, who first encountered the Lakota. Numerous cartoons made reference to the attractiveness of the Lakota men to British women. No doubt created and drawn by men, the images ridiculed women and Indians alike, both of whom were viewed as inferior beings. However, it is clear that in the stories and the cartoons the main objective was humor; there appears to have been no value judgment, and commentators were not overtly objecting to such relationships.[26]

The fascination of the British press with the Lakota performers meant that their every movement was reported, allowing us to see how they spent their free time. The Indians were understandably curious to explore their surroundings in the towns and cities that they visited, and they were also recorded as attending worship services. Several publications covered the visit by the Wild West's personnel to St. Paul's Cathedral for the morning service on a Sunday in May. The *Pall Mall Gazette* remarked, "The Indians were greatly impressed by the service, and particularly charmed by the music of the big organ."[27] On Sundays all the different groups attached to the exhibition were allowed to attend the churches of their choice. *The World* noted that the Indians "appear to visit with absolute impartiality the temples of every faith and creed and sect in turn, and declare that we are 'all Christians,' and worship the same Great Spirit who shapes their destinies and governs us all."[28] A Kensington clergyman testified that when the Wild West Indians attended his church, they behaved in a way that "might profitably be followed by many more fashionable worshippers. They are reverent and intelligent, and appreciate all that is taking place."[29]

In an interview with a reporter from the *Oracle*, Salsbury was asked if the Indians held their own religious services, to which he replied, "Yes, they do, but they never make no parade about it, and you would never know they were going on."[30] While the show was in Sheffield, a reporter from the *Evening Telegraph and Star* was privileged to witness such a ceremony on the morning of 14 August 1891. It was reported that the date coincided with the middle of the eighth moon, the season when the buffalo cast its hair and hunting was stopped, when the Indians would celebrate the Buffalo Dance Day.[31]

Standing discreetly at the back of one of the larger lodges, the reporter was allowed to witness the festivities in the company of the interpreter George Crager, who explained the proceedings and translated the songs.

> The hymn of praise to the Great Spirit is full of repetition, interspersed with dances, which, in that stuffy tent, with the wood smouldering in the centre, must have been, and certainly did appear to be, of a very fatiguing nature. All being assembled, the rude chant and wild music resumes. A literal interpretation is conveyed to the listener to be:—

> We thank the Great Spirit
> Who hast given us the buffalo,
> It gives us hides to cover our backs.
> It keeps us warm and makes our hearts glad.
> Now that its hair is coming off,
> It is no longer good to kill.
> In the spring we shall have good hides.
> For this we sing our praise.

> Loud, then low, and rising again to its full power the orchestra plays on in undulating waves of sound, accompanying its mechanical exertion with the drum stick, with full-throated sounds and those piercing whoops.[32]

The dance started with a representation of a buffalo stampede. The reporter described how the dancers commenced "an animated jerky dance, or shuffle, in which the whole body leaves the ground at the same time, quickening up with loud laughter and shouts as they endeavored to knock each other down in shocks of collision." This was then followed by a song lamenting the loss of the buffalo, which started in a slow and solemn fashion before quickening at the prospect of a good hunting season the next spring. The second dance was more vigorous than the first, and in addition to "their humorous efforts to render each other's foothold insecure," the dancers butted each other, illustrating the coming of the young buffalo in the spring.[33]

The ceremony lasted roughly two hours, and apart from the presence of the reporter and interpreter, it was attended exclusively by Indians, and was clearly an attempt on their part to maintain their ceremonial rituals. This and other such circumstances illustrate how the Lakota maintained their own religious and cultural practices while touring with Buffalo Bill's Wild West. For example, when the exhibition was performing at Earl's Court in London, a reporter for the *Million* described a sweat bath being used in the camp.[34]

The Lakota also found themselves the subjects of the familiar missionary impulse while the show wintered in Glasgow. The *Bailie* noted that "several ladies . . . from the Medical Mission Training Home, visit Buffalo Bill's redskins encampment daily, and talk seriously to the Indians."[35] Reflecting on her encounter with the Indians in Glasgow a few years later, one of the missionaries, who was described in the *New York Times* as a "society woman of wealth and position," recounted:

> They are very fond of singing either in English or Sioux: indeed, their demand for hymns is insatiable. As two books among forty or fifty [were] hardly enough, they promised to copy some of their favourites before another week, and when the next Sabbath came around Revenge, who was prominent in the rebellion, had undertaken to copy a good many hymns out. . . . They cannot be called heathen, as they believe in and worship the "Great Spirit." They accept what is told them implicitly, and several have said God has given them "white hearts," and many now say that they "talk to God." They were very anxious to hear about Jesus Christ.

The missionary found Short Bull to be "a most interesting character." He was "always one of the first to come forward," and although he could not speak English, was anxious to talk through an interpreter. Ironically, it was the Ghost Dancers, perceived by many to be backward-looking and pagan, who impressed the missionary most with their interest in and knowledge of religion.[36]

Raymond DeMallie noted that when Black Elk traveled with Buffalo Bill's Wild West to England on the exhibition's first visit, he "wrote a letter in Lakota to give his people news of his whereabouts. The letter was printed in the *Iapi Oaye* (the "Word Carrier"), a monthly newspaper published in the Sioux language at Santee, Nebraska." In the letter Black Elk stated, "Now I know the white men's customs well. One custom is very good. Whoever believes in God will find good ways—that is what I mean. And many of the ways the white men follow are hard to endure." When he returned to Pine Ridge in 1889, after having been left behind and lost in Europe for some time, Black Elk wrote a second letter, which was also printed in the *Iapi Oaye*. He stated that "of the white man's many customs, only his faith, the white man's belief about God's will, and how they act according to it, I wanted to understand. I traveled to one city after another, and there were many customs around God's will." Such statements betray a desire to understand the European perception of God, as was suggested by the missionary in Glasgow.[37]

Traveling with Buffalo Bill's Wild West enabled the Lakota performers to learn about the spirituality of the whites, and perhaps gave them a better understanding of white culture. Through the process of accommodation the Indians were taking on white religious concepts while also maintaining Lakota traditions. Intriguingly, it seems that the traditional Lakota, including the Fort Sheridan prisoners, rather than the more assimilated Indians, showed a keen interest in white religion and ritual.

The Lakota women with the exhibition received much less press coverage than the men, and such references as do exist are primarily concerned with their skilled beadwork, which occupied a great deal of the women's free time. The reporter for the *Sheffield and Rotherham Independent* was impressed by "the extraordinary brilliance of the colours which are used," and was interested to learn that "the dyes by which they are produced are entirely of native manufacture."[38] The Cardiff *Evening Express* commented on the fact that the women employed "neither needle nor thread, but simply buffalo sinew."[39]

The beadwork produced by the women could have been for use in the arena, or instead for sale to the public. Indians had been making items for sale or trade with whites for centuries. If the Lakota women were selling their wares to Europeans, this would clearly demonstrate their initiative and their efforts to take some control of their situation.

When it came to discussing the Indians who appeared in Cody's Wild West, the general perception of the British public is obvious from the press reports: there was a clear sense of cultural and racial superiority over the Lakota performers. Such a perspective is hardly surprising, for as a colonial empire, Britain had subjugated many native peoples around the world, including the many North American Indians they had come into contact with.[40] Moreover, Britons identified with the Euro-Americans who had defeated the Plains Indians, and therefore shared a perception of American Indians as "the Other."[41] The Lakota appeared as exotic "specimens"; according to the prevailing concept of Social Darwinism, they were representatives of an inferior and doomed race whose survivors would be integrated into the dominant world of white civilization.[42] Although nothing in the Wild West show contradicted such imperialistic and hierarchical assumptions, as Kasson has observed, "newspaper stories continued to assert [that] the Indians were special favorites with audiences, and human-interest stories about Indians . . . complicated the racial stereotypes and hierarchies."[43]

Reporters and other British observers made specific references to the physical appearance of the Lakota. A London paper noted that the former Fort Sheridan prisoners were easily distinguishable "by their disdainful glances at the palefaces," but that it was "very difficult to distinguish the average Indian brave from the average Indian squaw."[44] Similarly, the *Leeds Evening Express* remarked, "Nearly all the men have long hair like women, plaited and decorated with beads and 'wampum,' and this, with their bare faces, makes them difficult to tell, at a glance, from the women."[45] However, a reporter for the *Sheffield and Rotherham Independent* commented that while the "long black hair and the absence of any beard or whiskers gives the men a somewhat feminine look . . . there is nothing feminine in the determined act of the lips that divide the high and prominent cheekbones from the massive lower jaws, and their aspect as a whole fully confirms the published statements as to the dogged and unconquerable courage with which they have met their foes."[46]

The absence of any "vestige of a beard" appears to have been key to this supposedly feminine appearance, for Cody, who had long hair but also wore a beard, appeared to newspaper journalists as the epitome of masculinity. A correspondent for the *Manchester Chronicle* offered his readers a fantastic explanation for the Lakotas' lack of facial hair. "It is a fact that when the male Indian arrives at years of discretion, his mother plucks out every individual hair in his whiskers, beard and moustache with a pair of tweezers. This operation naturally lasts several weeks, and the hair cannot grow again."[47]

Other such flights of fantasy evolved from speculation about the origins of the American Indians. A correspondent for the journal *Science Siftings* speculated that the Indians were of either Jewish or Chinese origin. The journal had some similarly startling revelations to make about the Indians' language. "It is strange, but an actual fact, that the Manadad (Dakota) Indians use a Welsh dialect. At the present day a Welshman can understand them. It is presumed and is backed up by tradition, that some Welsh pioneer got stranded among these Indians and taught them their language."[48]

Other publications mistook the Lakota dialect for a bastardized version of English. The *Leicester Daily Post* suggested that their greeting of "'How' . . . [r]epresents their small stock of English, being a contraction of the ordinary salutation 'How d'ye do.'"[49] This idea was contradicted by the Glasgow *Evening Citizen*, which more correctly stated, "When the Indians shake hands . . . they say 'how, how,' but it is not English, you know."[50] The Lakota greeting of "Hau" can be translated as "hello," and therefore in meaning is not that dissimilar from the *Leicester Daily Post*'s suggestion, but it was not derived from English.

The preoccupation of the press with the language of the Lakota and their perceived desire to learn English shows the British sense of racial and cultural superiority, in the belief that "others" would naturally want to take on the language of the dominant society.[51] The

Lakota's use of the sign language was also of great interest, and reveals the same sense of cultural and racial superiority, contrasting "savages" conversing with hands with "civilized" people communicating with an advanced verbal and written language. There was occasion for comment on the sign language while the exhibition was in Glasgow. The incident amply demonstrates the perceptions of both the British and the white Americans of being a superior race, so that other races were not only inferior, but also "specimens" to be studied and compared.

On 26 December 1891 Cody wrote to his sister Julia informing her that he would return home in the near future. "Am sorry to say that I am off again. I have got the Hay fever or Grippe or something, & being so worn out and so much do to & to think of, its hard. I am now trying for new attractions to put in this place to fill my vacancy when I have to leave here for my trip home. I want to leave my company playing here while I am gone. And must strengthen them with other attractions."[52]

It was Lew Parker's job to find these new attractions, and in a piece entitled "A Peculiar Happening," in his book of reminiscences *Odd People I Have Known*, he detailed how he had acquired them. After booking a troupe of performing elephants in France, he learned that "Explorer Stanley and a wonderful tribe of Negroes . . . from Africa . . . had just landed at Hamburg."[53] Parker hurried across and engaged the African performers, returning to Glasgow with two new attractions for the exhibition.

On 15 January a personal reception was given by the Wild West to a large number of invited guests, including representatives of the local press, professors, and many of the city's leading clergy. They were invited "to witness the meeting . . . of a swarthy tribe from central Africa with the redskins of America." For the journalists who wrote about the reception, this meeting was "the most interesting part" of the gathering—a meeting, they speculated, "which perhaps has never had a parallel."[54] The "peculiar happening" to which Parker refers occurred when the Indians were encouraged to try to communicate with the Africans through sign language. To everyone's astonishment one of the Africans responded, "conveying . . . a perfect knowledge" of what had been said. "A few minutes afterwards both tribes were fraternizing and by signs getting along splendidly together."[55]

"The red men sent out chiefs No Neck, Short Bull and Kicking Bear," recorded the *Glasgow Evening News*, "who met three of the black chiefs, and soon the two tribes were upon most friendly terms, being also able to converse after a fashion with each other."[56] The *Evening Times* reported that the speeches, which were delivered "by the natives . . . indicated the bent of the mind of the speakers in an eminent degree. 'Kicking Bear,' speaking to the Africans, put the crux of the whole North American Indian question in a nutshell. . . . 'My heart is glad to see you today, and I shake your hand. Long ago, we had plenty of land, but civilisation has driven us from it. Make better treaties, and see they are kept.'"[57]

The reporter for the *Evening Citizen* remarked: "Two races differing widely in physique, in colour, in tradition, and in taste, are brought under the eye of the onlooker, and while they palaver and career through the mazes of their wild dances there is ample scope for reflection on the mysteries of race."[58] Almost all of the journalists who were present made comparisons between the two races on show. The comparison is informed and indeed framed by the assumption of difference between the white race and "the others."

None of the white performers in Buffalo Bill's Wild West was ever put under the same scrutiny as the Indians, and the appearance and customs of the American whites were never described in the same detail as those of the Indians. While the Lakota were undoubtedly novel and thus intrinsically interesting, the detailed descriptions of "the Other" and the concentration on their differences bolstered the idea of the white race as being more "civilized" and therefore superior. This is well illustrated by the *Birmingham Daily Post*, informed by "the views of a specialist like Major Burke," which reiterated that the Lakota are "unfit to mingle with the populations of the great cities, for they betray a congenital dislike for physical labour."[59] A correspondent for the *Sheffield and Rotherham Independent* had a different view: "the once simple-minded red men . . . who wondered at the civilisation of the New World, have at least in some degree been made familiar with the splendid history of the old."[60] Either way, the Indians were seen as essentially different from, and inferior to, European whites.

The American Indians were commonly perceived to be a race in decline, a race so backward that they were doomed to extinction or assimilation—that is, the race would die by becoming white. Buffalo Bill's Wild West played on this idea by promoting the exhibition as one of the last chances for the public to see a way of life that was vanishing. The *Nottingham Daily Express* proposed that "the children who watched with excitement . . . will have for their manhood a memory of wild phases of Western life in a time that is fast fading away."[61] Even more suggestive is the statement made by the *Manchester Weekly Times*, which referred to Lone Bull as being "a fine old specimen of the decaying red man."[62]

The British press reserved its main focus for those Indians perceived to be "hostiles." An article in the *Sheffield & Rotherham Independent* noted that a leather badge identified the former Fort Sheridan prisoners.[63] Yet the press often mistakenly identified any Indians from Cody's Wild West who featured in newspaper stories as "prisoners of war," automatically according them the dubious honor and infamy of being "Hostiles."[64]

Undoubtedly, the use of the former Fort Sheridan prisoners brought an unrivaled attraction into the exhibition. The *Glasgow Herald* remarked that "they constitute the most extraordinary company that has ever visited the city. . . . Among them are 'Short Bull,' the originator of the 'Ghost Dance'; 'Kicking Bear,' the redoubtable leader in the uprising and 'Scatter,' the Prophet of the 'Messiah' among the Sioux nation."[65] Not surprisingly, Short Bull and Kicking Bear were portrayed as the most prominent Indians in Cody's troupe, and the majority of column space was devoted to them.

Short Bull was described by one journalist as being "the noblest Indian of 'em all. He is a diplomatist and was leader of the 'Ghost Dancers,' and High Priest during the Messiah craze."[66] Although he was commonly perceived as a deluded religious fanatic, several reporters who had been introduced to Short Bull were impressed by his "acute intelligence and strong personal magnetism."[67] Such acumen could not be native, at least according to a reporter for the *Leeds Daily News*, who suggested that Short Bull's marked intelligence had been brought about by his influential travels with Cody and "showed that civilization had made him a philosopher."[68]

A reporter for the Cardiff *Evening Express*, who was fortunate enough to interview Short Bull, described him as "a great man among the Sioux, an orator and a holy man."[69] Through the press, the British public was able to learn more about the Ghost Dancer and his understanding of the events of the previous winter. The *Leeds Evening Express* reported that Short Bull "in his musical tones" told "how the war arose, how it ended, and how he comes to be now happy and contented with Gen. Cody, Major Burke, and Mr. Nate Salisbury." The occasion was reportedly even more interesting because "some of the 'hostiles' have not hitherto opened their mouths on the subject since they left their country."[70]

While Short Bull was portrayed as a dreaming, visionary "noble savage," Kicking Bear was given the mantle of "war chief of the Messiah craze."[71] The *Nottingham Evening Express* "gleaned from Major Burke" that "Kicking Bear is essentially a soldier from the Indian standpoint . . . and while . . . probably not a man who could direct any warlike operation on an extensive scale, it is thought he would be exceedingly valuable in arousing enthusiasm and inciting small bodies to heroic deeds."[72]

The opinions of the press about both Short Bull and Kicking Bear were reflected by Salsbury in a letter to General Miles; this may suggest that the British press were simply repeating what was being fed to them by the show's representatives. In his letter Salsbury stated that Kicking Bear "is turbulent and lawless," and he described Short Bull as "a religious enthusiast, but a decent fellow."[73]

When Buffalo Bill's Wild West traveled north to Scotland for its five-month winter stand in Glasgow, the show's influence reached outside the limits of the arena.[74] Cowboys were employed on local farms to tame unmanageable steeds, and the games of local children were transformed by imitating favorite parts of the exhibition.[75] Yet it was not just children who had a newfound interest in all things associated with the American West. On 19 January 1892 Glasgow

Museums acquired twenty-eight Native American artifacts from George Crager. Fourteen items were bought for the sum of £40, and fourteen items were donated.

Four of the twenty-eight articles were so called "historical souvenirs" that had been collected in the aftermath of the Wounded Knee Massacre. Of particular significance was a Ghost Dance shirt, or Ghost Shirt, allegedly removed from the body of a dead warrior.[76] Crager had been present at Pine Ridge in the aftermath of the massacre as a special correspondent for the *New York World,* and while there he had managed to add to his collection of "historical souvenirs."[77] In two newspaper articles written before the Glasgow acquisition, reporters visiting the Wild West who had been invited into George Crager's tent described artifacts in his possession, including several Ghost Dance shirts.[78] Not all of Crager's artifacts had been acquired in South Dakota, and some had been given to him by the Indian performers. During the exhibition's summer season in London, a journalist noted that the Indians had recently given Crager "some striking proofs of their affection," and that there was "an interesting collection of Indian curios in the Major's log cabin."[79]

The experiences of the Ghost Dancers as they toured Britain with Cody's Wild West introduced them to the world of the whites from a position of relative security. As Vine Deloria noted:

> As a transitional educational device wherein Indians were able to observe . . . [white] society and draw their own conclusions, the Wild West was worth more than every school built by the government on any of the reservations. Unlike the government programs, the Wild West treated the Indians as mature adults capable of making intelligent decisions and of contributing to an important enterprise. Knowledge of white society gained in the tours with Cody stood many of the Indians in good stead in later years, and without this knowledge, the government's exploitation of the Sioux during the period before the First World War might have been even more harsh.[80]

The 1891–92 tour of Britain gave the Indians an expanded view of the world, allowing them to gain a better understanding of white culture and religion, while at the same time relieving them of the monotony and poverty of reservation life.

But the British public was not so open to alternate perceptions of "the Other," and Buffalo Bill's Wild West did little more than reinforce their sense of racial superiority. This can be seen both in the British reporting of the Ghost Dance and the Wounded Knee Massacre and in journalists' comments about the Indian performers with Cody's Wild West.[81] The British accepted Cody's stereotype of the Indians as inferior, barbarous beings, and "a vanishing race as a result of disappearance into the dominant white society."[82] Because of the geographical distance involved, European audiences had no knowledge that would contradict the portrayal of the Indians in the press. Further, as Brian Dippie has noted, "distance made the mundane magical, the ordinary exotic."[83] Although British audiences may have accepted or even endorsed the Wild West's message, they remain fascinated with the Indians. "In all its complexity, the audience's encounter with the American Indian performers continued to be one of the Wild West's defining features."[84]

CHAPTER EIGHT

THE INDIANS' EXPERIENCES
ON THE BRITISH TOUR

There is no record of the Indians' experience of performing in the Wild West on the second British tour. Indeed, the only comment concerning an Indian's perception of the exhibition itself comes from Black Elk, who stated, "I enjoyed the Indian part of the shows that we put on . . . but I did not care much about the white people's parts."[1] From the few published accounts of the experiences of Indian performers with Buffalo Bill's Wild West, the actual performance seems to have had little impact. In contrast, all such chronicles by Indians who performed in Europe refer to their journey across the Atlantic, indicating that this experience had a much greater significance for them. Short Bull's comment was short and to the point: "Our trip across the water made me somewhat sea sick but as soon as I got on land again was in good health."[2]

The concept of the Atlantic Ocean was both new and frightening for the Lakota, and most of them seem to have suffered from seasickness.[3] Black Elk's first experience of crossing the Atlantic appears to have been even more traumatic than most, since a violent storm took place during the voyage.[4] Luther Standing Bear told of traveling in steerage, the difficulties posed by rough seas, and how he found sustenance in traditional Lakota food after days of seasickness.[5]

The crossing of the Atlantic Ocean appears to have been to some extent a test of endurance for the Lakota performers, and the experience was one not easily forgotten. After the voyage, performing in the Wild West must have seemed fairly tame to the Lakota, although the show was not without its own hazards. Short Bull received an injury to his foot during the inaugural performance at Aix-La-Chapelle. It was reported that he had fallen awkwardly "and was consequently compelled to remain in his tepee with his injured foot swathed in bandages."[6] However, the injury was apparently not too serious.[7]

The equestrian nature of the performance, especially the "bucking broncos" and the high-speed races, meant that accidents and injuries were far from unusual. Such dangerous elements added to the sensationalism of the performance.[8] The accidents came to be seen as part of the whole Wild West experience. At the opening of a performance in Sheffield, when the Indians and cowboys were "scampering out [of the arena] . . . at breakneck pace," an Indian was seen to sink under his horse. His companions "swooped down upon him, picked him up, and bore him out, without once slacking rein." It was perceived as a brilliant feat of horsemanship, and the spectators, thinking it part of the performance, "applauded vociferously." As it turned out, the drop from the steed's back was not a feature of the show, and the Indian in question, Paul Eagle Star, dislocated his ankle when the horse slid and fell, trapping his right foot under its belly.[9]

Eagle Star was immediately transported to the Sheffield Infirmary, where it was found that he was suffering from a compound dislocation. Tetanus set in, and just over a week later, it was decided to amputate the foot. The show having meanwhile moved on to Nottingham, George Crager was sent to Sheffield with instructions from Cody to "spare no expense, secure the best care, and save his life."[10] It was reported that with the patient's sanction the operation had been satisfactorily performed, but that Eagle Star "was unable to survive the shock." Two days later, on Monday 24 August, it was apparent that the end was near. He asked Crager, "who was at his bedside, to give him his hand. Shaking it feebly he said 'Jesus, Jesus' and died." On his return to Nottingham Crager found the camp in a condition of gloomy depression, the "Indians were walking among the wigwams chanting a requiem for their dead comrade."[11] A correspondent of the *Nottingham Daily Express* noted that "the death of Paul Eagle Star . . . did undoubtedly keenly affect the whole tribe."[12]

An inquest was held at the infirmary, at which Crager and the infirmary's house surgeon, Mr. Hugh Rhodes, both gave evidence, and the jury without hesitation returned a verdict of accidental death. Afterward, Eagle Star's body was placed in a coffin and loaded onto a train bound for Nottingham. All the members of the Wild West show met the train at the station, where the coffin was unscrewed and the Indians each took a last look at their comrade.[13] The body was then removed to London, where the funeral attracted "considerable attention." In an open hearse drawn by black stallions, the remains of Eagle Star were transferred from St. Pancras Station to West Brompton Cemetery.[14]

Eagle Star was only twenty-five when he died. He was a Brule Lakota who had been educated at the Carlisle Indian School in Pennsylvania, and was reported to be "a great favourite with Colonel Cody."[15] Although consistently referred to as being "a prisoner of war" in the many papers that covered his death, he had in fact been hired with most of the other Lakota performers at Pine Ridge.[16] John Shangrau wrote to a friend at the Rosebud Agency informing him of Eagle Star's death and requesting information on the whereabouts of his widow.[17] Eagle Star's wife and child later received $500 from Buffalo Bill's Wild West, plus his back pay of $120. Furthermore, Cody also agreed to pay the widow $25 a month "while the Wild West show remained in existence."[18]

This generous settlement was in stark contrast to the allegedly poor treatment injured and dead Indians had received the previous year while traveling with the show in continental Europe. In the light of the investigations of the year before, or perhaps out of genuine concern, the management of Buffalo Bill's Wild West "went to extraordinary lengths to meet the needs of their employees" during the 1891–92 tour of Britain. Indians who were taken ill obtained the "best medical care regardless of expense," and those too ill to continue were returned to their reservations, including five who had previously been Fort Sheridan prisoners.[19]

A journalist for the *Sheffield and Rotherham Independent*, who had been introduced to the Indian performers, recounted that the Indians "consider our climate abominable, and wonder how we can live in it. Cold they can stand, for they are accustomed to it, but the frequent rains and constant moisture in the air are terribly trying."[20] At the start of the tour in Leeds, it was reported that Long Wolf "the old chief of camp" had soon been reduced to a rheumatic patient by "the cold east wind of this country."[21] By the time the show reached Birmingham at the beginning of August, the ranks of the Indian contingent had been further reduced as the weather and the hazards of the arena began to take their toll. The *Birmingham Daily Post* remarked, "Ten more left the States, but one was killed at Sheffield, and the other nine have been suffered to return, ill of chest complaints contracted in our changeable climate."[22]

The Ghost Dancers who were too ill to continue posed a greater headache for Cody than the other Indian performers. He had been ordered to inform the War Department of their return, so he had each former prisoner who returned due to ill health sign an affidavit. Cody wrote to the secretary of war on 6 June 1891, informing him that "two of the Indian prisoners named 'Sorrel Horse' and 'Horn Point Eagle' are and have been sick." They were examined by physicians, who found that both were "suffering from 'Lung Troubles' contracted long ago from exposure." They asked to go home, and Cody was requesting that they both be allowed to return to their agency. He went on to state: "They have done no work of late with the company but have received full pay, food, clothing and medical attendance; more especially 'Sorrel Horse' who has done but two days work in all with my company. . . . P.S. Their conduct has been excellent."[23]

At the U.S. Consulate in Bradford, Sorrel Horse and Horn Point Eagle each signed an affidavit. Both acknowledged that they had suffered from consumption for some years, and that their condition had been "greatly enhanced by exposure last year in the troubles . . . and not bettered while a prisoner at Fort Sheridan." Fearing that they might die in Britain, they were being returned at their own request. The affidavits were more or less identical, and both performers went on to assert: "Since the time of my joining the 'Buffalo Bill's Wild West Co.' I have received proper medical treatment, care, nursing and medicines, good food, clothing and pay, while our treatment throughout has been most kind and considerate. . . . and I regret that my physical condition causes me to separate from them."[24]

After being translated by George Crager, the affidavits were sworn before the U.S. consul, John A. Tibbits, and witnessed by No Neck, Plenty Wolves, Short Bull, Kicking Bear, and Lone Bull. Salsbury wrote to the Pine Ridge agent on 23 June, informing him that the two were to "sail on the Steamship *City of New York*—2nd Cabin" the following day.[25] Less than a month later Scatter, who had been Short Bull's companion on his journey to see Wovoka in Nevada and had been imprisoned at Fort Sheridan, was also returned. In his affidavit Scatter confessed to having concealed the fact that he was suffering from consumption, "thinking that a change of climate would be favourable to his health."[26] Cody was granted permission to return the sick Indians to their homes in South Dakota, and on 4 August the Pine Ridge agent acknowledged the safe return of Sorrel Horse and Horn Point Eagle.[27] Two more Ghost Dancers, Run Along Side Of, and the Brule, Standing Bear, were returned to their agencies later that same month, bringing the total to five.[28]

While Buffalo Bill's Wild West was performing at Earl's Court in London, Dr. Maitland Coffin was the resident doctor of the camp. In an interview with the *Star* entitled "The Wild West Doctor," Coffin acknowledged that there had been one death in the Earl's Court camp. "He was an Indian chief called Shug-a-man-a 'o-Has-ka or Long Wolf, nicknamed by the tribe of Ogalallas, Lame Warrior."[29] Long Wolf had been admitted to the West London Hospital on 5 June, along with another Indian performer.[30] After a short illness "due partly to old age, and partly to trouble caused by numerous old wounds received in battle," Long Wolf died six days later.[31] His compatriot was more fortunate and was discharged on the same day after responding to treatment.

Long Wolf was a veteran performer in Cody's Wild West, having been in the show since 1886, and had been accompanied on this tour by his wife Wants and daughter Lizzie.[32] His photograph appeared in the exhibition's program, which referred to him as the "Head Chief of the 'Buffalo Bill' Wild West."[33] He was often named in press reviews of the show as it toured around the country, the *Birmingham Daily Post* being typical: "Long Wolf is an 'old time warrior,' with a great record, which served him in good stead as a conciliator of the rebels."[34]

Dr. Coffin's testimony that he was "a complete mass of gunshot wounds and sabre cuts" suggests that he was a courageous warrior, and he is believed to have taken part in many fights, including the Battle of the Little Bighorn.[35] Long Wolf was buried "with much picturesque ceremony" in West Brompton Cemetery, close to the Wild West's camp at Earl's Court, on 13 June. Unlike Eagle Star's burial, which had been in a common grave, Cody had paid £23 for a plot, and the grave was dug 13 feet deep.[36]

Two months later the grave was reopened to admit a small coffin, which was placed on top of Long Wolf's. It contained the remains of a twenty-month-old Indian girl called White Star, whose parents were performers in Cody's Wild West. In the section of the exhibition known as "Life Customs of the Indians," White Star had been "placed in a saddlebag, slung across the back of a horse and paraded around the arena with other small children from the camp." On 12 August she had fallen from the saddlebag and had died from her injuries later that evening.[37]

Following the child's burial a stone cross was erected on the grave, bearing this inscription:

Chief Long Wolf, North American Indian with Buffalo Bill's Wild West Co. Died June 11th, 1892, aged 59 years. Also Star, who died August 12th, 1892, aged 20 months.[38]

At the center of the cross was carved a wolf in keeping with Long Wolf's wishes. His daughter Lizzie later remembered "that he knew he was going to die, and that he drew a picture of a wolf, saying he wanted it carved on his tomb."[39]

The Wild West encampment also had causes for celebration as it toured Britain. Nate Salsbury's wife, Rachel, gave birth to twin girls shortly before Christmas 1891 while the exhibition was in Scotland, and there were also marriages on the tour involving the Indian contingent.[40] During the exhibition's visit to Manchester a marriage took place between two of the Lakota Indians traveling with the show. Black Heart, a veteran of the 1887 tour, and Calls the Name, one of the three women who had been prisoners at Fort Sheridan, were married at St. Brides Church, Old Trafford, on 8 August 1891. No

Neck, the bride's brother, "gave her away," and the interpreter
George Crager acted as best man. On the marriage certificate, Calls
the Name's father is given as Smoke, which might suggest that she
was also related to John Shangrau, who acted as witness.[41] After a
private ceremony attended by employees of the Wild West, a nuptial
feast was held in the camp at Whalley Range. A reporter for the
Brighton *Argus* perceived the marriage to be "evidence of the desire
on the part of these people to conform to civilised habits."[42]

This marriage has several points of interest, not least that of Calls
the Name's single status. If she was unmarried while traveling with
the show, her employment broke one of the company's cardinal
rules. All the Indian women who traveled with Cody's Wild West
were supposed to be wives of the male performers. Moses stated:
"At no time did Cody's show employ unmarried Native American
women as featured performers. . . . John Burke explained that corpo-
rate policy dictated that only married women participate so that
there could never be a hint of impropriety."[43]

The exception made for Calls the Name is perhaps understandable, as she had been one of the prisoners at Fort Sheridan, but even
that is intriguing when we recall that Black Heart was reportedly an
influential peacemaker who had been working for the interests of
the U.S. government in 1890–91. This would suggest that the so-
called "traditionalist-progressive divide" had been bridged in this
marriage.

Black Heart had been married before, to one of Red Cloud's
daughters, and had recently been divorced. Calls the Name had also
been married before. She was between seven and nine years older
than her husband and, according to the London publication the
Morning, was a grandmother, her daughter and grandchild having
also traveled with the show.[44] The other two women who had been
prisoners at Fort Sheridan were Medicine Horse and Crow Cane.
Medicine Horse was reported to be the wife of another prisoner,
with both Brings the White and Knows His Voice being named as
such. Crow Cane's marital status is unclear.[45]

It is hard to interpret how the traditionalist/progressive dynamic
played out during the tour. From the evidence of the returning Indians in the summer of 1890, it was not unusual for a certain amount

of rivalry to exist between differing groups of Lakota performers, as evidenced by the fallout between Red Shirt and Rocky Bear. Yet with the hiring of the Fort Sheridan prisoners, this tour would have thrown up greater tensions than any other. Cody had within his camp Lakota who had been on opposing sides during the suppression of the Ghost Dance. However, there appears to be only one mention of any competitiveness in all the press coverage, and it was not confined to the traditionalist/progressive dichotomy. The *Leeds Evening Express* reported: "There are rival chiefs, who each endeavour to draw around them a following—the man who has the greatest following having naturally the greatest influence and power. But whatever the inner hidden rivalries between them, they seem sufficiently friendly and amiable with one another."[46] Being so far from home and in an alien environment, it would seem likely that the Lakota would concentrate more on their similarities than their differences. Outside their reservations, such rivalries were perhaps less significant than at home. But this testimony could also be an indication that the traditionalist-progressive dichotomy on the reservations had been exaggerated by white interference.

Perhaps mindful of the close scrutiny that their business would receive in the wake of the recent investigations in America, the Wild West management routinely gave reporters access to the show's vast dining tent. The Portsmouth *Evening News* commented: "The meal sampled by the reporter was not found wanting. There were two kinds of soup and three kinds of meat on the table, and the visitor was informed that there was never any stint, for every member of the company could always have just as much as he wanted."[47]

The *Leeds Daily Mail* carried a report of speeches made by the Indian performers at the beginning of their tour of provincial England. They expressed their satisfaction with the treatment they received while traveling with Buffalo Bill, and "told with artless candour the satisfactory arrangements they were engaged under with regard to their food and pay."[48] Luther Standing Bear recalled that "many of the Indians would want to go out and buy trinkets and things to carry back home, such as nice blankets and shawls. But during the rainy weather some of them thought they had an excuse to drink. They said they thought it kept them warm."[49]

It was one of the functions of the Wild West's Indian police to keep the Lakota performers away from alcohol. The *Leicester Daily Post* noted that "the Indians have their own police, who look after the conduct of their compatriots."[50] The Portsmouth *Evening News* commented, "No Neck is the chief of police of the Wild West, under the constitution which the Indians observe among themselves."[51] The *Leeds Daily News* detailed the role the Indian police played:

> Throughout the whole camp there is a marvellous spirit of order and discipline. So much is this the case that there is actually an Indian Policeman, whose badge is a white star and ribbon, who has eight men under him to keep the peace. If any man proved refractory, summary punishment is dealt out in the shape of a fine. There is no such thing as imprisonment, but if one Indian injures another in some way or other he is deprived of a portion of his goods. It is, however, very rarely that any occasion arises for the services of the policeman.[52]

Standing Bear, who was placed in charge of the Lakota performers for their 1903–1904 visit to Britain, informed all the Indians with the exhibition, before they sailed from New York, that he would do all in his power to keep them from obtaining liquor. At the beginning of his employment with Buffalo Bill's Wild West, Standing Bear had "heard that when any one joins this show, about the first thing he thinks of is getting drunk."[53] Such a reputation among the Lakota would surely belie Cody's claims of abstinence among his Indian performers.

While the exhibition was wintering in Glasgow, several instances that involved Indians somewhat worse for drink were reported in the local press.[54] In March 1892 a correspondent, who signed himself as "R. L. McG.," wrote to the editor of the Glasgow *Evening News* detailing his experience with a couple of inebriated Indians the previous night when he had been assaulted in the street, and warning the public to be on their guard.[55] Had the police become involved in the incident, it would surely have been a great embarrassment to the management of Buffalo Bill's Wild West, not only because of the Indians' state of drunkenness but also for the assault on a member of the public. Indeed, a similar incident, which occurred on Hogmanay,

resulted in one of the Lakota performers being incarcerated in Barlinnie Jail.

On the very same day that John Shangrau and Lillie Orr were
married, another party from the Wild West show appeared before
the sheriff at the County Buildings, but under completely different
circumstances. Charging Thunder, one of the Indian performers, was
remitted to the sheriff from the Eastern Police Courts "on a charge of
having committed a serious assault with an Indian club upon the
interpreter, behind the scenes of the Wild West Show on the 31st
ult."[56] George Crager had been chatting with Cody behind the
scenes while the performance was in progress. It was alleged that
Charging Thunder had then come stealthily up behind the interpreter and struck a smart blow on the back of his head with a 2-
pound club. The blow fell just about an inch below "a vital part,"
and although the injury inflicted was slight, the force of the stroke
rendered Crager insensible, and he fell prone. Cody quickly secured
Charging Thunder and handed him over to the police. He was put in
a cell, where he reportedly "lay down on the plank bed, pulled his
blanket over him and declined to speak to anyone." The next morning he was roused for a remand, which was extended until the following Monday, as Crager was unable to appear in court. At first no
reason could be assigned for the attack, Crager being unaware of
having acted in any way that might have roused the anger of his
assailant. Charging Thunder had already been through the hands of
the police of the Eastern Division, having been previously found
guilty of disorderly conduct in Duke Street and admonished. Of the
large number of Indians in the company, he was reported as being
the only one who gave serious trouble.[57]

Charging Thunder made a declaration before the Sheriff at the
County Buildings on 4 January.[58] He traveled up from the County
Buildings to Duke Street Jail, in a van along with a gang of twenty
other untried prisoners. In the prison he had been stripped of his
own clothes and provided with clothes made of dark moleskin. The
North British Daily Mail remarked, "He has, however, been allowed
by the authorities to wear his ornaments," and patronizingly went
on to note that "he relished the warm bath as a luxury not often
enjoyed."[59]

On 12 January Charging Thunder was bought before Sheriff Birnie in the County Buildings. He was charged "with having . . . assaulted George Crager . . . by hitting him severely on the head and neck with an Indian club." His sister and an Indian man wearing a medal bearing the words "Lieutenant of Police" accompanied the prisoner to court. In answer to the charge, Charging Thunder replied through an interpreter that he was guilty. Mr. F. R. Richardson, addressing the court on behalf of the prisoner, then stated that "Charging Thunder was only 23 years of age, and usually one of the quietest members of the Wild West show, but in common with other Indians, the slightest drop of drink was sufficient to infuriate him." On the night in question Charging Thunder had entered a public house and asked for lemonade, but by mistake, whisky was put into it. On returning to the show, he had become very much excited, and during the performance "the boy came up and raised an ordinary club, not a war club and struck the interpreter with it." The agent stated that Charging Thunder entertained no malice whatever toward the interpreter—indeed, they were friends. The sheriff asked where the shop was that supplied the whisky. Charging Thunder replied through the interpreter that it was in Duke Street, but he did not know the name. The sheriff then commented that if Charging Thunder had not been a stranger, he would have sent him to prison for a long time, but in the circumstances he would make the term short, sending him to Barlinnie Prison for thirty days as a warning to others. The sentence was translated to Charging Thunder, who left the court in a melancholy mood.[60]

At the time of Charging Thunder's incarceration, Barlinnie Prison was relatively new, having been completed in 1886. The original four buildings consisted of four-story cellblocks with accommodation for 200 prisoners in each block. Despite improvements, it remained a place of much hardship.[61] Charging Thunder is referred to as one of Barlinnie's "famous guests," in a book on Glasgow's underworld entitled *Such Bad Company*, which also claims that "[Buffalo] Bill had to make a personal visit to the prison to 'get the Chief the hell outa here.'"[62] While this latter statement seems highly unlikely, this reference to Charging Thunder does suggest that his brief spell inside Barlinnie became part of the jail's folklore.[63] Charging Thunder was released on 11 February and escorted back to the Wild West show by George Crager, the interpreter he had assaulted. He admitted to reporters that he had not enjoyed the food and prison life, but despite his incarceration he was in excellent health and "destroyed a very comprehensive breakfast."[64]

Cody publicly maintained a policy of abstinence as an example to his Indian employees, and was quoted as saying: "I cannot very well hold up my face before my large family on this drink question unless I practice what I preach, and so, while traveling at anyrate, I prefer to do without touching drink."[65]

This was no small concession for a man known to enjoy a tipple. Buffalo Bill had been fined one dollar for being drunk and incapable two years earlier, after celebrating the New Year in North Platte.[66] Glasgow was also no stranger to the problem of the "demon drink," and drink-related crimes were a regular feature in papers of the day. Indeed, after Hogmanay excesses in 1891, 250 drink-associated cases were brought up before the Glasgow courts.[67]

At a complimentary dinner for the Wild West's personnel in December, a correspondent for *Quiz* observed Cody's strict regime to keep the Indians from drinking. No Neck, Short Bull, and Kicking Bear, along with about fifty others, had been entertained by Mr. Galloway in his restaurant in West Nile Street. "Their taciturnity was only equalled by their keen desire for something short of a drink. They couldn't get it however, for fire-water risks cannot be run by Colonel Cody."[68]

The stereotype of the intoxicated savage Indian had quickly become established in the wake of European contact, and had given rise to the notion that the slightest drop of drink would drive an Indian crazy. In the nineteenth century, white experts claimed that alcoholism of many Indians resulted from a biological flaw and that their low resistance demonstrated a racial defect. At the time this seemed further evidence of the inherent weakness and inferiority of Indians, and in a sense legitimized their status as a vanishing race.[69] Such prejudice helped to distance Buffalo Bill from responsibility in the Charging Thunder affair, for many whites accepted without question Richardson's report that Charging Thunder had become so drunk after imbibing one "whisky-spiked" lemonade that he had attacked a "friend" without provocation.[70] Thus, the Wild West's management was relieved of embarrassment, and after Cody's assertion that he could control the alcohol consumption of the Indians in his employ, the blame was transferred to whichever public house had "mistakenly" served the drink. Moreover, with careful "spin" the Charging Thunder incident emphasized the "wild" nature of the participants in Cody's Wild West.

One possible reason for some of the excessive drinking while touring with Cody's Wild West was boredom. There was not a lot for the Indians to do when they were not performing. Perhaps in order to combat low morale brought about by inactivity, but also to satisfy General Miles's wishes that they would be taught "the power and numerical strength of the white race, and the benefits and advantages of civilisation," the Wild West management arranged visits to local places of interest for the Indian performers. In an interview with a journalist, Crager spoke lyrically about the positive effects of touring with the Wild West. "There is no place of interest in any town we visit that they are not taken to see. . . . They have been over the Portsmouth Dockyard, and were taken to the Gun Works at Birmingham, and a point is made of letting them visit all such places whenever the opportunity occurs. . . . We find that the Indians who were the most aggressive during the campaign [are] the most docile under Colonel Cody, and very anxious to learn the arts and industries of civilisation."[71]

Short Bull welcomed the outings arranged for the Lakota, and he commented that "we go everywhere and see all the great works of the Country through which we travel. It learns us much."[72] A correspondent for the *Birmingham Daily Post* remarked that the Indians took "an eager interest in seeing the processes of manufacture, and none of these impressed them so much as the great steam hammer."[73] Some trips were as entertaining as they were educational, as in the case of a visit to the steel works of Messrs. Joseph Rodgers & Sons in Sheffield, where the Indians were delighted by the "wonders of Electro-plating."[74]

There appears to have been a certain amount of Lakota manufacture going on during the tour as well. Some of the Indian men were reported to have been making drums or shields, perhaps for use in the arena or even for sale to the public. Short Bull carved a cane (*sagye*) depicting nine of his own war exploits, and also drew in pencil and crayon a total of forty-three images, including a self portrait. This might suggest that Short Bull used his spare time for reflection, possibly inspired by scenes he was participating in or witnessing each day in the Wild West arena.[75]

Being absent from their reservations for such a length of time made it particularly difficult for the Lakota to deal with problems back home. There is plenty of evidence that the Indian performers were corresponding with relatives in South Dakota, and although this personal correspondence does not survive, the letters written on behalf of the Lakota to the Indian agents illustrate some of their concerns. This correspondence also shows what lengths Cody was prepared to go to, in order to help his Indian employees, in some instances going far beyond what was required of him in their employment contracts.

The vast majority of communications dealt with money being forwarded to family and friends. Not long after Buffalo Bill's Wild West arrived in continental Europe, George Crager wrote on behalf of Cody and Salsbury to Capt. Charles Penny, the acting Indian agent at Pine Ridge. "I have this day sent in your care two money orders, one for $10 payable to Mrs. John Shangrau and one for $5 payable to Mrs. Kicking Bear (Kills Pawnee Woman). Will you kindly deliver same and send receipts. . . . We expect that many Indians will send their friends money from time to time and we will consider it a great favor if you will personally distribute it to the parties named."[76]

Captain Penny was very happy to cooperate with this scheme, but it was not without problems, and on 6 August 1891 the agent remarked with some frustration, "I wish, in remitting money, you would send draft. This is not an International Money Office here, and the Post Master here declines payment."[77] Penny also encountered problems distributing the money when people from outlying districts were not able to come in to the agency to collect it.[78] Not all of the money was posted back to the agency; when Indians returned from the show, they might carry with them larger checks, to be cashed and distributed by the agent.[79] By December 1891 Penny had been replaced by Capt. George LeRoy Brown, and the management wrote asking if he too would "confer this favor" of distributing the money, which he did.[80]

As well as making it possible for the Lakota to send money home to their families and friends, Cody also wrote to the acting agent on their behalf in relation to a variety of specific concerns. In May 1891, while the exhibition was in Brussels, Crager wrote on behalf of Cody "confidentially and in the interest of the Pine Ridge Indians who are with us . . . relative to lands heretofore occupied by them."

> They tell me that their families write, that the lands formerly occupied by some of them were taken up by other Indians; of course I don't know exact states of affairs, but would like to protect the interests of those who are absent with us. Of course you . . . [have] a list of Indians now with us and if there is any method of protecting their interests I would like to assist in doing so even at some expense. If they are giving land in severalty and any of our Indians have located lands heretofore I think it would be right that it should not be trespassed upon, . . . They are traveling by authority of the Department and have not forfeited their rights at home.[81]

On 3 July the agent forwarded a list of those Indians traveling with Cody to the "Additional Farmer" at the Wounded Knee District. He further stated, "You are requested to give their representatives special care and attention, to see that their rights are in no way trespassed upon or interfered with in the matter of their locations, farms, houses &c."[82]

There was also the matter of claims for cattle that had been taken by Ghost Dancers, when they fled to the Badlands during the military suppression of the religion. The claims were referred to Special Agent Cooper, who then wrote to the commissioner of Indian affairs.[83] "The claimants are in England some of their wives are with them and some are single men. I have allowed the wives of claimants to make proof in some cases where the husband was gone by making the claim in the wife's name. But I cannot see how proof can be made when all the claimants are in England."[84]

It appears that Agent Cooper was able to come up with some kind of accommodation for the Indians touring Britain with Cody, for on 22 April 1892 Capt. LeRoy Brown wrote on behalf of Red Cloud, concerning Black Heart's claim. Red Cloud informed the agent that "his daughter married Black Heart; that they lost many things during the trouble, that Black Heart put in a claim for these things and he and his wife were afterwards divorced." Red Cloud wished to have the claim money divided, so the agent requested that Cody bring the matter before Black Heart and "ask him to authorize someone to draw the money and divide it equally" between the two.[85]

No Neck was looking for reimbursement for losses he had sustained as far back as 1876. On 5 June 1891 he swore an affidavit before the U.S. Consul in Brussels, stating that when all the horses had been taken from Red Cloud's band in 1876, he had lost nine horses. During his absence while touring with the Wild West show, all the other Indians who had sustained such losses had been reimbursed by the government. Therefore, No Neck requested that the money due to him should now be left in charge of the Pine Ridge agent.[86]

The affidavit was forwarded to Agent Penny by Cody, who requested that if he himself had not forwarded it "thro the proper channels will you do so and inform me as to the amount left in your trust."[87] Penny replied on 30 July, informing Cody that "Special Agent Cooper . . . cannot pay over to me the money due to No Neck on his claim."[88] The following week Penny elaborated, informing Cody that No Neck would have to apply directly to the Treasury, further advising him to apply in person on his return.[89]

On 4 September, Penny wrote again to Cody, stating that Yankton Charlie had arrived bearing No Neck's affidavit and a letter from Cody inquiring "upon what grounds does Cooper refuse to pay this money."[90] Cody also urged Penny to use his influence with Cooper to have the money deposited with the agent, but Penny explained: "Of course I do not expect, hope or desire, to remain here for any considerable length of time if I have any sort of luck I shall be out of this business before No Neck returns. Under these circumstances I should think it certainly better that the money should be in the treasury than here in the Agency safe. The money is certainly his, and in safe keeping; much safer than it would be in the hands of an irresponsible Indian Agent."[91]

Captain Penny was appointed acting Indian agent for Pine Ridge Reservation at the close of the military suppression of the Ghost

Dance. He was a military appointee and wished to return to his military career. Penny clearly empathized with the Lakota, and on 4 August 1891 he wrote a note of reassurance with specific reference for Kicking Bear and Short Bull: "their families have full permission to remain here and . . . I will look after them and their interests, so long as I am here."[92] Two days later he repeated his assertion that "all the late prisoners of war have been turned over to me and taken up on the rolls for rations and other supplies," further promising that "they will receive the same care and treatment as the Ogalalla's who have always lived here." Those now traveling with Cody "need pay no attention to any disquieting rumors or reports that may reach them."[93]

One of the former Fort Sheridan prisoners had troubles back home that took up the time of both Penny and his replacement, George LeRoy Brown. In September 1891 Calls the Name received word from George Sword that a mare and colt given to her by the government had been taken "by the 'boss Farmer' and given to another Indian."[94] Cody requested Penny to "kindly investigate this matter and confer a great favor on me."[95] Penny responded on 2 November, asserting that investigation had found that the person who had been left in charge of the animals had neglected them, so they had been placed in the charge of another Indian. Penny concluded that "the trace of these animals is not lost and is not likely to be, and when Calls the Name returns, the matter of ownership can be easily and satisfactorily adjusted."[96]

Not satisfied with this response, Cody wrote on 12 November to Gen. Miles to request his "intercession," so that Calls the Name "may have restored to her, her rightful property." Cody laid the facts as he saw them before Miles. "The said mare and colt were held in keeping by her nephew Wm. Shangrau until her return to America, but the 'boss farmer' told Mr. Shangrau that as . . . 'Calls the Name' was away from the agency she 'could not have the mare and colt' besides 'she had no rights off the agency.'"[97]

Cody reminded Miles that Calls the Name was absent with Miles's permission and with authority granted by the secretary of the interior, and respectfully asked his assistance to secure "her rights and justice." The following day Cody wrote again to Penny reiterating that Calls the Name had not "left the agency of her own accord," much along the same lines as in his letter to Miles.[98]

On 18 December Calls the Name received two more letters informing her that her horses and cattle had also been taken away by "Boss Farmer Davidson." This spurred Cody to write again to Agent Penny "or [the] Acting Indian Agent," to request "that her rights be not infringed upon." He went on to state: "'Calls the Name' informs me that the reason the boss farmer is now venting spite on her is that she absolutely refused to cohabit with said Boss Farmer who has made many overtures to her regarding this and she says that your Chief of Police Major Sword is well acquainted with all the facts as is herein stated."[99]

George LeRoy Brown, the new agent at Pine Ridge, replied on 4 January 1892. His stance was not that dissimilar from Commissioner Morgan's, which might indicate Morgan's influence. The new agent reported that the regulations of the Indian Department stated that a person receiving stock from the government was held to a strict accountability for the good care and treatment of the animals. If they left their reservation for any purpose without making provisions for the proper care of their stock, they would forfeit all right to them. "The case in question . . . needs no explanation. Calls the Name left the reservation without providing any means of caring for the mare and colt."[100]

Calls the Name and her brother No Neck were unsuccessful in sorting out their respective problems back home while touring with Cody. But Cody's efforts on their behalf show his commitment to his Indian employees. In some instances, Cody may have been inspired by personal friendships between himself and the Lakota involved. No Neck had been chief of Cody's Indian police for some years, and the trust and respect between them quite probably transcended their employer-employee relationship. Unfortunately for No Neck, when he returned to Pine Ridge and applied to the Treasury for his money, he was informed that "no claim . . . appears to have been presented."[101] It is quite possible that Commissioner Morgan's personal policy of noncooperation may have adversely affected the interests of the Lakota performers.

In the wake of the investigations a year before, the management of Buffalo Bill's Wild West went to great lengths to care for the Indian employees during their 1891–92 tour of Britain. Crager, who had been so disturbed by the death of Kills Plenty that he had written to the secretary of the interior criticizing the exhibition, now told British reporters of the "splendid treatment" the Indians received in Cody's employ.[102] Indians who were injured or taken ill received the best medical care, and those too ill to continue were returned home. Furthermore, the death rate for the tour of Britain was down to 2 percent, one from old age and two from accidents within the arena.

Cody still remained unable to prevent the Indians from drinking and gambling while on tour, but they were not held under duress and were given freedom to come and go as they pleased. It is also possible that despite what he publicly proclaimed, Cody was unwilling to strictly police the Indians with regard to alcohol. He did not take a paternalistic stance with the Indians, and on a later tour of Britain, Luther Standing Bear recorded that Cody did not punish those caught drinking.[103] Whatever his attitude, it remains clear that the Indians enjoyed the independence offered by touring with Buffalo Bill's Wild West.

The Wild West's management attempted to alleviate the Indian performers' boredom between appearances, by arranging trips to places of interest. This was also perceived to be an object lesson to subdue hostile tendencies, by showing the Indians the great achievements of the white race. The humbling effect of being gazed upon by so many thousands of white faces night after night would also contribute to the object lesson, as it would clearly illustrate the numerical strength and permanence of white society.

Vine Deloria has noted that "Buffalo Bill's prestige enabled him to arrange for individuals otherwise regarded as dangerous characters to leave the reservation and participate in his tours."[104] The Ghost Dancers had a great deal more freedom than they would have enjoyed at Fort Sheridan, and were able to avoid much of the hostility they might have faced in America. Through performing in the Wild West, the prisoners also achieved a certain amount of status and recognition, and were treated with relative equality to the other performers in the exhibition. Deloria maintained that Cody "recognized and emphasized . . . [the Indians'] ability as horsemen and warriors and stressed their patriotism in defending their home lands. This type of recognition meant a great deal to the Indians who were keenly aware that American public opinion often refused to admit the justice of their claims and motivations."[105]

It is hard to ascertain what influence the 1891–92 tour had on the Indian performers in general, and more specifically on the Fort Sheridan prisoners. It undoubtedly made a real impression on those Indians who had never before visited the immense centers of white urban population, let alone crossed the Atlantic. Kasson has suggested that "performing for the Wild West may have satisfied other purposes, obscure to white observers: preserving their culture, securing leadership and status, even perpetuating spiritual traditions."[106] This sentiment was echoed by Frederick Hoxie when he suggested that the early experiences of some American Indians "exposed them to the scale and technology of modern society, and . . . [that in response] they chose to devote themselves to the preservation of indigenous traditions." In part these Indians were inspired by the "misconception of Indian life and character so common among the white people."[107] It remains a possibility that in a similar vein, the perceived misrepresentation of Lakota life in Buffalo Bill's Wild West could have motivated Short Bull to speak in such detail about his Ghost Dance experiences to George Crager, and in later life to anthropologists and other recorders.

CHAPTER NINE

RETURN TO AMERICA
AND THEREAFTER

When the Glasgow season ended, twelve of the Wild West show's Ghost Dance prisoners, including Short Bull and Kicking Bear, resolved to return to America. Buffalo Bill's Wild West gave its final performance at Glasgow's East End Exhibition Buildings on 28 February 1892, and Kicking Bear chose this moment to recount "his deeds of valor," a traditional Lakota practice also known as "counting coup."[1] George Crager later told a Chicago reporter that this performance had been "just as he would have done on his native soil if he had been preparing to enter into war."[2]

Kicking Bear had already resolved to sever his connection with the show, and in Nate Salsbury's opinion had persuaded some others that if they accompanied him, "they will go straight to the Reservation, and that if they neglect this chance they are foolish."[3] It is possible that Kicking Bear based this belief on the fact that those prisoners who had previously left through ill health had been permitted to return to their homes. Neither the management of the Wild West nor the U.S. government was altogether happy about the imminent return of some of the Ghost Dancers. Buffalo Bill's Wild West was losing its main attraction just before its return engagement at London's Earl's Court, while the U.S. government was regaining some burdensome prisoners six months earlier than anticipated.

Salsbury had used every possible argument in his attempt to keep the Ghost Dancers with the show, including translating the order from the War Department, which contradicted Kicking Bear's claim that they would immediately return home. In a letter to General Miles, written following the exhibition's close in Glasgow, he acknowledged that he was "compelled by circumstances to disregard your advice concerning the Indian prisoners in our employ. . . . as their natural perverseness is a bar to any policy that would operate to their well being." He further noted: "After an experience of eleven months with Kicking Bear I am forced to the conclusion that you have formed a just estimate of his character. He is turbulent and lawless. Has no fear of consequences and will promote trouble on the Reservation *sure*. The war spirit is evidently on him at present, as only last night he indulged in a long harangue filled with menace and bravado known as 'Counting the Koo' [Coup]."[4]

It seems unlikely that Salsbury was writing out of spite against all of the Ghost Dancers, since he went on to commend Short Bull as "a decent fellow, amenable to reason" with "a sense of honor utterly lacking in 'Kicking Bear.'" Believing that Short Bull's days were numbered, Salsbury recommended that he be sent home to "die among his people." He went on to warn that "another man among them that will bear watching is 'Revenge,' he is as full of vice and meanness as any *educated* Indian can be, he don't appreciate kindness and don't deserve it." He concluded, "The rest of them are just plain every day trouble breeders who expect to go back to the reservation and do as they please."[5]

Nine days earlier Salsbury had written to Stephen B. Elkins, the secretary of war, to inform him that some of the former Fort Sheridan prisoners wished to return to America, and asking whether he should "send them to Washington or Chicago?" Salsbury went on to advise Elkins that the Indians would leave Glasgow on 4 March, by the steamship SS *Corean*, and were due to arrive at New York City "on about March 15th (perhaps sooner)." George Crager had traveled ahead of the returning prisoners to act as the Wild West's agent, and Salsbury notified Elkins that Crager could be contacted at an address in New York if the secretary of war had "any special instructions" he wished carried out.[6]

On 5 March Elkins informed Crager that he should take the Indian prisoners immediately to Fort Sheridan.[7] Upon receiving Elkins's letter, Crager replied that he requested "the services of about four (4)

Enlisted men," to assist him "in properly turning said prisoners over to Genl. N. A. Miles," since the prisoners were "very much dissatisfied that they must return to Fort Sheridan." He further remarked, "Some of the men especially 'Kicking Bear' the chief and leader is a wicked and malicious man and would stop at nothing to get away and for this reason I appeal to you for assistance."[8]

Miles directed that Crager was to be furnished with a noncommissioned officer and three enlisted men by the commanding general at Governor's Island in New York, and that the entire expense was to be met by Crager. Miles directed that the Indians were to be "treated with all kindness" en route, and that they should be informed that the decision of the return to their reservation had gone before the Interior Department for consideration.[9] From his ranch in North Platte, Nebraska, Cody sent a telegram to the secretary of war on 11 March, in which he too drew attention to Kicking Bear, who "requires watching."[10] As a result of these negative reports, Miles was particularly concerned about Kicking Bear and Revenge. On 14 March he wrote to the adjutant general of the U.S. Army, informing him of the prisoners' pending return. "It was understood they would be occupied and kept in Europe until next October, but influences have been at work to draw them back to the reservation. They are a disturbing element, and if they return trouble may be anticipated. . . . [and] the presence of 'Kicking Bear' would tend to promote serious trouble within twelve months."[11] Miles went on to recommend that Kicking Bear and Revenge should be retained under the control of the military for the time being.

The SS *Corean* docked at the Brooklyn pier on Friday, 18 March, and the twenty-four Indians on board were met by Crager, Sgt. Christian Peterson of Battery H, and three enlisted men from Governor's Island. The soldiers at once surrounded the Indians and placed the twelve former Fort Sheridan prisoners under arrest.[12] The *New York Herald* reported that "in the party were chiefs Kicking Bear, head of the Sioux; Short Bull and Lone Bull, together with eight warriors and one squaw."[13] The paper believed that recent reports "of a possible revival of the ghost dances at Pine Ridge" would make it likely that the prisoners would be returned to Fort Sheridan, basing this opinion on the rumor that the Lakota had "been waiting for the arrival of the three chiefs to again put on their war paint." Short Bull acknowledged that he had heard of a revival of the Ghost Dance, but refused to talk with the press about it.[14] A reporter for the *New York Tribune* laid the blame for the alleged revival at the feet of the Indians who had been in Europe, alleging that they had been "writing letters to other Indians on the Western reservations, telling of the great things they would do when they got back."[15]

"The Indians took the matter in their usual stoical manner," commented one journalist, while another noted that they had "expressed their desire of an early release." The guard was due to accompany them to Chicago, where they would be handed over to another military escort from Fort Sheridan. The *Chicago Daily Tribune* mistakenly assumed that the escort had been ordered by the War Department, "to prevent the noble red men from getting drunk on the money they had gathered from the foreigners."[16] Instead it would appear that the soldiers were more than happy to allow the Indians to drink, as a report in the *New York Tribune* appears to illustrate. "The stern corporal and his three blue-coat soldiers marched the 12 captives from the steamer to an immigrant boarding house . . . to await the time when they should take the train to Chicago. The other Indians followed those under arrest, and all of them assembled in the bar-room of the hotel. . . . The Indians smoked cigarettes and drank lager beer to an unlimited extent, and all the while the four blue-coated soldiers stood about and watched them with immovable faces."[17]

Crager informed the journalists that forty-one Indians were left in Glasgow, where the Wild West Show had gone into winter quarters. He went on to confirm that he expected to get sixty more warriors and thirty-five cowboys for the show, which was due to open in London on 7 May. After treating the Indians to a feast at the Stuttgart House in Greenwich Street, Crager and the party left at midnight on the Baltimore & Ohio Railroad, bound for Chicago.[18]

Accompanied by Crager and the four-man guard, the returning performers from Buffalo Bill's Wild West arrived in Chicago at noon the following Sunday. Crager told the gathered pressmen that while abroad "there had been very little trouble with the Indians, notwithstanding the stories that have been sent back." Contrary to Crager's private statement to the secretary of war, he related to journalists that although Kicking Bear "had a bad reputation and was supposed to be sore about his arrest," he had been a model man. However, Crager also noted that "he and Short Bull have been constant companions since they left Pine Ridge, and whenever they had the chance they were always to be seen talking earnestly together. We were not able to find out what their scheme was because they did not confide in any one and when approached would cease talking."[19]

The Indians were then divided into two groups, with the former Ghost Dancers being turned over to a detachment of troops from Fort Sheridan.[20] The prisoners left for Fort Sheridan in the early afternoon, after which Crager and the other twelve Indians started out for Pine Ridge.[21] Newspaper reports suggested that the fate of the Ghost Dancers lay with the Interior Department, but given that Kicking Bear and Short Bull had appeared "to be conniving at some deviltry," it seemed likely that they would be incarcerated for some time.[22] On 23 March the *Chicago Daily Tribune* stated that Miles planned to interview Short Bull and Kicking Bear about their "present attitude toward the Messiah," after which he would decide their fate. If he concluded that they were still enthusiasts of the Ghost Dance, the paper suggested that "in all probability they will be kept prisoners until the summer opens." However, as there was no great excitement among the tribes at present, it remained possible that the prisoners would return home in April.[23]

Miles sent a telegram to the adjutant general of the U.S. Army on 23 April, in which he stated that after a personal examination of the prisoners and in view of the peaceable conditions on the Lakota reservations, "if there is no objection, I will send back all but three Indians, namely: Kicking Bear, Short Bull and Bring the White." Clearly, these Indians had demonstrated either a negative attitude or a continuing belief in the Ghost Dance. Revenge, who had earlier been a cause for concern, was sick with consumption. The post surgeon had recommended his immediate repatriation without delay, and Miles hoped to return the other nine prisoners with him.[24]

However, Thomas Morgan, the commissioner of Indian affairs, did not concur with Miles's belief, and instead asserted that "affairs at Pine Ridge Agency have been in a very unsettled and unsatisfactory state ever since the disturbance." He deemed it "of the highest importance that nothing should interfere" with the progress he believed had been made in their assimilation programs. "I cannot help fearing that their presence and their stories will have a very decided tendency to unsettle the minds of the Indians and to interfere with the forces now at work which make for peace."[25]

John Noble, the secretary of the interior, was more inclined to agree with Miles. The reports he had received from both Miles and the Pine Ridge agent had led him "to different conclusions from those arrived at by the Commissioner."[26] He said he was not at all apprehensive that any harm would result in the prisoners' return as proposed by Miles, acknowledging, "I have every confidence in his judgement in this matter and prefer to be guided thereby." Furthermore, he concluded that "as he confined these Indians as prisoners of War I see no reason why they should not be returned whenever, in his judgement, the exigency under which he took them shall have passed."[27]

Nevertheless, Noble's decision did not immediately result in authorization to return the prisoners, so on 6 May Miles again sent a telegram to the adjutant general. He suggested that with the exception of Kicking Bear, Short Bull, and Brings the White, the military could no longer be justified in retaining the Ghost Dancers. He was particularly concerned with the state of Revenge who was now in hospital and would "soon die" unless he was immediately returned to the more suitable climate of South Dakota.[28] Authorization was received the following day, and two days later Miles contacted Captain Brown, the acting agent at Pine Ridge, to inform him of the nine prisoners' imminent return.[29]

On 11 May Miles penned a letter to Young Man Afraid of His Horses, American Horse, Broad Trail, "and all other chiefs and Sioux Indians." The letter was in response to one sent on 13 April, asking about the Indians still held at Fort Sheridan.[30] Brigadier General Brooke had reported on 2 April that "the retention of Short Bull and Kicking Bear . . . causes dissatisfaction [among the Indians], their presence being desired at Pine Ridge for the spring medicine making."[31] Miles reassured the Lakota that the three remaining prisoners would

only be held for a few months longer and cautioned them "not to listen to anyone advising you to go to war again."[32]

Miles was unwilling to make Brings the White "prominent by
holding him as a prisoner with Kicking Bear and Short Bull"; therefore, in a letter to the adjutant general dated 7 June 1892, he proposed
to return the Indian to the reservation. "He was at Carlisle school,
has some intelligence, but is reported to be a bad young Indian. If
there is no objection, I will send him to visit some of the jails or court-
rooms and to the State Penitentiary at Joliet, Ills., in order to impress
upon his mind the restraint and punishment for evil doers, and then
send him back to his tribe quietly and alone."[33]

The proposition was forwarded to the Interior Department, and
Commissioner Morgan, who this time had no objection to the action
recommended, suggested that it would "doubtless have a very salu-
tary effect upon the Indian and will doubtless accomplish the end
sought."[34] The action was approved and authorized by the secretary
of war on 8 July, and Brings the White was released eight days later.
He was accompanied to Pine Ridge by E. L. Huggins, captain in the
2nd U.S. Cavalry, who notified the Pine Ridge agent on 17 July of
their pending arrival.[35]

Two days later Miles wrote to the adjutant general that "the time
has arrived to send the two remaining Indian prisoners . . . back to
their tribe; and if there be no objection, I will send them one at a time
to Pine Ridge Agency during the last of this month or the first part of
August."[36] Morgan concurred, stating "there is reason to hope that
hereafter they will conduct themselves in such a manner as to not
again necessitate their incarceration in the interests of peace and
good order."[37] George Chandler, the acting secretary of the interior,
also approved Miles's suggestion, informing the secretary of war on
2 August.[38]

It is unclear when the last two imprisoned Ghost Dancers were
released from Fort Sheridan to return to their families at Pine Ridge,
but it was certainly later than Miles had hoped. Nate Salsbury was
granted permission to visit them at Fort Sheridan on 20 August, and
on 6 September the London *Evening News and Post* reported that
Kicking Bear had been brought down from Fort Sheridan "to pose as
one of the figures in a group which will commemorate the Fort Dear-

born massacre of 1812."[39] Ironically, the Indian performer with Buffalo Bill's Wild West who had been portrayed and accepted as the epitome of a hostile Indian, had been selected to represent "the friendly Pottowattomie chief." The distraction of being a sculptor's model no doubt gave Kicking Bear some slight relief from the boredom of his incarceration at Fort Sheridan.[40]

It appears that Short Bull and Kicking Bear continued to forward money to their families while they remained imprisoned. When Crager arrived at Pine Ridge at the end of March, he gave the agent $30 to be passed on to Kicking Bear's wife, and $10 for Short Bull's wife. The agent wrote to Kicking Bear at Fort Sheridan to acknowledge that the money had been distributed as requested.[41] On 13 May the agent wrote again to Kicking Bear, enclosing a receipt showing that his wife had received the $10 he had forwarded. It is unclear if the agent, Capt. George LeRoy Brown, had been previously acquainted with Kicking Bear, whom he referred to as "My Dear Friend," but he clearly went some way to offer the imprisoned man a degree of reassurance:

> Your wife is in very good health. She was in here this morning to get the $10.00 and she was very much pleased. She is fat and her cheeks shine and her eyes were bright because you had not forgotten her, and she was glad to hear that you were also well. She is a good woman and has a good reputation among the people and deserves a good husband. I shake hands with you, my friend, in my heart and hope you will keep well and that you will tell my other friends that the people here have not forgotten them.[42]

On 12 October 1892 Brig. Gen. John R. Brooke referred to Short Bull and Kicking Bear as having been "released from confinement . . . and returned to their people." Brooke, who was the commander of the department that encompassed the Pine Ridge and Rosebud Agencies, had recently been "unofficially" made aware of their release, and was both disturbed and slighted that he had not been informed of the decision.[43]

Once Secretary Noble was satisfied that the Indian performers who had returned at the close of the Glasgow season had been well treated, he granted Cody permission to hire another fifty Indians.[44] Noble's only stipulation was that the men must not be under twenty-five years of age and the women not under the age of twenty, and he wrote to the Pine Ridge agent on 14 April 1892 informing him of the decision.[45] Shortly after, the new Indian performers hired for the exhibition's return to Earl's Court, London, for the upcoming summer season left by train from Rushville, but not without incident.

On 18 April Agent Brown was compelled to write to Cody care of the Leland Hotel in Chicago. The tone of the letter was angry, and the Pine Ridge agent opened with the words, "You will pardon me writing to you in a very plain straight way in regard to the manner in which the Indians were taken away from Rushville."

> I have but one rule in dealing with Indians; that is never to deceive them, and I am forced to the conviction that those in charge of the matter . . . did deceive these Indians with reference to Rocky Bear's going with the party as head chief. He returns this morning to the Agency, and I am told by reliable parties, that the balance of the Indians . . . knew nothing about the matter, but supposed that he was on the cars and going with them. It may be that this matter can be satisfactorily explained, but as it stands now I confess that I do not like it.[46]

Furthermore, Rocky Bear had leveled serious charges against the interpreters in Cody's employ, complaining that they were "not men of strong character, capable of controlling themselves." Neither, he claimed, did they help the Indians by giving good advice about how they should conduct themselves or by "explaining to the Indians the habits, manners, etc., of the White people, with whom they are brought in contact." Agent Brown hoped that Cody would give the matter serious consideration, because he himself was as responsible as Cody for the future welfare of the Indians who had recently joined Buffalo Bill's Wild West. He suggested that the Wild West should employ an independent interpreter "not connected by ties of kinship or otherwise, with the Indians whom you employ."[47]

Cody replied from New York four days later and immediately asserted that "the argument offered to you by Rocky Bear is entirely false." Instead, he laid out events as he saw them, claiming to have "a dozen witnesses" who could confirm that this version was "true and just." At Rushville Rocky Bear had demanded higher wages, which had been refused. After holding a brief conference, Rocky Bear then decided that he would "steal silently away and say no more about it," and he and Little Warrior had never arrived at the train depot. Cody recalled, "As soon as the train left all the Indians were informed of the matter, each and everyone being told that Rocky Bear was not going and all save *one* Indian were unanimous in saying *they were glad*."[48]

The controversy may well have resulted from Rocky Bear's request that he should "be head chief at a salary of $125.00 per month," and that his old friend from the 1889–90 European tour, Bronco Bill, should be employed as interpreter. Cody further maintained that Rocky Bear had been paid handsomely to go to Rushville, but as soon as he arrived, had begun to gamble and drink. Turning to the question of interpreters, Cody argued that at the council held in Brown's own Council Room "not one word was breathed against Mr. John Shangrau being chief Interpreter." Moreover, he said, "[m]y chief Interpreter does not drink or Gamble, he is a sober honest man and [I] can vouch for him and his reliability, he is married and settled down."[49]

Cody's explanation of the incident satisfied the Pine Ridge agent's disquiet, and he wrote to Cody in England to thank him for his "full and complete report on the matter."[50] The agent's opinion was significant, for the management of the Wild West relied on his good report to the secretary of the interior. Secretary Noble had consulted both Miles and Agent Brown on the condition of the returned Indians before granting Cody permission to hire an additional fifty performers for the show's summer season in London. If Brown had complained about Buffalo Bill's Wild West and its treatment of the Indian performers, Cody might once again have been faced with a ban on their employment. Their participation was crucial to the exhibition, and Cody had already set his heart on playing Chicago's World Fair the following year. Therefore, it was essential to maintain a good relationship with the Pine Ridge agent.

On 28 September Cody wrote to Secretary Elkins with the news that the last five of the former Fort Sheridan prisoners would be returning to America when the show closed in October. As all the other former prisoners had now returned home, Cody hoped that there would be no objections to the last five being returned straight to their agencies, "as they are all well-disposed and good Indians."[51] Permission was granted, and the remaining five Ghost Dance prisoners were returned to their homes and families. The SS *Mohawk*, which carried the Wild West's personnel, landed in New York on 24 October. The arrival marked the end of almost four years of touring in Europe. The Indian performers were returned to their reservations, and after traveling up from Rushville in Nebraska by wagon, they reached Pine Ridge on 1 November.[52]

The acknowledged Lakota Ghost Dance leaders, Short Bull and Kicking Bear, had made two significant journeys between late 1889 and the summer of 1892. The first took them west, when they traveled at the request of the Lakota as part of a delegation seeking to find out all they could about Wovoka and his new religion, which later became known to the Lakota as the Ghost Dance. The second journey took them east, initially as prisoners of General Miles who had them brought to Fort Sheridan, Illinois, at the end of the military suppression of the Lakota Ghost Dance. After two months' confinement they were released into the custody of Col. William F. Cody, and as performers in Buffalo Bill's Wild West, Short Bull and Kicking Bear accompanied another twenty-one Ghost Dance prisoners across the Atlantic to Europe. Their second journey was in part meant as an object lesson, to teach the Ghost Dancers the superiority of the white man and the futility of their opposition to the U.S. government's programs of assimilation. However, it was their first journey, across the Rocky Mountains to Nevada, which apparently had the greatest impact upon them. Clark Wissler noted: "After the collapse of the movement, they withdrew to different parts of the reservation, where they lived quietly with their respective bands. Short Bull seems to have been the abler of the two and quietly followed the precepts of the Ghost Dance Religion for a long time. His band remained the most conservative and the most pagan, yet gave the officials the least trouble."[53]

Both Short Bull and Kicking Bear maintained their belief in the Ghost Dance, and by all accounts they were not alone in this. In 1902

Kicking Bear once again journeyed west to visit Wovoka, and was just one of several Plains Indian delegations to do so.[54] Four years later the *Lyon County Times* reported that three Lakota men—Cloud Horse, Chasing Hawk, and Bear Comes Out—had traveled to Mason Valley from the Rosebud Reservation "to see Jack Wilson [Wovoka] . . . on some important business."[55] "They held a pow-wow at the Indian camp above Bovard's Sunday night, talked with Jack Wilson and smoked the pipe of peace all round. They made Wilson a present of a beautifully carved stone pipe, and, having accomplished their end . . . left for their homes Monday morning."[56]

1906

Grace Danberg noted in her anthropological paper, "Letters to Jack Wilson, The Paiute Prophet, Written between 1908 and 1911," that letters from both Cloud Horse and Bear Comes Out were found among a cache of twenty that had been left in a vegetable cellar constructed by Wovoka on a ranch in Nevada. Another Lakota who wrote to Wovoka during this time period was John Short Bull of Allen, South Dakota.[57] John, who would have been aged twenty-four when he wrote the letter in 1911, was the son of Short Bull and Plenty Shell, the older of Short Bull's two wives.[58] He sent Wovoka a $5 money order, and asked his advice on appropriate medicines and prayers for various illnesses. It is clear that this letter was part of an ongoing correspondence.

After Kicking Bear's return visit to Wovoka in 1902, he and Short Bull went on to instruct Fred Robinson, "a prominent young Assiniboin," in the religion.[59] Richmond Clow maintained in his article, "The Lakota Ghost Dance after 1890," that the two men traveled to the Fort Peck Reservation, Montana, in the autumn of 1902.

At Poplar, they taught the Ghost Dance to residents who later sent them "goods and money for their instructions and (for) different kinds of things that are used in these dances." . . . From these Lakota roots, Robinson molded the Ghost Dance into "New Tidings," a version of the religion that instructed the people to lead a "clean, honest life" and promised them that the souls of their relatives gathered to greet them after death. Taking this gospel to the Dakota of Canada, Robinson found believers on the Sioux Wahpeton Reserve on the Round Plain in Saskatchewan, where a Ghost Dance congregation existed as late as the 1960s.[60]

Short Bull's importance in Lakota history was not restricted to his association with the Ghost Dance, but also encompassed some significant ethnographical works. In his article "Short Bull: Lakota Visionary, Historian and Artist," Ronald McCoy asserted that "Short Bull's status and influence as a shamanic figure among the Lakota remained intact, as James R. Walker, agency physician at Pine Ridge, learned."

> Setting himself the goal of preserving knowledge of vanishing tribal ways, Walker spent nine years convincing Oglala elders of the wisdom of imparting important ritualistic information. The principal actor in this drama of the empowered members of one culture passing sacred knowledge to someone from another culture was Short Bull. In 1905, the elders announced that conversations could take place, but only if Short Bull received a vision sanctioning the sessions. Walker never learned the details of this vision, but the former Ghost Dance leader eventually approved of the endeavor. The resulting flow of information formed the basis for important works by Walker.[61]

When interviewed by Frederick Weygold in 1909, Short Bull also agreed to pose for a photograph. The image shows Short Bull wearing a Ghost Dance shirt, which Haberland suggests substantiated Weygold's report that the Brule medicine man had maintained his belief.[62]

The Wounded Knee orphan, Young Cub or Cub Bear, who appeared as Johnnie Burke No Neck in Buffalo Bill's Wild West, went on to tour with the exhibition for some years, accompanied by his adoptive parents, No Neck and his wife Ellen. The other child who had survived the Wounded Knee Massacre, and whom Burke had haggled over with Brig. Gen. Leonard W. Colby, was raised by Colby's wife, Clara, a leading proponent of women's rights. In 1896 Kicking Bear traveled to Washington as part of a delegation, and while there the group called upon the Colby household in order to pay a visit to the young child, Zintka or Lost Bird.[63] Perhaps the sight of this young Lakota girl reminded Kicking Bear of his own daughter, whose death had first motivated him to seek out Wovoka; the significance of the meeting would no doubt have been heartfelt.[64] Kicking Bear is reported to have died eight years later, in 1904, and given his return trip to see Wovoka in 1902, it is more than likely that he continued his belief in the Ghost Dance religion right up to his death.

Short Bull lived well into the twentieth century, and there has been some speculation about the actual date of his death. It has been said that he was interviewed in 1924 and photographed as late as 1933.[65] Yet an examination of the Pine Ridge Census Rolls suggests that by the time the 1924 census was taken, Short Bull had already died. Up until that time he had been listed consistently, first as Short Bull No.2 (as opposed to Short Bull No.1, who later became known as Grant Short Bull), and then in 1898 and after, under the name of Arnold Short Bull. Therefore, it seems likely that Short Bull died in 1923 or 1924.[66]

For Buffalo Bill's Wild West, new acts were continually being incorporated into the show, as it went on to embrace the Congress of Rough Riders, but the Indians remained as essential to the show as Buffalo Bill himself. Cody never again faced a ban on his employment of Indians for his Wild West show, which continued more or less until his death in 1917, in various guises. Indeed in 1894 the then commissioner of Indian affairs, D. M. Browning, visited the show at Ambrose Park, New York. Not only was the commissioner reportedly "delighted" with the performance, but he was "equally pleased at being afforded an opportunity to note the effect of civilization upon the Indians, and . . . expressed himself as being delighted at the manner in which Messrs. Cody and Salsbury care for those in their employ."[67]

The journey west to see Wovoka was clearly of much greater significance to Short Bull and Kicking Bear than their tour with Buffalo Bill's Wild West, but perhaps Cody did them a great favor, and touring with the exhibition was infinitely better than being held at Fort Sheridan. That Miles still perceived the Ghost Dance to be a threat is evidenced by his decision to keep Short Bull and Kicking Bear imprisoned when they returned to America, on the basis that they had maintained their faith. Miles also recognized that by removing and incarcerating the Ghost Dancers, he had given the Indians a certain amount of status. Unwilling to confer such notoriety on Brings the White, he had argued for his early release.

Miles's object lesson of dissuading the Ghost Dancers from believing in the religion seems to have been unsuccessful. It was certainly pointless, as belief in the Ghost Dance had not made the Lakota hostile, as Miles supposed. Instead, the Lakota Ghost Dance had been a peaceful religion that incorporated traditional Indian practices with elements of Christianity. It was an example of accommodation during a time of great transition for the Lakota. Those Lakota who embraced the Ghost Dance saw the religion as an accessible way forward, something that connected the old life with the future without denying them the right to an Indian identity. It became a resistance movement only when the government forcibly tried to suppress it. Ironically, the closest the Fort Sheridan prisoners got to actual rebellion was when they performed Cody's interpretation of Indian-white relations in the Wild West arena.

APPENDIX

Five Short Bull narratives were recorded between 1891 and 1915; all five are presented here. The first, which was transcribed and translated by George Crager in 1891, is presented as written, with its limited punctuation, and all words that appear in parentheses are Crager's. This handwritten document is held in the archives of the Buffalo Bill Museum and Grave, Golden, Colorado. James Walker, the Pine Ridge agency physician, recorded the second narrative, which includes two parts. The original manuscript is in the collection of the State Historical Society of Colorado, Denver. It was published in James R. Walker, *Lakota Belief and Ritual*, ed. Raymond J. DeMallie and Elaine A. Jahner (1980; reprint, Lincoln: University of Nebraska Press, 1991). The third was recorded by Natalie Curtis around 1906 and was published in *The Indians' Book: An Offering by the American Indians of Indian Lore, Musical and Narrative, to Form a Record of the Songs and Legends of Their Race* (1907; reprint, New York: Gramercy Books, 1994). The note at the beginning appeared in Curtis's publication. The fourth was initially recorded in English by Frederick Weygold, but survives only in German translation. It was included in Wolfgang Haberland's article "Die Oglala-Sammlung Weygold im Hamburgischen Museum für Völkerkunde (Teil 4)," *Mitteilungen aus dem Museum für Völkurkunde zu Hamburg*, N.F. 7 (1977). Haberland stated that "according to Weygold's notes, he talked in the summer of 1909 a few hours with Short Bull, supported by an interpreter, probably . . . Herbert Bisonette." I have translated this narrative back into English; all the parenthetical insertions are Weygold's explanations. Ivan Stars transcribed the final narrative in Lakota in 1915, for Eugene Buechel. The original manuscript is held in the Holy Rosary Mission, Special Collections and Archives, Marquette University Libraries, Milwaukee, Wisconsin. Raymond DeMallie translated it for this publication, with assistance from Dennis Christafferson and Rani-Henrik Andersson.

1. AS NARRATED BY SHORT BULL (1891)

In the fall of 1889 I was at Cheyenne Agency and returned to Rosebud Agency in time for the issue. I then went to carrying freight for the Government between Valentine Neb. & Rosebud Agency. I had made one trip and getting ready to make another, when a messenger handed me a letter. I asked for whom the letter was, his answer was, "Take it to the Council house," I done so, the Council house was full of people as they were dancing "Omaha" at the time—I went at night to the council house again, and saw two Brules searching through the crowd as if looking for some one. One of the men was "Eagle Pipe"—When they saw me, they pulled off my blanket & placed me in the centre of the circle, at this time I did not know what they meant, they then selected "Scatter" whom they said was to go with me on a great mission—Standing Bear (Brule) gave me a new Blanket and leggins—saying "We have a letter from the West saying the Father has come and we want you to go and see him (meaning the Messiah)—"You must try and get there, see him, recognize him and tell us what he says and we will do it. Be there with a big heart. Do not fail." (These were the expressions of the entire council.) It may here be said that those present in the council room were all armed because "Two Strikes" son had choked one of the Indian Police, and a fight was going on outside. I said nothing but thought a good deal—The next morning another Council was held and here they told me what my mission was to be.—Men and women were assembled and my Uncle spoke, saying—"I am not afraid to tell you what this letter contains," it was read—and the wind was blowing so furiously that the whole house was filled with dust, but as soon as the reading of the letter began the wind ceased—this gave me confidence—I had faith to go—I had no belief in it before but now my mind was made up—My people know I was a man of Truth and could be relied on—I stood up and said "My brothers—you are all sitting here with your guns, this is not what the Messiah wants us to do, and when I leave here I ask you to drop your arms, follow my trail, watch my movements and have no trouble with the whites or Police, be as one, drop no blood; If I have to stay two years I will try and see him myself and bring you his words—

"Sore Back" arose and said "My boy—I select you to go West, you ask me to drop my arms and be peaceful and I will do it; I look to you to bring us the good word. Don't think we will shed any blood, we will do right."—

Two days after this Council Scatter and I started, we went to Pine Ridge Agency, (but before starting "High Hawks" brother gave us a buggy). We found at Pine Ridge that "Kicking Bear" "He Dog" "Flat Iron" "Yellow Knife" "Brave Bear" and "Twist Back" had left two days before for the West—and on the night previous "Yellow Breast" and "Broken Arm" had left. We were delayed one day at Pine Ridge to have the buggy repaired—We then started off and after hard travelling for two and one half days we caught up with the Ogallalas at Sage Creek near Casper Mountains—Here we also met "Man" and his two nephews Louis and John Shangrau who were returning to the Agency from a trip to Fort Washakie—we told them we were travelling West to meet the Messiah—We then traveled on to the Arapahoes at Shoshone Agency where we stayed until one week after Christmas, when we started on horseback to the end of "Painted Rock" here we boarded a Rail Road train and arrived at a point where only Chinamen were. The Agent at Fort Washakie gave us Rail Road Passes, Sitting Bull gave me 25 Dollars and I sold one of my beaded vests for $10, while we were at Shoshone Agency we danced the "Omaha" and got presents of money—We stayed three days at the Chinamans town, we then boarded another train travelling one day and night, but owing to a "hot box" we had to get out at the forks of a large creek where we camped for the night, the next morning we walked about 1½ miles reaching a small town, and once more began to travel by rail—The snow was so deep that plows were used to clear the road which delayed us three days in a small town, on the fourth night the road was open so that we could travel again; after spending the night on the train we came to a creek which was lined on either side by Lodges, a town was near so we got off the cars, travelling by foot to this Indian Village—The snow was very deep—Two of the men of this camp had been to see the Messiah. The Chief of the tribe was the brother of "old Washakie," who set up a teepee for us, we stayed nine days and nights, five of which were spent in "Ghost Dancing"—despite the snow, but a rainstorm came up and melted the snow shortly after the dancing began. Here 10 Bannocks came over and took us with them, horses were provided for us at an Agency named "Pocktella"—Here we met two big Indians, one with long black hair and the other with a black beard which looked so strange, they were both holding horses, the bearded mans name was "Botee" and the other "Elks Tusk Necklace"—At the request of Washakies Brother "Yellow Breast" and myself remained with him, while the others left—We went to his house and here I saw a Dakota woman who was married to a white man—Washakie's brother told me that the Messiah would talk to me, but he wanted to say something to me first—saying—"Once I went to Washington and had a talk with "Spotted Tail," "Two Strike" and "Red Cloud" (speaking in the sign language) pay no attention to what some people say, the Messiah will tell you the truth. I shook hands with all the Sioux Chiefs and dropped my arms against them for good and am their friend—Don't be afraid, no one will harm you here we are all friends—you will not die." Here the Bannocks came in for their rations and they gave us rations too also horses and took us with them to the other party who had gone on ahead, and we held a Council at the house of "Elks Tusk Necklace" who said—"My heart is glad to see all of you people today—my people here always do as I ask of them—we shake your hands and are glad—that fighting we done in the past is dropped—We are friends and hope we will always be so—Now we will go together to the Messiah—He sent for me three times and I went, he has now sent for me again and I will go with you.["]

After remaining here ten days over one hundred boarded the cars and travelled from the evening till the next night, where we changed cars to arrive at another Agency of the Shoshones. From this point "Sitting Bull" of the Arapahoes, "Short Bull" of the Sioux "Porcupine" of the Cheyennes, and several Bannocks started for the Messiah by rail, after travelling from town to town for two days, we came to an Indian Villiage whose teepees were made of Bark & willows—The chiefs name was "Owns the people" of the "Rabbit Skin tribe", (their blankets and bedding being made of rabbit skins), the women were dressed like the white women and they lived on fish, they have an Agency—their rations are small and one beef suffices for the whole band—they are rich—they fish continually and sell it.

From this point we moved in wagons and other conveyances for one day to the Puites where we remained thirteen days and then began to travel West, camping on a large creek the first night, and then following the Railroad to a station where some young men and women of the "Rabbit Skin" tribe met us who told us to go to the right of a large house in the distance and there remain two days which was done.

After waiting two days the party started overland all but one Gros Ventre, a chief of the "Rabbit Skins" Two Bannocks and Short Bull who boarded a train at about 3 O'clock in the morning and at Sundown reached a white mans villiage where an Agency was—This was the supposed home of the Messiah—they met some Indians who told them the Messiah would come in three days. Short Bull here found out that the letter that was sent to all Indian reservations asking them to gather at this point was written by an Indian.

The spot selected was a lovely one, a heavy growth of Willow all around it, and a Circle had been cut down in the centre with entrances North, South, East and West—Short Bull was put at the West End with a Gros Ventre and Sitting Bull (Arapahoe)—In this circle were only a few Indian Chiefs all the rest camping outside. In 2 days the wagon party came, besides every train bringing more and more people to this great gathering who had been sent for from all parts of the United States, there were, Sioux, Cheyenne, Arapahoes, Puites, Gros Ventres, Bannocks, "Rabbit Skins", Indians with rings in their nose and others, names of which Short Bull did not know—Being tired Short Bull laid down but the next day got in a wagon and went out to a ridge which would be the spot where the Messiah would arrive, after looking for some time could see no signs of him when finally a messenger arrived asking for a conveyance to bring the great man in—It was given him, the crowds then mounted their horses to go and meet him, but in a short time the wagon appeared from which direction it came no one knew, it contained two persons—The driver, an Indian, dressed in

white mans clothing; and another man who had on a broad brimmed
brown hat with two Eagle feathers in it, and a striped blanket.—The
person with the blanket on was the Messiah—Short Bull wanted to
shake hands with him but the Chief told him not to saying "Wait till
you go back then he will shake hands with you"—at dusk I went out
and told all my people to come in—inside the circle a small Teepee
was put up for the Messiah he entered with his face toward the
south—the teepee was opened and we all stood before him, everybody crowding to get a glimpse of him—he took off his hat laying it
on the ground with the crown down and brim up and said "How"—
an old man sat infront of him with his arms extended on his knees
and another behind him in the same position, these were his interpreters, while the Messiah spoke these men would stand up and
interpret what he said—Short Bull sat directly in front of the Messiah
and looked him all over from head to foot.

(At this stage of the story "Short Bull" went into a trance remaining so for quite a while and then continued.) One of these interpreters talked in English to one of the Arapahoes named "Singing
Grass" a son of old Chief "Friday" who spoke to me in the sign language—The Messiah said—"I have sent for you and you came to see
me. I will talk with you tomorrow—today I will talk to these people
who have been here so long—We will now pray"—here all who were
assembled crowded in with their faces turned toward the west, the
Messiah made a "speech" but they did not tell me what he said—I
got a good look at him, he was dark-skined, talked in a language
similar to Indian and I believe he was an Indian.—After he had
ceased talking dancing began in which he joined. Men, women, and
all were singing and dancing with hands joined in a peculiar way,
knuckle to knuckle, going round and round. Keeping it up for a long
time.

The next morning a crier called out for all to assemble as the Messiah was coming—The Inner Circle was spread over with white
sheets for the people to sit on—Everything was quiet—The Messiah
stood up and looked toward the west and began to talk (through 4
Interpreters) he said to "Short Bull." "I have sent for you to tell you
certain things that you must do. There are Two Chiefs at your Agencies and I want you to help them all you can. Have your people work

the ground so they do not get idle, help your Agents and get farms this is one chief—The other Chief is the Church—I want you to help him for he tells you of me; when you get back go to Church. All these churches are mine, if you go to church when you get back others will do the same. I have raised two bodies of men on this earth and have dropped one of them that is the Army, I want no more fighting. take pity on one another, and whenever you do anything that is bad something will happen to you—I mean fights between the Indians and whites—all over the world one should be like the other and no distinction made, always sing and pray about me, for it is right, 2 days from now all nations will talk one tongue (Short Bull thinks he meant 200 or 2 years) the sign talk will be no more. Educate your children send them to schools"—He prayed again and stopped. These are all the words I got from him—While they were dancing the Ghost dance I saw White men, women and girls joining in the dance. I saw the Messiah daily for five days, he [his] name was tattoed on the back of his left hand; On the fifth day I shook hands with him and all he said was that "soon there would be no world, after the end of the world those who went to church would see all their relatives that had died (Resurection). This will be the same all over the world even across the big waters."

He advised us to return again in the fall of the following year when he would have more to tell us, but for reasons we did not go.

Our party returned by the same route we came, only one accident occurring, the train was overturned and fell over an embankment but no one was hurt.

When I reached Rosebud Agency everybody looked for me, on the second day after my arrival I went to the Council house to tell them all about what I had seen and heard, but was stopped by Indian Police by order of the Agent, they arrested me and took me before the Agent to whom I told my story—he told me if I would tell this story to the Indians I would be a dead man—I laughed and said it was good—"I wanted to tell the Indians what I have told you but the Police stopped me—

When the "Ghost dancing" began I did not go there but went afterwards, it was not started by me but by "Scatter"—Once one of the Indian Police and Interpreter Louis Rubadeau insulted me, I did not say much to them but said this "The Messiah told me not to fight and I will not you may take a gun and kill me if you want to.["]—Louis Rubadeau said to me "See if one of the dancers who are in a fit see the Messiah, I[f] you can't do it you will be lost." at this Louis' brother who was nearby, grabbed him and dragged him away. Louis told "Turning Bear" if you will kill "Short Bull" the Agent will give you One hundred Dollars, two horses, a cow and a yoke of oxen. "Turning Bear" told this to "Short Bull" who laughed and said nothing. "Turning Bear" was told to rush into the teepee, grab "Short Bull" and if he had him help would rush in to assist him to finish the job. This was in May and the "Ghost" dancing had well begun. One day while a dance was in progress I stood up in the centre and told all my people what the Messiah had done and said—the people kept the dancing up with a good will. My funds were now getting low so I applied to the Agent for an order to get some freight at Valentine this was refused me, I was somewhat angered but said nothing. I then went to live with my uncle "Hawk Eagle." I lived with him sometime occasionally visiting the dances and finally participated in them, becoming in time a "regular" dancer—day and night—I kept telling my people of the Messiah and they had faith in him—this was good—While in the ring dancing one day one of the Indian Police, a son of "Rope Necklace" (a cut off) caught hold of my shoulder and turned me around [and] said "You have you ears, (the dancing stopped) and "White Horse" told the Policeman "to go away, as the Messiahs words were right, he only wanted the people to do two things, Farm and go to Church. We should not fight but be friends—I do not see any wrong in that—it is right and true, Short Bull has told the Agent all these things—We sent him to see the Messiah and we believe the words he has brought—he speaks the truth—the Indian Police are making trouble and soon plenty of whites will come here and make us trouble"—that is all I have to say—and the Policeman left and dancing was resumed—The next day "Sore Hip" sent for me and I went to him—he told me "that he had seen "Red Cloud" sometime ago in reference to transferring a number of families to Pine Ridge Agency and that he was going to see him again and that he would be back in five days, but requested me to go to my home and stay there until he should return," which I done. But while enroute from the Agency to my home I was met by a band of Ogal-lalas who had come over for the purpose of dancing—So we camped all the young men (Brules and Ogallalas) danced the "Ghost Dance" among the young men was a brother of "Iron Foot" who took quite a lively interest, he said "he had seen the Messiah and was much "worked up" over it (Short Bull does not know if this young man saw the Messiah in person, or if he had only seen him in a "trance" while dancing the "Ghost Dance.")

On the 5th day I went to "Black Pipe" Creek and waited for "Sore Hip" all those who wanted to be transferred to Pine Ridge Agency going along—We met "Sore Hip" who told us "that all had been arranged for our removal and that we were to start in four days.["] So on the night of the third day those who had no wagons moved to Pass Creek—and the main body was to move the next day, but before moving we had a great Ghost dance that night—In the middle of the night I was awakened by a friend who told me that many of my peo-ple were moving toward Pine Ridge Agency which surprised me, and some Indian freighters who had just returned from Valentine sent me word that soldiers were moving toward Rosebud Agency. I did not know why this should be, and it made me angry. One of these freighters "Rescuer" son of Elk Road told me that they were coming to arrest me and if I was not given up they would fire on us all. It was on account of many lies spread by others that I was to be arrested for. "Rescuer" said all the freighters heard the same, this was in November—I called my people together on Pass Creek and told them "to move forward and I would stay here alone, as I did not want them to have any trouble on my account. I want nothing but what was right for myself and my family. I had done as they wanted me to, and now have no rest, day or night—My brother "White Thunder" and my Cousin "Thumb" had been killed for jealousy and now they want me—Go on, I will stay here if they want to kill me they are welcome." that night they moved, all save myself and a few young men, my family who were on Pass Creek moved also; that night my brother came to me and said it was all lies that the freighters said, and the next morning some of the young men came back for me and I followed them camping that night on "Crow Creek," we broke camp the next morning, moving to "Medicine

Creek" where we rested, camping that night at the forks of "Medicine Root Creek"—The next morning an Ogallala came to us telling
us to move our camp to the crossing by "American Horses" villiage
which we done. having settled our camp we went in a body to the
home of "Little Wound" singing (which signifies a Treaty of friendship"). An old man known as "Issowonie" rode around our circle
and stopped in the middle saying to us, "My boys, save your Pow-
der, Guns, Bows, Arrows and Ammunition, for the Agency is full of
Soldiers—Red Cloud says if they do anything we will fight them,
and Little Wound says the same, our own people have caused the
soldiers to come here by telling lies, American Horse, Charging
Thunder, Fast Thunder, Spotted Horse and Good Back told these
lies, tomorrow morning we will go to Wounded Knee Creek." The
Agent had sent for Little Wound to bring Short Bull and his people
to the Agency, so Little Wound started with Short Bull and ten
Brules, they halted at the house of "Cherry Cedar" where they eat
some dried meat, continuing afterward to the Agency bluffs and
resting. Little Wound going on ahead to the Agency, it was sundown
when Cheyenne Creek was reached, and afterwards going to the
lodge of "Twist Back" on the Agency—While in this lodge I was
called out by some of my young men who told me the Indian Soldiers were about to surround us, at this we remounted our horses
and rode back to our camp on Wounded Knee Creek—Our people
were surprised and feared something was wrong—the old crier then
told me to move my people who were poorly mounted to the Bad
Lands, as his people had told him to bring me this word, and should
anything happen Red Cloud and the rest would join us there with
plenty of horses. The Ogallalas brought a large lot of horses to us,
saying that they belonged to a white man ("Big Bat") who lived up
the creek, we went to him and he told us that "if there is going to be
fight he could not take his horses with him as he had so many all
over the country and if we wanted to ride them we could" so some
of the Brules did take them; "Sore Hip" "High Hawk" and "Chief of
the Black Hills" (a white man who is a judge) came out to us to have
a talk. I did not go to the Council and don't know what was said—
The next morning we moved toward the Bad Lands and camped
there that night. "High Hawk" and the others returning to the

Agency, no good being done by them. After we went into camp some half breed Indians came to us, "No Ear" was in charge asking us for stray horses, they looked through our herd and while picking some out one of our Indians was kicked in the head so we killed the horse that kicked him—The shot caused an excitement in the camp which only proved to be some wrangling among the Indians. I called them together and bid them to stop saying "I wanted no trouble"— "You must stop, you should do right, have no fighting, You have taken and butchered other peoples cattle and stolen horses, we will move back to the Agency, sell our ponies, pay for these cattle and have no more trouble, the Ogallalas must listen to what I say as well as the Brules, you have plenty of dried meat now, but do as I ask you"— they would not listen but moved toward White River—I again asked them to listen, they had no ears, telling them to go to the Agency and that as soon as I got over being mad I would come in too—At this the young men surrounded me, I covered my head with my blanket so I could not see who would kill me for I heard their guns cock, one of them spoke up bidding me to uncover my face so I done it—I told them the reason I covered my face was that I did not care to see who would kill me, and wanted no trouble, the women then came in crying, the warriors left to recall the party who had started for the Agency and brought them back to my camp, which was on the hill by the Bad Lands. Five of our men were then sent to Cheyenne River to buy sugar and other things for our use and as they neared a house, at the end of which was a haystack they were fired upon by a party of whites and my nephew "Circle Elk" a young boy who had been to school at Carlisle was killed—he could speak English and for that reason was sent with the party—When the four returned all of the young men mounted their horses to bring back the body of my nephew. I could see them in the distance going backward and forward when finally one of them returned saying they had met a band of Ogallalas from Pine Ridge Agency and they had taken away their guns. I told him to go back and return the guns, they had not been sent out to make trouble but to bring back the body of my nephew; he went back to the place and they all came back to the camp. "Roaming Walk" who had a "Medicine Pipe" (made of bone) laid it before me to fill and smoke but "Porcupine Belly" shot it (which means I break the treaty). "Crow Dog" and "Roaming Walk" were very much dissatisfied all the time, so we took their guns from them, and some of the Ogallalas who said they would return to Pine Ridge Agency and kill us all—

The next morning we all assembled on the dancing ground and "Knob Arrow" said "Let us ditch this hill and if anyone comes here they cannot get to us. I told them to do as they pleased, but to first get my nephews body, whereupon some of the young men started, the remainder digging the ditch—They found the body partly burned by prairie fire so it was wrapped up and left—We then went over to where the fire was and were met by White Soldiers who fired on us, so we turned back. I then told my people if these soldiers fire on you, fire back and when we got close to them again they fled. (The soldiers here mentioned were Cowboys). Again while a party of my men were out on foot one day they were attacked by soldiers, no one was killed but one was wounded, they had but one gun with them and in their flight lost that. After this my people stole more horses, "Lone Bull" getting a fine Grey horse which he rode—The next day a delegation of Ogallalas came to us from Pine Ridge to make a treaty. Among the Chiefs were No Neck, Yankton Charlie, Standing Bear, and Crow Dog. they brought us presents, we killed one of the stolen cattle and made a feast; I told these Chiefs that if my people would be allowed to go to Pine Ridge to live and draw rations there they would all be satisfied to go in—at this "Fast Thunder" arose pointing to me said "You are the man who wants to get your people in trouble" to which I asked him "What do you mean?" he said "You are trying to have your people fight. Now I ask you to do something wonderful that this Messiah told you to do if you can do it I will also believe in him." I then said "My people do not want to fight they want peace—I told them what the Messiah said—He did not invest me with any spiritual power—but here is a "Ghost Shirt" take any Gun and shoot it if you can"—He asked for my gun but I told him "to use his own gun and cartridge.["]

Here young Jack Red Cloud my cousin came between us and said "pay no attention to this man he is crazy, or else he would not speak as he does["]—I said "You ask me to stop and I will do it—this shooting at the shirt is only a trick and now I will not let him shoot at it["]—

The next morning we held a council at which it was decided that we all move in together toward the Agency on the following day—but some starting that same day—The next morning at daybreak the main camp moved, all but Short Bull and his uncle "Come away from the crowd"; during all this time we were being watched by some Cheyenne Indian Soldiers, watching all of our movements, but they could not get to us—That night my uncle and I started to reach our main body that had gone away in the morning, but as we failed to reach them we camped by ourselves on a large hill—at daylight the next day we heard the firing of guns and cannon, so we started off in the direction of the firing and before we got there heard more firing, we met a white man who was driving in the woods after fire wood and we asked him the cause of this firing, he told us it was "the soldiers (of whom there were many at the Agency) practicing at targets, and they shoot all the time"—So we moved on and as we reached the "big hill" we could look down and there saw the villiage, everything was in a fearful state. Further on were other Indians coming toward the villiage and it looked as if trouble was near—I went into the villiage and was there told that "Big Foot" (or Spotted Elk's) Band had been all killed—I saw my cousin "Many Wounds" who was there and confirmed this report in a measure as he himself been wounded in the shoulder; he told me that "all his relatives Father, Mother, all had been killed, all of their guns were taken from them and then they were fired on, and could do nothing["]—he continued saying "I do not know how it happened, I was in my lodge putting on my shirt and leggins when the firing commenced; this will make our hearts bad for a long time and we will fight the soldiers." I told him "It is not right, even if all our relatives are killed we will do right, they blame us when we are not to be blamed, we will now wait and see, if the soldiers continue to fire on us after three days we will try and protect ourselves and families the best we can; I am not to blame the whites fired on us first, Twenty-three of my own relations were killed in this fight, men, women & children, this is like butchery—Why do they kill helpless women and children? This shows the soldiers want us all to die off—When our Indians fought against an enemy of their own color you know what kind of a man I was, I laughed and feared nothing, but now I do not want you to fight, take care of the women and children, I am not looking for trouble, but if I am angered I am the worst among you—I have put all badness from me and want to be a good man—I will go over to where the battle was fought in the morning and see the bodies of my relatives—When I return if the soldiers fire on you, I will remember my old feelings, stand up and be a soldier once more."

The next morning with four others we started for the battle-field. I was looking over the dead bodies and while so doing heard cannons in the distance, in the direction of Clay Creek—I found one of my uncles who had been badly shot in the leg but not dead, who told me this—"that all of the Indians had their Guns and Knives taken from them and as I went to my lodge to get my knife to surrender it, the firing began, I was shot in the leg and have laid here ever since, I do not know where the women and children are," so we "hitched up" four of the wagons we found here and put the horses to them picking up all that we could find who were not dead (some forty odd) taking them to a deserted house nearby on Wounded Knee Creek—Those whom we thought fatally wounded we left here and with the rest we started for our Camp.—It began to snow during the night and by morning a heavy snow had fallen, but we started for Wounded Knee about noon, when we reached the house we saw our friends were gone, but afterwards ascertained that they had been taken to the Agency by the friendlies in charge of "No Neck"—during all this time my heart was bad, yet I did not want my people to fight the Government—I might have done much harm but always kept my people from it, I wanted no fighting, I wanted to do as the Messiah bid me"; Some 10 days afterwards a delegation was sent out to see us from General Miles, asking us to return to the Agency so as to save anymore bloodshed, Genl. Miles sent to us several times but we paid no attention, but now I told my people "Pack up everything you have and we will move toward the Agency and I hope we will be allowed to live there in peace General Miles said we shall not be fired on and I believe him, we will surrender our guns and have peace" this message I sent to General Miles. So the next morning we went to the Agency—We were asked to surrender our arms, I had a good Winchester Rifle which I surrendered freely and so did my people—General Miles asked me if I had any more guns, I told him "I had an old patched up gun the stock and barrel being wrapped with buckskin and not worth anything" he asked me to turn it in, which I done. Some ten days afterwards—General Miles asked me to go to Fort Sheridan, with "Kicking Bear" and some twenty-five others (in all twenty-four men and three women)—We started at the same time that a delegation went to Washington to hold a Council with the "Great Father." When we reached Chicago we got off the train and were taken to Fort Sheridan—While there we were often visited by Genl. Miles who with all the officers there made us as comfortable as could be, doing all in their power for us.

In the spring "Long Hair" (Col. Wm. F. Cody, "Buffalo Bill") came to see us and made us a proposition to join his company across the "big water," we said we would consider the matter, and later on Major John M. Burke came to see us, we held a Council and he made us such grand offers to see the "great Country beyond the water" with good salary that we all consented to go, and started with sixty of our friends and relatives (from Pine Ridge Agency.)—Our trip across the water made me somewhat Sea Sick but as soon as I got on land again was in good health. Ever since I have been with the Company I have been well treated and cared for, all of the promises made have been fulfilled. Col. Cody, Mr. Salsbury and Maj. Burke as well as the entire Company are our friends, and do all they can for us in every way. We get good food three times a day, good clothing, warm bedding and plenty of wood—If our people have any complaints it is fixed at once, if we do not feel well, a doctor comes and looks after us—besides we go everywhere and see all the great works of the Country through which we travel. It learns us much, we see many people who are all kind to us, I like the English people but not their weather as it rains so much.

Source: Handwritten document recorded by George C. Crager, "As Narrated by Short Bull" (MS [1891]) 1, BBMG.

2A. "I WAS CALLED BY JOCKO WILSON"
(INTERPRETER UNKNOWN)

[Interpreter's comment:] Wants to prove that he was not the cause of the trouble of 1890–91.

He saw a woman. It was told that a woman gave birth to a child and this was known in heaven. This was told to him and he wanted to see the child when they heard this. This man professed to be a great man, next to God; [he] told them that he wanted to be their interme- diator and that they should dance and be together and he would be with them.

He had a look. He said as many nights and days as it would take to do that he knew all about it. He said Indians [are] like grass and flowers and they learn and they sing and pray. He said "Do nothing wrong." He said people can't take away anything when they die. Whiskey is bad. Who drinks, they cause murders and suicides.

Across the ocean is a great church where he came from. "That church belongs to me. You may go as you please, but one church, one belief, one faith. When you listen to me when I pray or teach from my church all good people will come with me. The whole world will sing. The whole earth is now filthy and stinks. These murders and suicides are that which stinks. You say, 'Father, oh Father, is that you?['] All that will say, say that the Father, God will look at you. Those that have done wrong, he will shake the earth. This part of the earth will get it."

First heard of this man at Rosebud in the year When Red Shirt's Sister Committed Suicide. I did not see the child. I do not know where it was born. I was called by Jocko Wilson to go and I went to see him. I went to the Rabbit Blanket [Paiute] Indians. I went in March. I was a long time in going. I first went to the Arapahoe Agency. I do not know how long I was there. I was six days at Pocatello. I went to the Bannocks and was there nine days. Then I got on a train. I was on the train two days and the third day in the evening, I came to the Fish Eaters and I was there eight days. There were many whites and Indians there. I left there.

I left there on [a] train and on the hills above Porcatello there was an accident. Big river washed out [the] bridge and [the] train upset. [I] came to Arapahoe Agency [Wind River Reservation], came from Arapahoe Agency on horseback. To my home it took fourteen days.

Red Star went. At Rosebud heard that this man had sent representative[s] to Rosebud and Pine Ridge and told them to have Short Bull come over there. He wanted a man who would be straight and would not lie. Rosebud Indians called a council and tried to pick out a man to go and they chose me. There was a paper at Rosebud that called for such a man made by the Oglala chiefs.

I first heard that this was a holy man. Said that God's daughter had given birth to a child and we should go and see it. I do not know where. I did not see this woman. All I saw was the man and his wife. Dance for five days; first pray and address. The other four all dance.

2B. GHOST DANCE

First: purification by sweat bath. Clasp hands and circle to the left. Hold hands and sing until a trance is induced, looking up all the time. Brought to a pitch of excitement by singing songs prescribed by the Messiah. Dressed as prescribed. Froth at mouth when in trance. They must keep step with the cadence of the song. The[y] go into trance in from ten minutes to three quarters of an hour. Each one described his vision. Each vision is different from others. Men, women, children have visions.

The Ghost shirt is *wakan*. It is impervious to missiles.

Source: James R. Walker, *Lakota Belief and Ritual,* edited by Raymond J. DeMallie and Elaine A. Jahner (1980; reprint, Lincoln: Bison Books, University of Nebraska Press, 1991), 142–43.

3. SHORT BULL'S NARRATIVE (DICTATED C. 1906)

Note.—The white reader should bear in mind that this is the narrative of a seer. As is usual with Indians, the language is often figurative. In the English rendering, the attempt has been made to reflect the rhythmic dignity and simplicity of the Dakota. The narrated visit to the spirit-camp was probably a vision, or was made in a trance. To the Indian, such a vision is as real as a waking event. The visit to the other camp was a reality. The Paiute Indians wear blankets or robes of rabbit-skin. He who is referred to as "this one of the rabbit-robe" is the prophet, known to the people as "the Father." "The land where the sun sets" is Nevada, the home of the prophet. "Rosebud" is an Indian reservation in South Dakota.

Who would have thought that dancing could make such trouble? We had no wish to make trouble, nor did we cause it of ourselves. There was trouble, but it was not of my making. We had no thought of fighting; if we had meant to fight, would we not have carried arms? We went unarmed to the dance. How could we have held weapons? For thus we danced, in a circle, hand in hand, each man's fingers linked in those of his neighbor.

Who would have thought that dancing could make such trouble? For the message that I brought was peace. And the message was given by the Father to all the tribes. Thus it happened:

I journeyed to the land where the sun sets, and then I went to the spirit-land, where I saw the spirit-encampment. I drew near and stood outside a spirit-tipi. A spirit-man came out and stood beside me. He spoke to me and said:

"Behold, I give you something holy!" Then he said, "Whence come you?"

And I answered, "I come from Rosebud."

Then said the spirit-man, "Go we together in a cloud, upward, to the Father."

So we rose in a cloud to where were other camps, and there we saw those who wear the blanket of rabbit-skin. As we passed through the camp of these, there came towards us a man and his wife. Said this one of the rabbit-robe:

"I would speak with you now. Behold, I tell you something for you to tell to all the people! Give this dance to all the different tribes of Indians. White people and Indians shall all dance together. But first they shall sing. There shall be no more fighting. No man shall kill another. If any man should be killed it would be a grievous thing. No man shall lie. Love one another. Help one another. Revile not one another. Hear me, for I will give you water to drink. Thus I tell you, this is why I have called you. My meaning, have you understood it?"

Thus spoke he of the rabbit-blanket, and holy red paint he gave to me. In the spirit-camp I had seen those who had died, and when I came homeward there came with me two spirit-companions, invisible to all but me. These journeyed with me and stayed ever with me. I heard their counsel.

Alone in my tipi I dreamed, and saw visions, and communed with the spirits. And I went forth and taught the people and told them of the Father's word and of the help that should come to the Indians. There were others who taught as well as I. The Father had commanded all the world to dance, and we gave the dance to the people as we had been bidden. When they danced they fell dead and went to the spirit-camp and saw those who had died, those whom they loved—their fathers, their mothers, and their little children. Then came trouble. Yet in our dance we harmed no one, nor meant we ill to any man. As the Father had commanded, so did we.

It is true, all men should love one another. It is true, all men should live as brothers. Is it we who do not thus? What others demand of us, should they not themselves give? Is it just to expect one friend to give all the friendship? We are glad to live with the white men as brothers. But we ask that they expect not the brotherhood and the love to come from the Indian alone.

In this world the Great Father has given to the white man everything and to the Indian nothing. But it will not always be thus. In another world the Indian shall be as the white man and the white man as the Indian. To the Indian will be given wisdom and power, and the white man shall be helpless and unknowing with only the bow and arrow. For ere long this world will be consumed in flame and pass away. Then, in the life after this, to the Indian shall all be given.

Source: Natalie Curtis, *The Indians' Book: An Offering by the American Indians of Indian Lore, Musical and Narrative, to Form a Record of the Songs and Legends of Their Race* (1907; reprint, New York: Gramercy Books, 1994), 44–47.

4. SHORT BULL INTERVIEW
WITH WEYGOLD (1909)

"I was chosen at a council at the Rosebud Reservation to go and to collect everything about the Ghost Dance (that is, he was sent by the Brule and Oglala to the "Messiah" in Nevada in order to teach his people about that doctrine)

"I could see that apparently [a] lot of people were glad when I left, but later they lied in regard to this.

"Lots of the Indians were malevolent towards me and did not want the [to?] see me elected, but I had to go.

"I said to them (that is: before the Ghost Dance he said to his followers)

"Paint your faces!

You have to have good hearts!

Close your eyes and bow your heads towards the earth, then you will only have one way to think (that is: your thoughts won't wander to other things)."

"I said to them, I wanted them in that position to say a prayer, but also I said to them that I would like to speak some words at first:

"Your children should go to school and learn. The old people should attend some religious worship and say prayers.

"I said to them they should draw something (from) the earth, too (that is: do some farming) and they should build houses to live in, and take good advice from respectable white men, too.

Then do not kill each other!

"In the old times there were lots of wars, blood and a bad odour (that is: from blood and corpses).

"I said this to the old people, that they should draw advantage from previous experiences.

"Then I said that they should listen to my words, and that I would say a prayer.

"Take down all your finger-rings, ear-rings and all iron before you start dancing.

"If they would carry iron (with them) they would be tempted to do something bad.

"One thing someone (probably the "Messiah") wants to explain to you: (The following statements are probably meant to be views from the "Messiah")

"The white people know the praying. I said to them: They should pray and dance.

"All humans on earth, the Whites, too, if they have got intellect and heart, would come for praying with us in our way.

"From the rising to the sinking sun will (or should) all humans be one in this kind of praying.

"After that, only one thing will occur that will be bad.

"Indians and white people should have pity with each other.

"The man who sent me (that is: the "Messiah" Wovoka) said that the people should pray honestly, like he taught it. If somebody would neglect this order, he would be hit by much misfortune.

"He (that is: Wovoka) said to the people:

"I gave up the way of the Whites." He then took a pole and threw it away in front of the people. That means the following:

"We Indians did not know well the language of the Whites. Sometimes they cursed us, and we did not understand. Therefore he told the Indians, they should abandon the way of the Whites and not consider it further.

"The Indians were made by the Great Mystery and only for living in a certain way and they should (therefore) not accept the ways of another people.

"I thought, that this was misunderstood a lot."

Source: Wolfgang Haberland, "Die Oglala-Sammlung Weygold im Hamburgischen Museum für Völkerkunde (Teil 4)," *Mitteilungen aus dem Museum für Völkurkunde zu Hamburg, N.F. 7* (1977): 19–52.

5. THE GHOST DANCE AS TOLD
BY SHORT BULL (1915)

Translated by Raymond J. DeMallie with the assistance of Dennis M. Christafferson and Rani-Henrik Andersson, American Indian Studies Research Institute, Indiana University, Bloomington, Indiana.

This is the story of the Ghost Dance, in which these men went to the place of ghosts; and some of them have died, and I know about it. These are the ones who went to the place of ghosts: Short Bull, Kicking Bear, Brave Wolf, Thunder Horse, Turn Over Back, Scare Them, and Gray Horse.

In the year 1889, in June, we went from Pine Ridge; four of us were from Rosebud, and from Pine Ridge there were three, so we were seven. And after eleven nights we reached Arapaho Agency, Wyoming, and there we rested seven days. And then from there we went to the Bannock (Wabanaka) Agency and after nineteen nights we reached there and the people came together and held an Omaha Dance, and we took part in it.

Then a man who was said to be holy participated, a Bannock (Banake); he spoke to us as follows: "Three days from here is the place of God (Wakan Tanka) so four tribes will go see him. So, my friends, you will join them, so later when the time is right I will come again and I will speak to you," he said. Thus he spoke to us.

And then the dance ended and then the next morning a man came making an announcement. Then the man in whose tipi we stayed spoke to us as follows: "My friends, there will be a holy dance. At midday there will be a feast," and then he said, "so you will take part in it." So, "Yes," we said.

And then when it was a little past midday again a crier came and made an announcement. Then that man said, "Now put on red earth paint, we are going to go there." So then we painted ourselves. And then we went with him and all the people gathered in the circle were painted a reddish color. So then we went there and the men and women, too, completely mixed together, were standing in a circle, and there was room so we stood there.

And that man who was said to be holy who had spoken to us stood there in the middle, and he told of his vision, and when he finished they danced. And I did not understand how it was done so even though I participated in some of the dances I was not overcome; but for some of them it was different, and they lost their senses and fell into a faint.

And then they rested and sat in a circle and some of those who had fainted came to and five men sat in the center and they came back there and when they sat down a big man, one of those who had revived, told of his experience. So then he stood up and spoke to the people in a loud voice. Well, I counted those who had fainted. Then there were eleven of them. Well, they all told of their experiences. And then after they finished we danced for a short while and we stopped.

Then when it was morning that man came and said, "My friends, now they will go together so you should join them. Hurry!" Then we saddled our horses and then we went. Then we went on a road along a creek and we caught up with them. And then we went with them for six nights and we arrived there at the Paiute (Rabbit-skin Blanket Wearers) Agency and stayed two days. And from there we went with four Paiutes and after three days we camped; we arrived at the foot of the Rocky Mountains (White Mountains).

Then one of the Paiutes spoke to us as follows: "We will stay here for two days, waiting for two tribes to arrive here, then they will reach us here at midday," he said. Then we stayed right there. And then on the second day some Cheyennes and Shoshones, these two, arrived; there were three Cheyennes and five Shoshones, and so eight arrived.

Well, then we went and they stopped at midday, and when they finished eating they said this: "We will sit on this hill and then he will arrive," they said. And then we went to a hill, the biggest and highest one in the Rocky Mountains. So then I was the last one to join them and then we stopped beneath it. And then we dismounted and we tied our horses to little pine trees. And then we put on red earth paint. And then, one behind the other, we climbed the hill. And then we climbed to the top. And in the middle there was a huge flat rock and around it was a grove of pine trees, and everything was visible in all directions. And then they sat in a circle.

And one of the Paiutes sat down in the middle where we were sitting and shouted something. After a while a white man came and stood in the middle of them, but not one of us looked steadily at him. He stood with his head bowed and all at once, surprisingly, he made a speech in the Lakota language. He said as follows:

"My pitiful children," meaning these, "because you come to me suffering you will hear those things that are right and you will act accordingly," he said. "By means of a dance you will see again those of your relatives who died long ago; but only if you do it properly will you truly see your people. And because father told me these things, remember me! Behold me, my sons, I myself was killed long ago by the white men, and therefore now there are many holes in me. They went away, and now they honor me," he said, "but because you Indian people are suffering I am paying you this visit so in the future you and your relatives who have died will see one another. From this time on, by dancing and those things that I will say, you will live well.

"My beloved sons, do not murder one another! Whoever commits murder does evil. And love one another! And take pity on one another! If you act in this manner I will give you more concerning the ceremony. And those people should take sweat baths. While you are dancing you must not eat any at all of the white man's food! And fast! And you must not wear any metal. And while you dance you must dance with your eyes closed. If you think about one of your relatives who died long ago you will see him.

"Well, it is not possible for you Indians and the white to become the same as long as your generations continue. Therefore my father made you of a different nature and also gave you a country. And he will see any bad things that you do, so from this time on whatever you do, I will watch over and keep. The Indians are far below because my father made you last. Now I will help you and you will live well. In the future these things will be fulfilled. Behold! There is a village. These are your relatives of past generations so you will go there," he said, and turning around he looked to the west, so we looked there.

Then there was a village of people and many were walking about and the village was smoky. And some were coming this way on horseback. And on this side there was a hill so they were coming up on the other side. Then he said as follows: "You will be with them, but then you will not truly be with them; then you will see your relatives, so then you will see them in the normal way," he said, "and from now on, do not forget this visit! And whatever the whites with whom you will live want, do it accordingly! This will not be for long. Well, I give you these things, so remember them well!"

He sang:

My son, hold my hand!
My son, hold my hand!
You will grow up, you will grow up.
My father says so, my father says so.

He sang:

My father says so, my father says so.
I am bringing a pipe to you
So you will live.
My father says so, my father says so.

"Well, my sons, do not overdo these things! And do them properly! Everyone close their eyes!" he said. So I sat there with my head bowed and I sat with my eyes closed. And then I looked. Then he was gone, so, "Look there!" I said. Then one of them looked up furtively, pointing behind, so I looked that way. Then he was standing high up. And the land and that village of people, too, were slowly disappearing. So those whom I had joined were crying.

"Come on! Now we will go down," I said. And then they stopped crying so we went together back to where the horses were tied and we sat down there in the shade of the pine trees. And then I asked them, "Did you understand clearly what he said?" "Yes," they said. Then I asked the Cheyenne named Porcupine, "My friend, did you understand what father said?" Then, "Yes," he said. Then I asked a Shoshone and he, too, said they understood him. So I told them how we understood him and when I finished they all said it was right.

So again I spoke as follows: "When you return and arrive home, will you dance?" Then, "Yes," they said. So before that, the Arapahos (Blue Clouds) and Bannocks, those two tribes, already knew about it and danced.

So then we went back and we arrived at the Paiute Agency. And we stayed there four days and from there again we went back and arrived at the Bannock Agency and we stayed there six days. And from there we went to Pine Ridge, South Dakota; we arrived there and at White

Clay we told our story. There in the middle of a flat prairie a dance ceremony was to be held by Brave Wolf and High Horse. And among those who took part there was Kicking Bear.

And from there we returned to Rosebud, and at once we danced. And those who longed for their relatives and danced in earnest fainted. And then when I was first about to be overcome, suddenly something flashed in my face a bright light that turned blue. And then I really felt that I was going to vomit and so I was frightened and lost consciousness. And it seemed that I was brought down in a land of green grass and I set out walking and I went up a big hill and stood on the top.

Then beyond there was a big village of only tipis and so I went there. Then a horseback rider came from there, galloping fast, and reached me. Then it was my father as a very handsome young man, and speaking, he said this to me: "Alas! I see you, my beloved son, but you smell bad, so go back home, and when you get there, wash yourself and come back! So you will go among the lodges and there we will see you," he said.

So therefore I turned around. Then that was all. I came to. Then I was actually sitting in the middle of the dance circle. Right there I came to and I was very sad. Anyone who was overcome and fainted told about what he learned, and did not lie. So then I myself told of my experience. And then we finished. So then I went swimming and washed myself thoroughly.

And in the morning we danced again. Then again I was overcome. And all at once I fainted and again I was standing on top of a hill. Then there was a man standing there, so I went to him. Then it was the Son of God, the one whom we came back from visiting, who was standing there, so I went to him, but, in the village beyond, the center of the camp circle was buzzing, and the man said this: "My son, you have not related my words properly. So these customs that I tell you about I have established for the future, so therefore tell them to the people! And under your clothes, always paint your bodies like this! And wear this! And do not forget! By means of these, in the future you will see one another. So behold! These and their people have come together here crying and talking sorrowfully. So I want you to live well, but in the future, when the time is near to see one another, you will hear the sound of the land. And this earth is now completely worn out, so you will live on a new land. So rejoice!

"So listen now to these things that I tell you and remember them well! I am the one, so by and by you will pray to me for things and I will hear it.

"Well, you want to see your relatives, so go there!"

Thus he spoke to me, so then I went straight there. And from the hill I went toward the village. And then as I neared it a rider came galloping from the village and came near me and dismounted. Then it was my father as a small young man and he said: "My beloved son," and he hugged me around the neck and said, "we live in that big tipi over yonder, so we will go there." So then I went there with him. And then we arrived at that tipi. And then I went inside. And there were no women there. Nine big young men were sitting inside and they said "Hau!" and they made room for me at the place of honor and I sat down there. And they gave me a wooden dish of pemmican and put it in front of me and I took it, ate, and gave the dish back to them.

And then a big man spoke to me as follows: "Grandson, I am your grandfather, and these are your grandfathers, one after the other. And we are without women. Father decreed it so. We of one blood are gathered together here. The people of the village are all camped here. And those in the tipi next to where we live are your grandmothers, so go there! They will see you," he said.

And none of the men with him in the tipi said anything; they sat in silence. And so then I came outside and went to the other tipi. And then there were only women there, twelve of them, and so I went inside. And so a woman hugged me around the neck and said, "Grandson, these are your grandmothers, and we are not with your grandfathers, and this is what father decreed so this is how we are," she said. And she said "Grandson, eat this!" She gave me some honeycomb tripe and a marrowbone so I took them and ate. And none of the other women said anything. So I ate it up and I started back and I went up and stood on the hill.

Then I started to wake and I came to lying right there in the middle of the dance circle and I was very sad and I stood up at the sacred tree and the people sat around me. And so I told them what I had seen and what had been told to me and I instructed them to do things properly.

Well, that is the way it was, and because of it there was fighting, but there was nothing about that in the ceremony. Twelve times I fainted and each time an eagle carried me and took me to where my relatives lived and with great joy I saw all my fathers, mothers, sisters, and brothers.

Well, that is the way it was and more than this cannot be told. This was the Indians' religion so in the future the people and the ghosts would see one another and in the future the Indians would be strong because of the things that he would give them. These are the things I know.

Short Bull—Chases Insect

Source: Translated from the original Lakota manuscript in the records of Holy Rosary Mission, Special Collections and Archives, Marquette University Libraries, Milwaukee, Wisconsin.

ABBREVIATIONS

BBHC	Buffalo Bill Historical Center, Cody, Wyoming
BBMG	Buffalo Bill Museum and Grave, Golden, Colorado
CIA	Commissioner of Indian Affairs
CS	Crager Scrapbook 1890–92
DPL	Denver Public Library, Colorado
FARC	Federal Archives and Record Center, Kansas City, Missouri
HRM	Holy Rosary Mission, Special Collections and Archives, Marquette University Libraries, Milwaukee, Wisconsin
IRA	Indian Rights Association Papers, 1864–1973
LR	Letters Received
LS	Letters Sent
NARA	National Archives and Records Administration, Washington, D.C.
NSHS	Nebraska State Historical Society, Lincoln
PR	Pine Ridge Reservation
RG	Record Group
SC 188	Special Case 188, Ghost Dance, 1890–98
SDSHS	South Dakota State Historical Society, Pierre
SHSC	State Historical Society of Colorado, Denver

NOTES

INTRODUCTION

1. *Evening Times* (Glasgow), 16 January 1892.
2. For further information on the Lakota, see chapter 1.
3. Frederick Hoxie has identified 1890 as the year when the American nation "adopted a new approach to Indian affairs and created the machinery for effecting a campaign of total assimilation" (Hoxie, *Final Promise*, 41). For information on paternalistic attitudes toward Indians, see Prucha, *Indians in American Society*.
4. For discussions of American racial theories, see the following: Gossett, *Race*; Stanton, *Leopard's Spots*; and Horseman, *Race and Manifest Destiny*.
5. See Adams, *Education for Extinction*; Hoxie, *Final Promise*; Bolt, *American Indian Policy and American Reform*.
6. Perhaps the best known of the "separate but equal" decisions, in which the Supreme Court upheld the right of a railroad in Louisiana to segregate black passengers, setting a precedent for legally sanctioned segregation. See Gossett, *Race*, 274–75.
7. For both the process and facts of evolving Indian dependency, see White, *Roots of Dependency*. An unidentified Rosebud Indian agent stated in 1889: "The time has arrived when it is absolutely cruel to treat the Sioux as children and wards. Public sentiment is restive under the (budgetary) strain and will not long permit them to retain their present status; they must become individualized and acquire the rights of citizenship. The strain of civilization will deplete their numbers, as in the case of the Omahas, Winnebagos, and other semi-civilized tribes, but the principle of the survival of the fittest will apply, and such may acquire a reasonable degree of independence." Quoted in Biolsi, "Birth of the Reservation," 121.
8. Hoxie, *Final Promise*, 33–34, 38–39.
9. Lewis, "Reservation Leadership and the Progressive-Traditional Dichotomy," 201–19; Adams, *Education for Extinction*; Riney, *Rapid City Indian School, 1898–1933*;

Child, *Boarding School Seasons;* Osburn, *Southern Ute Women;* Lewis, *Neither Wolf nor Dog.*

10. Thomas Biolsi has noted: "The Lakota in particular and Plains Indians in general have been recognized in the anthropological literature as particularly 'individualistic' societies in which political power was not centralized but tended to cohere around self-made leaders, and individuals competed for wealth, prestige, and power" (Biolsi, "Birth of the Reservation," 112). Raymond J. DeMallie noted: "The Oglalas remained a deeply factionalized people whose lack of unity made them especially vulnerable to manipulation by government officials and other outsiders" (DeMallie, review of Robert W. Larson, *Red-Cloud: Warrior-Statesman of the Lakota Sioux* [1997], in *American Historical Review* [December 2000]: 1749–50).

11. Lewis, "Reservation Leadership and the Progressive-Traditional Dichotomy," 201–19 (quotations on 203 and 214).

12. Ibid., 215.

13. For further information on Wovoka, see Hittman, *Wovoka and the Ghost Dance,* ed. Lynch.

14. Richard E. Jensen noted that "only the Lakotas believed the garments were bulletproof. The general concept was both old and widespread on the plains, for warriors often invoked supernatural aid to protect them from an enemy's weapon" (Jensen et al., *Eyewitness at Wounded Knee,* 10).

15. Phister, "Indian Messiah," 108.

16. Mooney, *Ghost Dance,* 149.

17. Utley, *Last Days of the Sioux Nation,* 86–87. In the preface to the second edition (2004), he has changed his interpretation somewhat. See xi–xv.

18. DeMallie, "Lakota Ghost Dance," 395, 387; Kehoe, *Ghost Dance,* 13. For an overview of the literature, see Osterreich, *American Indian Ghost Dance, 1870 and 1890;* and Sievers, "Historiography of 'the Bloody Field . . . That Kept the Secret of the Everlasting Word,'" 33–54.

19. DeMallie, "Lakota Ghost Dance," 389.

20. This source is analyzed in depth in chapter 2.

CHAPTER ONE: LAKOTA CULTURE
IN AN ERA OF CHANGE

1. The Seven Council Fires represent the seven Siouan Tribes: the Lakota (or Teton), Mdewakanton, Wahpekute, Wahpeton, Sisseton, Yantons, and Yanktonai. They share a language (with dialectal differences), customs, and geographic origins. For further information see Raymond J. DeMallie, "Sioux until 1850," in *Handbook of North American Indians,* vol 13: *Plains,* ed. DeMallie, 718–60; Price, *Oglala People, 1841–1879,* 5–6; and Hassrick, *Sioux,* 3–6.

2. DeMallie, "Sioux until 1850," 755–60.

3. Price, *Oglala People, 1841–1879,* 2.

4. Ibid., 5.

5. Prucha, *Indians in American Society,* 24.

6. Utley, *Last Days of the Sioux Nation,* 31.

7. Prucha, *Indians in American Society,* 36–37, 43.

8. Walker, *Lakota Belief and Ritual,* ed. DeMallie and Jahner, 138. DeMallie noted that Red Cloud had made this speech when he "abdicated his position as head chief in favor of his son, Jack Red Cloud." See p. 297n.41.

9. Washburn, *American Indian and the United States,* vol. 1, 424–25.

10. Utley, *Last Days of the Sioux Nation,* 27. See also Coleman, *Voices of Wounded Knee,* 17.

11. Utley, *Last Days of the Sioux Nation,* 26–29.

12. Washburn, *American Indian and the United States,* vol. 1, 435.

13. The Dawes Act of 1887 authorized the president to survey the Indian reservations, and classify them for farming and grazing. Each head of family could receive 160 acres of farmland; each single male adult, 80; and each child, 40. For lands suited mainly for grazing, the amounts could be doubled. The actual title would not be conveyed immediately, but rather would be held in trust by the government for twenty-five years, to prevent alienation to greedy whites "until the civilization process equipped the Indian to make enlightened decisions." After allotments—or before, at the discretion of the secretary of the interior—the government could negotiate the purchase of surplus reservation lands and throw them open to white homesteading. The proceeds from the sale of these lands would then be used for the benefit of the Indians. Finally, Indians who took allotments automatically became U.S. citizens, subject to both civil and criminal laws of the state or territory in which they lived.

14. The six new reservations were Pine Ridge, Rosebud, Cheyenne River, Standing Rock, Lower Brule, and Crow Creek; see Utley, *Last Days of the Sioux Nation,* 63.

15. Utley, *Last Days of the Sioux Nation,* 48.

16. The signatures collected for the Sioux Act of 1889 were achieved through coercion and confusion, and therefore can be described as being fraudulent. For further information see Utley, *Last Days of the Sioux Nation,* 49–54.

17. Ibid.

18. Mooney, *Ghost Dance,* 201–2.

19. Utley, *Last Days of the Sioux Nation,* 54–55.

20. Ibid., 55.

21. William T. Selwyn to Col. E. W. Foster, U.S. Indian Agent, Yankton Agency, South Dakota, 25 November 1890, SC188, 2041, Records of the Bureau of Indian Affairs, RG 75, NARA.

22. Mooney, *Ghost Dance,* 159.

23. See DeMallie, ed., *Sixth Grandfather,* 256–57.

24. Selwyn to Foster, 25 November 1890, SC 188, 2041, RG 75, NARA.

25. Crager, "As Narrated by Short Bull" (MS [1891]), 1, BBMG. See text of Crager's account, reproduced in the appendix to the present volume.

26. See, for example, Overholt, "Short Bull, Black Elk, Sword, and the 'Meaning' of the Ghost Dance," 187.

27. Eli S. Ricker, quoted in McCoy, "Short Bull," 57.

28. The name "Tatanka Ptecela" is given in Walker, *Lakota Belief and Ritual*, 284. A narrative by Short Bull is accredited to "Chases Bug [Wabluska Kuwa], otherwise known as Short Bull," in Buechel, *Lakota Tales and Texts in Translation*, 518. Raymond DeMallie has retranslated this text for the purposes of this publication, and has interpreted the given name as "Chases Insect"; see appendix. For a discussion of Short Bull's date of birth, see McCoy, "Short Bull," 55; and Wildhage, "Material on Short Bull," 35.

29. McCoy, "Short Bull," 59–60; Vestal [Walter Stanley Campbell], *Sitting Bull*, 113–17; Wildhage, "Material on Short Bull," 35; Haberland, "Adrian Jacobson on Pine Ridge Reservation 1910," 13. Not to be confused with the Oglala (Grant) Short Bull who rode with Crazy Horse; see Michno, *Lakota Noon*.

30. Clow, "Rosebud Sioux," 17–18; Wildhage, "Material on Short Bull," 35; McCoy, "Short Bull," 55. This commitment is also illustrated by the Short Bull narrative "Sending Spirits to the Spirit World," in which he protests against the arrest of a member of his band, who had given away his property in accordance with the traditional Lakota custom when his son died. See Walker, *Lakota Belief and Ritual*, 141–42.

31. Crager, "As Narrated by Short Bull," 1, BBMG.

32. Walker, *Lakota Belief and Ritual*, 142–43.

33. This list is taken from the 1891 document "As Narrated by Short Bull," which differs from the later list given in the Beuchal document; see documents 1 and 5 in the appendix. Short Bull's list corresponds only in part to previously published lists, but this might simply mean that Short Bull knew some of the Oglala by different names. Black Elk states, "So Kicking Bear, Short Bull, Bear Comes Out and (Mash the) Kettle and a party started out to find out more about this sacred man and see him if possible" (DeMallie, *Sixth Grandfather*, 257–58). Sword states: "Good Thunder, Cloud Horse, Yellow Knife, and Short Bull visited the place again in 1890 and saw the messiah" (Mooney, *Ghost Dance*, 159). Mooney concluded: "The delegates chosen were Good Thunder, Flat Iron, Yellow Breast, and Broken Arm, from Pine Ridge; Short Bull and another from Rosebud, and Kicking Bear from Cheyenne River agency" (ibid., 182). Utley states: "In all there were eleven and they travelled together. From Pine Ridge went Good Thunder, Yellow Breast, Flat Iron, Broken Arm, Cloud Horse, Yellow Knife, Elk Horn, and Kicks Back. Short Bull and Mash the Kettle represented Rosebud, and Kicking Bear represented Cheyenne River" (Utley, *Last Days of the Sioux Nation*, 61). Luther Standing Bear calls Short Bull's companion "Ce-re-aka-ruga-pi, or Breaks-the-Pot-on-Him." This might suggest that Scatter and Mash the Kettle are one and the same. See Standing Bear, *My People, the Sioux*, 218.

34. Crager, "As Narrated by Short Bull," 8–9, BBMG.

35. See Wildhage, "Material on Short Bull," 38–41.

36. For the history of Buffalo Bill and his Wild West exhibition, see Russell, *Lives and Legends of Buffalo Bill*; Rosa and May, *Buffalo Bill and His Wild West*; Reddin, *Wild West Shows*; and Kasson, *Buffalo Bill's Wild West*.

37. Pegler and Rimer, *Buffalo Bill's Wild West*, 12.

38. Cody and Salsbury's partnership was by no means an untroubled one; in one of his reminiscences, entitled "Secret Service," Salsbury noted that when he came to write his "famous book," he intended to call it "Sixteen Years in Hell with Buffalo Bill." Nathan Salsbury Papers, Series II, Personal Papers, Box 2, Folders 63/64, "Reminiscences," Beinecke Rare Book and Manuscript Library, Yale University, New Haven, Conn.

39. Russell noted that Burke was "one of the founders of the art of press-agentry, and to him goes much of the credit for making the name of Buffalo Bill a household word. It is also possible that the subsequent deterioration in the reputation of Buffalo Bill is due to Burke's exaggerations, his inconsistencies, his flagrant misquotations, and his lazy carelessness" (Russell, *Lives and Legends of Buffalo Bill*, 203).

40. See Russell, *Lives and Legends of Buffalo Bill*, 322.

41. Moses, *Wild West Shows and the Images of American Indians, 1883–1933*, 18.

42. Ibid., 19, 21.

43. "Major Frank North, Chief of Pawnee Scouts." *Buffalo Bill's Wild West*, 1884 program, William F. Cody Collection (MS. 6), Series VIA—programs, Box 1, McCracken Research Library, BBHC.

44. Moses, *Wild West Shows and the Images of American Indians, 1883–1933*, 23.

45. Pegler and Rimer, *Buffalo Bill's Wild West*, 11.

46. Moses, "Wild West Shows, Reformers, and the Image of the American Indian, 1887–1914," 193.

47. Moses, *Wild West Shows and the Images of American Indians, 1883–1933*, 32–33.

48. Vilas to CIA, 1 March 1889; Vilas to CIA, 18 February 1889; both in PR General Records, Miscellaneous Correspondence Received, January 1882–December 1890, Box 27, RG 75, FARC.

49. Moses, "Wild West Shows," 201–2.

50. Oberly's argument was based on "the case of Standing Bear in 1879, in which the court had acknowledged the right of a peaceful Indian to come and go as he wished with the same freedom accorded to the white man." See Prucha, *American Indian Policy in Crisis*, 321; Moses, "Wild West Shows," 203.

51. See Moses, "Wild West Shows," 199; and Rosa and May, *Buffalo Bill and His Wild West*, 147.

52. Moses, "Wild West Shows," 203.

53. CIA to Gallagher, 1 November 1889, PR General Records, Correspondence Received from Office of Indian Affairs, October 1880–December 1890, Box 9, RG 75, FARC.

54. Ibid.; Moses, "Wild West Shows," 203–4.

55. Moses, "Wild West Shows," 204; Vilas to CIA, 18 February 1889, PR General Records, Box 27, RG 75, FARC.

56. CIA to Indian Agents, circular, 8 March 1890, PR General Records, Box 27, RG 75, FARC.

57. Ibid.

58. Prucha, *Indians in American Society*, 24.

CHAPTER TWO: THE LAKOTA
AND THE GHOST DANCE RELIGION

1. Michael Kilian, "At Last, U.S. Returns Sacred Wounded Knee Relics to Sioux," *Chicago Tribune*, 27 September 1998, 7.

2. Hittman, *Wovoka and the Ghost Dance*, 7.

3. Ibid., 234–35.

4. Mooney, "Ghost Dance Religion and the Sioux Outbreak of 1890." All citations of this article are from the 1996 reprint (see bibliography). DeMallie, "Lakota Ghost Dance," 386. Michael Hittman describes Utley's book as an "excellent history of the 1890 Ghost Dance Religion among the Lakota" (Hittman, *Wovoka and the Ghost Dance*, 22). My examination focuses on Mooney's interpretation of the Lakota Ghost Dance, and I maintain that his work on the Ghost Dance as a whole remains a vital source of great significance. It is also worth noting that Utley has amended his interpretation of the Lakota Ghost Dance in the second edition of his book, which was published in 2004.

5. Stewart, "Contemporary Document on Wovoka (Jack Wilson) Prophet of the Ghost Dance in 1890," 219.

6. Michael Hittman, for example, argued that Mooney had a "Plains bias," which colored his interpretation of the religion. Hittman, *Wovoka and the Ghost Dance*, 98. See also Utley, *Last Days of the Sioux Nation*, 76n.22.

7. Mooney's sources were Casper Edson, an Arapaho, and Black Short Nose, a Cheyenne, both of whom traveled to see Wovoka in August 1891. Mooney reproduces the letters in full, and most subsequent publications on the Ghost Dance use the letters as the major source for the doctrine, many quoting from them directly. Mooney, *Ghost Dance*, 142–45. Richmond L. Clow argued that the Lakota continued to practice the Ghost Dance long after the military suppression; see Clow, "Lakota Ghost Dance after 1890," 323–33. See also Jensen et al., *Eyewitness at Wounded Knee*, 7.

8. Utley, *Last Days of the Sioux Nation*, 69.

9. Mooney, *Ghost Dance*, 421–22.

10. See Moses, *Indian Man*, 72.

11. Hagan, *Indian Police and Judges*, 82–103; Overholt, "Ghost Dance of 1890 and the Nature of the Prophetic Process," 57.

12. Mooney, *Ghost Dance*, 150–51. U.S. Secretary of War, *Annual Report, 1891*, 142–43; McDermott, "Wounded Knee," 253; see also DeMallie, *Sixth Grandfather*, 267n.13.

13. While ostensibly inspecting government beef cattle at the Rosebud Agency, Earnest had also been forwarding confidential reports detailing the movements and the temperament of the various groups on the reservation. Capt. C. A. Earnest to Assistant Adjutant General, Dept. of the Platte, 19 November 1890, LR, 6601, Record of Adjutant General's Office, 1780–1917, RG 94, NARA.

14. Earnest to Assistant Adjutant General, Dept. of the Platte, 19 November 1890, LR 6601, RG 94, NARA. See also Secretary of War, *Annual Report, 1891*, 140; and E. B. Reynolds, Special U.S. Indian Agent, to T. J. Morgan, CIA, 2 November 1890, SC 188,

50–51, RG 75, NARA. Reynolds outlines in his communication the efforts of the Indian police to arrest those Ghost Dancers responsible for killing cattle without authority, noting that on their third attempt he sent "the Chief of Police with an interpreter." He also makes specific references to the advancement for "the inauguration of the new era. . . . to the new moon after the next one," which corresponds directly with Short Bull's reported statement, "I have told you that this would come to pass in two seasons, but since the whites are interfering so much, I will advance the time from what my father above told me to do, so the time will be shorter. . . . [W]e must dance the balance of this moon, at the end of which time the earth will shiver very hard" (Mooney, *Ghost Dance*, 150–51).

15. See Crager, "As Narrated by Short Bull," 9–10, BBMG.

16. Thomas Overholt uses this sermon to illustrate that the Lakota had introduced "a warlike twist in the doctrine." See Overholt, "Short Bull, Black Elk, Sword," 175. See also Secretary of War, *Annual Report, 1891*, 142; Earnest to Assistant Adjutant General, Dept. of the Platte, 19 November 1890, LR 6601, RG 94, NARA.

17. Earnest to Assistant Adjutant General, Dept. of the Platte, 19 November 1890, LR 6733, RG 94, NARA.

18. Mooney, *Ghost Dance*, 158–60. George Sword's statement was also published as "The Story of the Ghost Dance," *Folk-Lorist* 1 (1892–93): 28–31. See also Utley, *Last Days of the Sioux Nation*, 73; Overholt, "Ghost Dance of 1890," 53–54.

19. Sword quoted in Mooney, *Ghost Dance*, 160. Good Thunder reportedly gave an account of his visit to Nevada to Elaine Goodale, who later reproduced it under her married name. See Eastman, "Ghost Dance War and Wounded Knee Massacre of 1890–91," 31.

20. Hyde, *Red Clouds Folk*, 174; Overholt, "Short Bull, Black Elk, Sword," 181.

21. Sword quoted in Walker, *Lakota Belief and Ritual*, 74–75. Hagan gives his name as "Man-Who-Carries-the-Sword"; see Hagan, *Indian Police and Judges*, 92.

22. Hyde, *Sioux Chronicle*, 264; Overholt, "Short Bull, Black Elk, Sword," 189.

23. Mooney, *Ghost Dance*, 161–63.

24. Ibid., 160–61. Agent Foster described Selwyn as "a full-blooded Indian being the son of Medicine Cow, an old chief of this tribe; he is fairly well educated having been a protégé of Hon. John Welch, of Philadelphia, with whom he lived as a member of that gentleman's family" (Foster to CIA, 25 November 1890, SC 188, 2042, RG 75, NARA).

25. Selwyn was not employed as a policeman as such, but rather as assistant farmer; the agent sent him with the arresting party "to obtain what information he could from the stranger." Furthermore, Selwyn himself stated, "[B]y your order of the 21st instant, I went up to White Swan and have arrested the wanted man (Kuwapi, or one they chased after)" (ibid., 2042–43).

26. Mooney, *Ghost Dance*, 149; Commissioner of Indian Affairs, *Annual Report, 1891*, 125–26.

27. Commissioner of Indian Affairs, *Annual Report, 1891*, 126; McLaughlin, *My Friend the Indian*, 184–90; Utley, *Last Days of the Sioux Nation*, 97n.13.

28. DeMallie, "Lakota Ghost Dance," 394.

29. Commissioner of Indian Affairs, *Annual Report, 1891*, 125–26.

30. Vestal [Campbell], *Sitting Bull*, 272.

31. Vestal [Campbell], *New Sources of Indian History, 1850–1891*, 340–41.

32. Walker, *Lakota Belief and Ritual*, 142–43. The date and interpreter for these two texts are unknown. Another text by Short Bull included in the publication, entitled "Sending the Spirits to the Spirit World," was interpreted by Thomas Tyon on 11 February 1898. James R. Walker spent eighteen years in South Dakota as the agency physician at Pine Ridge, during which time he collected material relating to almost every facet of the old Lakota way of life. See Walker, *Lakota Belief and Ritual*, 3–50.

33. Curtis, *Indians' Book*, 45–47. Natalie Curtis was a noted folklorist and collector of ethnic songs, who collected more than two hundred songs from eighteen tribes, which formed the basis of her book. The book also included a photograph of, and a drawing by, Short Bull. See McCoy, "Short Bull," 57.

34. Haberland, "Die Oglala-Sammlung Weygold im Hamburgischen Museum für Völkerkunde (Teil 4)," 19–52. Wolfgang Haberland stated that "according to Weygold's notes, he talked in the summer of 1909 a few hours with Short Bull, supported by an interpreter, probably . . . Herbert Bisonette." See also Draeger, "Einige Indianische Darstellungen des Sonnentanzes aus dem Museum für Völkerkunde in Leipzig," 80.

35. Buechel, *Lakota Tales and Texts*, ed. Manhart, 277–89; translated into English in a later edition, Buechel, *Lakota Tales and Texts in Translation*, 508–39. Raymond DeMallie has retranslated this account for the purposes of this publication, and I have used DeMallie's translation throughout the book (see document 5 in the appendix). Eugene Buechel emigrated from Germany, arriving in the United States in 1900, and was later a Jesuit missionary among the Lakota stationed at the St. Francis Mission. He is best known for his work on the Lakota language, having translated a Bible history and prayer book into Lakota. He self-published *A Grammar of Lakota: The Language of the Teton Sioux Indians* (1939).

36. Overlooked for many years, the document has recently been published in Coleman, *Voices of Wounded Knee*. Coleman uses the text throughout his book, but has put his own interpretation upon it. See document 1 in the appendix.

37. Crager, "As Narrated by Short Bull." For further information about the interpreter, George C. Crager, see Maddra, *Glasgow's Ghost Shirt*, 14–17.

38. DeMallie, "Lakota Ghost Dance," 395.

39. Crager, "As Narrated by Short Bull," 20, BBMG.

40. I have been conducting archival research on George Crager for several years. For a published example of Crager's handwriting, see Maddra, *Glasgow's Ghost Shirt*, 12.

41. *Evening Express* (Cardiff), 23 September 1891, 2. See also *Evening Express* (Cardiff), 26 September 1891, 4.

42. It is recorded that Crager was the only journalist permitted to witness the Lakota Council on 17 January 1891 and that he "gave Gen. Miles a copy of his ver-

batim report of the event, which the latter forwarded to the War Department in Washington as an official document." "In Indian Guise," *New York World*, n.d., CS, William F. Cody Collection (MS. 6), Series IX: scrapbooks, Box 2, McCracken Research Library, BBHC.

43. Walker, *Lakota Belief and Ritual*, 142. See also Haberland, "Die Oglala-Samm-lung Weygold . . . (Teil 4)," 38.

44. Haberland, "Die Oglala-Sammlung Weygold . . . (Teil 4)," 21. Words in paren-theses are Weygold's.

45. For a discussion of the religion's evolution, see Kehoe, *Ghost Dance*, 41–50.

46. Maj. Henry Carroll, who was in command of Camp Crook, at Tongue River Agency, Montana, transmitted Porcupine's statement to the War Department, which forwarded it to the Indian Office. Published verbatim in Mooney, *Ghost Dance*, 155–58. Short Bull makes reference to Porcupine in two of his narratives: Crager, "As Narrated by Short Bull," 4, BBMG; Buechel, "Ghost Dance. Told by Short Bull," transcribed by Ivan Stars (1915), HRM (translated by Raymond DeMallie, 2005). Porcupine also gave a statement about the religion to J. A. Gaston, first lieutenant, 8th Cavalry, command-ing the department on Tongue River, at a council held with the Cheyenne on Tongue River, Montana, 18 November 1890. See SC 188, 117–21, RG 75, NARA.

47. See Crager, "As Narrated by Short Bull," 3–4, BBMG; Buechel, "Ghost Dance," HRM; and Mooney, *Ghost Dance*, 155–56.

48. Hittman, *Wovoka and the Ghost Dance*, 236.

49. Ibid., 231–33, 271–72.

50. Crager, "As Narrated by Short Bull," 6, BBMG.

51. Mooney, *Ghost Dance*, 157.

52. Crager, "As Narrated by Short Bull," 7, BBMG.

53. Mooney, *Ghost Dance*, 157. Porcupine's description compares well with Arthur Chapman's description, which appeared in an article, "Circle of the Shades," in *Spokane Review*; Hittman, *Wovoka and the Ghost Dance*, 107. Kicking Bear and Good Thunder's descriptions were very different. Good Thunder described Wovoka as "a man of surpassing beauty, with long yellow hair, clad in a blue robe" (Eastman, "Ghost Dance War," 31). Kicking Bear, as quoted in McLaughlin, stated, "[W]hen we were weak and faint from our journey, we looked for a camping place, and were met by a man dressed like an Indian, but whose hair was long and glistening like the yel-low money of the white man. His face was very beautiful to see, and when he spoke my heart was glad and I forgot my hunger and the toil I had gone through" (McLaughlin, *My Friend the Indian*, 186).

54. Crager, "As Narrated by Short Bull," 6, BBMG. Mooney stated that Wovoka "speaks only his own Paiute language, with some little knowledge of English. He is not acquainted with the sign language, which is hardly known west of the moun-tains" (Mooney, *Ghost Dance*, 133). Hittman quoted an acquaintance of Wovoka's, Ed Dyer, as stating, "Wilson [Wovoka] was known to have a good working knowl-edge of English but not quite up to explaining obscure points of Indian theology" (Hittman, *Wovoka and the Ghost Dance*, 253).

55. Crager, "As Narrated by Short Bull," 6–7, BBMG; Mooney, *Ghost Dance*, 157.

56. Crager, "As Narrated by Short Bull," 7–8, BBMG. Words in parentheses are Crager's.

57. Mooney, *Ghost Dance*, 157–58.

58. Curtis, *Indians' Book*, 45–46; Haberland, "Die Oglala-Sammlung Weygold . . . (Teil 4)," 38.

59. Walker, *Lakota Belief and Ritual*, 142.

60. Buechel, "Ghost Dance," HRM.

61. Mooney, *Ghost Dance*, 159.

62. Ibid., 158.

63. Standing Bear, *My People, the Sioux*, 218.

64. Mooney, *Ghost Dance*, 315.

65. Ibid., 183.

66. Shoemaker, ed., *American Indians*, 8.

67. Buechel, "Ghost Dance," HRM.

68. Haberland, "Die Oglala-Sammlung Weygold . . . (Teil 4)," 38. Words in parentheses are Haberland's.

69. Curtis, *Indians' Book*, 46–47.

70. Moses, "Jack Wilson and the Indian Service," 306; Vestal [Campbell], *Sitting Bull*, 272.

71. Coleman, *Voices of Wounded Knee*, 57.

CHAPTER THREE:
FROM ACCOMMODATION TO RESISTANCE

1. DeMallie, "Lakota Ghost Dance," 390; Josephy et al., *Wounded Knee*, 17.

2. Hyde, *Sioux Chronicle*, 258–59; Moses, "Jack Wilson and the Indian Service," 309.

3. Overholt, "Ghost Dance of 1890," 57.

4. Crager, "As Narrated by Short Bull," 11–12, BBMG; Jensen et al., *Eyewitness at Wounded Knee*, 13.

5. Standing Bear, *My People, the Sioux*, 217, 220. Despite having a close relationship with the agent, whom he described as "a nice young man," in the aftermath of the Wounded Knee Massacre Standing Bear and two friends "were ready to fight if it came to a 'show-down.' While we three were Carlisle graduates, we determined to stick by our race" (Standing Bear, *My People, the Sioux*, 225).

6. Yet to assume that the different departments of the government were in unison would be wrong. Both the War Department and the Interior Department, or more specifically the Bureau of Indian Affairs, tried to distance themselves from any responsibility, and each attempted to put the onus for the situation on the other.

7. Jensen et al., *Eyewitness at Wounded Knee*, 43.

8. Moses "'The Father Tells Me So!'" 342.

9. Jensen et al., *Eyewitness at Wounded Knee*, 47.

10. Hyde, *Sioux Chronicle*, 258.

11. Moses, "Jack Wilson and the Indian Service," 301.

12. Commissioner of Indian Affairs, *Annual Report, 1891*, 411.

13. Haberland, "Die Oglala-Sammlung Weygold . . . (Teil 4)," 37.

14. Haberland, "Die Oglala-Sammlung Weygold . . . (Teil 3)," 22–24; Mooney, *Ghost Dance*, 160, 150.

15. Mooney, *Ghost Dance*, 160, 150; Haberland, "Die Oglala-Sammlung Weygold . . . (Teil 3)," 22–24; Haberland, "Die Oglala-Sammlung Weygoldellipsis (Teil 4)," 21.

16. Walker, *Lakota Belief and Ritual*, 143.

17. Crager, "As Narrated by Short Bull," 7, BBMG.

18. Buechel, "Ghost Dance," HRM.

19. Ibid.

20. Ibid. For examples of other Lakota visions, see Utley, *Last Days of the Sioux Nation*, 89–91; and DeMallie, *Sixth Grandfather*, 260–66.

21. Hyde, *Sioux Chronicle*, 258.

22. Mooney, *Ghost Dance*, 153.

23. Phister, "Indian Messiah," 108; Hittman, *Wovoka*, 235. Hittman quotes numerous people with regard to this demonstration of Wovoka's invulnerability, some of whom were witnesses to the event, while others reported what they had heard. Furthermore, while some saw the incident as proof of Wovoka's greatness, others told how he pulled off an illusory trick. See Hittman, *Wovoka*, 82–84, 250–51, 263, 306, 308–9, 326, 332, 336. Short Bull makes a similar statement with regard to shooting at a Ghost Shirt; see appendix.

24. Hittman, *Wovoka*, 198. The demand for Wovoka's clothing also included hats; it would appear that Wovoka was responding to written requests, and that what followers desired were articles that he himself had worn (ibid., 252).

25. Jensen et al., *Eyewitness at Wounded Knee*, 12.

26. Vestal [Campbell], *Sitting Bull*, 277.

27. "A comparison of the interpretations of shield-designs and ghost-dress designs seems to leave little opportunity for any other conclusion than that the protective designs used in the ghost-dance were essentially the same as those used in former times upon shields and other objects. The garments may be foreign; but the idea of protective designs is most certainly not peculiar to the ghost-dance religion, since it was widely distributed among American tribes, and associated with ceremonial objects that were in use at least a century before the ghost-dance religion appeared" (Wissler, "Some Protective Designs of the Dakota," 22–23, 39–40).

28. Utley, *Last Days of the Sioux Nation*, 78.

29. Ibid.

30. Mooney, *Ghost Dance*, 202.

31. Bland, ed., *Brief History of the Late Military Invasion of the Home of the Sioux*, 20–21.

32. Utley, *Last Days of the Sioux Nation*, 78–79. See also Clow, *Rosebud Sioux*, 71–74.

33. Crager, "As Narrated by Short Bull," 10–11, BBMG.

34. On 21 November 1890 the acting commissioner of Indian affairs, R. V. Belt, wrote to the secretary of the interior stating his "request that the military be directed to cause the arrest of the Indians named in Special Agent Reynold's telegram, should the military authorities concur . . . arrest and detention is absolutely necessary." Short Bull headed Reynold's list, which included twenty other Brule Lakota. See R.V. Belt, Acting CIA, to John Noble, Secretary of the Interior, 21 November 1890, SC 188, p89, RG 75, NARA.

35. Bland, *Brief History of the Late Military Invasion*, 8.

36. Crager, "As Narrated by Short Bull," 11–13, BBMG. On 27 November 1890 Miles reported that Little Wound was at Pine Ridge Agency "and his following coming. Short Bull of the Rosebud Agency, came in night before last; reports his people coming in; estimated at about 500 lodges and 2,500 people" (Miles, Chicago, to Adjutant General, 27 November 1890, SC 188, p268, RG 75, NARA).

37. Crager, "As Narrated by Short Bull," 11–13, BBMG.

38. Ibid.; Bland, *Brief History of the Late Military Invasion*, 8.

39. Bland, *Brief History of the Late Military Invasion*, 8.

40. Mooney, *Ghost Dance*, 246.

41. Utley, *Last Days of the Sioux Nation*, 115–17.

42. Crager, "As Narrated by Short Bull," 13–14, BBMG. Utley paints a very different picture of Short Bull's role, instead suggesting that it was Crow Dog who defused the situation by placing his blanket over his head. However, it is worth noting that Utley's source was "press dispatches . . . summarized in . . . [Boyd, *Recent Indian Wars*,] pp. 205–10"; see Utley, *Last Days of the Sioux Nation*, 140–42.

43. Crager, "As Narrated by Short Bull," 14–15.

44. Ibid., 16–17.

45. Ibid., 16–17, 18.

46. Ibid.

47. Ibid.

48. DeMallie, "Lakota Ghost Dance," 396.

49. Curtis, *Indians' Book*, 45.

50. Crager, "As Narrated by Short Bull," 19, BBMG.

51. Those removed to Fort Sheridan were the following: Short Bull, One Bull, Scatter, Good Eagle, High Eagle, Horn Eagle, Standing Bear, Sorrel Horse, Wounded With Many Arrows, Run Along Side Of, Close To Home, Hard To Hit, Crow Cane, Kicking Bear, Revenge, Knows-His-Voice, One Star, Standing Bear, Coming Grunt, Brings The White, Brave, Calls The Name, Medicine Horse, White Beaver, Little Horse, His Horses Voice, and Take the Shield Away. There were two individuals known as Standing Bear who were removed to Fort Sheridan; one was an Oglala, the other was a Brule. The prisoner One Bull should not be confused with Agent Mclaughlin's informant on Kicking Bear's speech, the Hunkpapa Indian policeman who was also Sitting Bull's nephew. Agent Charles Penny (Acting), Pine Ridge, to CIA, 28 March 1891, Microfilm M1282, LS to Office of Indian Affairs by Pine Ridge

Agency, 1775–1914 (hereafter cited as M1282 LS), 179–81, RG 75, FARC; passenger list of SS *Switzerland* sailing from Philadelphia to Antwerp, 1 April 1891, CS, MS6.IX, Box 2, McCracken Research Library, BBHC; Russell, *Lives and Legends*, 264; Green, ed., *After Wounded Knee*, 92. Major Lauderdale also informed his sister Francis that Miles had sent a telegram three days later stating "that the party reached there [Fort Sheridan] all right and that the Indians are very happy. This message was communicated to the Sioux families here and I have no doubt that there is great rejoicing in the tepees and homes where they live" (Green, ed., *After Wounded Knee*, 98).

52. Miles to Adjutant General, telegram, 26 January 1891, File 5412-PRD-1890, RG 94, National Archives Microfilm Publication M983, *Reports and Correspondence Relating to the Army Investigations of the Battle of Wounded Knee and to the Sioux Campaign of 1890–1891* (hereafter cited as M983, RG 94, NARA), 1077.

53. *Chicago Daily Tribune*, 28 January 1891, 1 ("Miles Talks of His Charges: The General Satisfied That There Will Be No More Trouble").

54. *Chicago Daily Tribune*, 27 January 1891, 2 ("To Be Rounded Up Here: Miles Will Take the Hostile Indians to Fort Sheridan").

55. Agent J. George Wright, Rosebud, to CIA, 12 February 1891, SC188, 9–11, RG 75, NARA.

56. Jas. G. Wright to Herbert Welsh, Secretary, Indian Rights Association, 17 June 1891, Series I-A. Incoming Correspondence, 1864–1968, Reel 7, IRA, Microfilm 42 357, Western History Collections, University of Oklahoma.

57. Miles, *Serving the Republic*, 245.

58. *Chicago Daily Tribune*, 31 January 1891, 8 ("Not Imprisoned by Morgan's Orders: The Commissioner Denies That He Sent the Indians to Fort Sheridan").

59. Vestal [Campbell], *New Sources of Indian History*, 59.

60. "Statement of Mary Collins," 2, Mary Clementine Collins Family Papers, Folder #48, Box 3, SDSHS.

61. Utley, *Last Days of the Sioux Nation*, 271.

62. With regard to the women, it seems from later newspaper articles that at least two were married to male prisoners, which appears to support the idea that the Lakota themselves selected who went. Furthermore, it seems that such a practice was not unique. David Wallace Adams has noted that when seventy-two Indian prisoners were removed to Fort Marion, Florida, following the so-called Red River War of 1874, "for some unexplained reason Black Horse, a prominent Comanche, was allowed to take his wife and daughter" (Adams, *Education for Extinction*, 37n.22). See chapters 8 and 9 for a more in-depth discussion of the women prisoners.

63. *New York World*, 25 January 1891, 2.

64. *Chicago Daily Tribune*, 27 January 1891, 2. The use of Indian prisoners as scouts was not that uncommon; for further information see Smits, "Indian Scouts and Indian Allies in the Frontier Army," in *Major Problems in American Indian History*, ed. Hurtado and Iverson, 332.

65. *Chicago Daily Tribune*, 28 January 1891, 1.

66. *Chicago Daily Tribune,* 29 January 1891, 3.

67. *Omaha Morning World-Herald,* 6 February 1891 ("Called on Ghost Dancers"). The same was true for the Indian prisoners under the charge of Lt. Richard Henry Pratt at Fort Marion. Adams noted, "The Indians, although initially feared by some, were an object of great curiosity" (Adams, *Education for Extinction,* 38, 41).

68. *Chicago Daily Tribune,* 29 January 1891, 3.

69. *Omaha Morning World-Herald,* 6 February 1891 ("Talking for the Hostages").

70. Two sources suggest that the Fort Sheridan prisoners were considered by the military as prisoners of war. First, a telegram from Maj. Gen. J. M. Schofield to Brigadier General Brooke, sent on 1 December 1890, stated: "By direction of the Secretary of War you will regard as prisoners of war all Indians whom you think it necessary under present circumstances to detain under your control, and as such furnish them with necessary food from the Army supplies, in addition to that furnished by the Interior Department." See SC 188, 1709, RG 75, NARA. Second, the remaining four prisoners at Fort Sheridan, after the majority had joined Cody's Wild West, appeared on a list of all "Indian Prisoners of War." See SC 188, 1470, RG 75, NARA.

71. Crager, "As Narrated by Short Bull," 19, BBMG.

72. Unidentified newspaper clipping, n.d., "Braves Go to Europe—Buffalo Bill to Take the Indians from Fort Sheridan," Buffalo Bill Scrapbook, 1891–1927, Microfilm FF18, William Frederick Cody Papers 1887–1919, SHSC.

73. Jensen et al., *Eyewitness at Wounded Knee,* 7.

74. Prucha, *Indians in American Society,* 36–37, 43.

CHAPTER FOUR: INDIAN PERFORMERS IN BUFFALO BILL'S WILD WEST

1. *New York World,* 21 July 1890, CS, MS6.IX, Box 2, McCracken Research Library, BBHC.

2. John M. Burke to CIA, telegram, 26 October 1890, LR 33009–1890, RG 75, NARA; Moses, *Wild West Shows and the Images of American Indians, 1883–1933,* 100; Russell, *Lives and Legends,* 351; Rosa and May, *Buffalo Bill and His Wild West,* 149.

3. U.S. Commissioner of Indian Affairs, *Annual Report, 1890,* 3–4.

4. Moses, "Wild West Shows," 194.

5. Prucha, *American Indian Policy in Crisis,* 320.

6. Moses, "Wild West Shows," 199.

7. Ibid., 198–99.

8. Unidentified newspaper clipping [New York], 16 June 1890, CS, MS6.IX, Box 2, McCracken Research Library, BBHC.

9. Ibid.; George C. Crager to Noble, 21 June 1890, LR 19021–1890, Box 634, RG 75, NARA.

10. *New York Herald,* 19 June 1890, and unidentified clipping, n.d., CS, MS6.IX, Box 2, McCracken Research Library, BBHC.

11. *New York Times*, 19 June 1890, CS, MS6.IX, Box 2, McCracken Research Library, BBHC; Crager to Noble, 21 June 1890, LR 19021–1890, Box 634, RG 75, NARA. *New York News*, 18 June 1890; *New York Journal*, 18 June 1890; *New York Press*, 19 June 1890; and *New York Times*, 19 June 1890; all in CS, MS6.IX, Box 2, McCracken Research Library, BBHC.

12. Crager to Noble, 21 June 1890, LR 19021–1890, Box 634, RG 75, NARA. Father Francis M. J. Craft, S.J., was a long time missionary to the Indians. See Jensen et al., *Eyewitness at Wounded Knee*, 136; and Clow, *Rosebud Sioux*, 45. George Crager had lived among the Brule Lakota for years, and appears to have been employed by Buffalo Bill's Wild West in 1886. See Maddra, *Glasgow's Ghost Shirt*, 14–15; *New York Sun*, 2 January 1891, CS, MS6.IX, Box 2, McCracken Research Library, BBHC; unidentified newspaper clipping [*New York World*?], n.d.[c. 1886, when Wild West show did six-month stand at Erastina, Staten Island], CS, MS6.IX, Box 2, McCracken Research Library, BBHC. Clipping not only refers to Crager "the Sioux interpreter," but also talks about Pawnee as well as Sioux performers, which helps date it to 1886.

13. Crager to Noble, 21 June 1890, LR 19021–1890, Box 634, RG 75, NARA; *New York Tribune*, 19 June 1890, CS, MS6.IX, Box 2, McCracken Research Library, BBHC. See also Moses, *Wild West Shows and the Images of American Indians, 1883–1933*, 95.

14. See CS, MS6.IX, Box 2, McCracken Research Library, BBHC.

15. Crager to Noble, 21 June 1890, LR 19021–1890, Box 634, RG 75, NARA.

16. Moses, "Wild West Shows," 206; Vilas to CIA, 1 March 1889 and 18 February 1889, PR General Records, Box 27, RG 75, FARC.

17. CIA to Louis L. Robbins, Superintendent of Indian Warehouse, telegram, 23 June 1890, LB 200, 410, RG 75, NARA.

18. O'Beirne lists the pallbearers as "Rev. Father Groff [Craft], Mr George C. Cregar [Crager], Capt. McGee, formerly interpreter and scout, Mr. Hank Clifford, Mr. Pierre Barguet, and James R. O'Beirne." See Jas. R. O'Beirne, Assistant Superintendent, Office of Immigration, to Agent Hugh D. Gallagher, PR, 4 July 1890, PR General Records, Box 27, RG 75, FARC.

19. Clifford was later employed by Buffalo Bill's Wild West as the show's orator when it toured Britain in 1891–92. Unidentified newspaper clipping, n.d., and *New York Journal*, 23 June 1890, CS, MS6.IX, Box 2, McCracken Research Library, BBHC; Gallagher to O'Beirne, 28 June 1890, PR General Records, Misc. LS 1890, vol. 6, p. 152, Box 54, RG 75, FARC; O'Beirne to Gallagher, 4 July 1890, PR General Records, Box 27, RG 75, FARC; Gallagher to CIA, 28 July 1890, LR 23464–1890, Box 646, RG 75, NARA. See also Moses, *Wild West Shows and the Images of American Indians, 1883–1933*, 95.

20. Charles B. Trail, Marseilles, to William F. Wharton, Assistant Secretary of State, 27 January 1890, PR General Records, Box 27, RG 75, FARC; Moses, *Wild West Shows and the Images of American Indians, 1883–1933*, 94.

21. Edward Camphausen, Naples, to Wharton, 19 February 1890, LR 7465–1890, Box 602, RG 75, NARA. See also Moses, *Wild West Shows and the Images of American Indians, 1883–1933*, 94.

22. Augustus O'Bourn, Rome, to Wharton, 12 March 1890, PR General Records, Box 9, RG 75, FARC. See also Moses, *Wild West Shows and the Images of American Indians, 1883–1933*, 89, 94; and Napier, "Across the Big Water," in *Indians and Europe*, ed. Feest, 397–400.

23. O'Beirne to Gallagher, 4 July 1890, PR General Records, Box 27, RG 75, FARC. See also Moses, *Wild West Shows and the Images of American Indians, 1883–1933*, 95.

24. Gen. James R. O'Bierne had been a special agent sent from Washington "to induce the Rosebud and Pine Ridge Indians to scatter out on farming land" (Hyde, *Sioux Chronicle*, 70).

25. O'Beirne to Gallagher, 4 July 1890, PR General Records, Box 27, RG 75, FARC. See also Moses, *Wild West Shows and the Images of American Indians, 1883–1933*, 95–96. Moses erroneously mixes this group with another, subsequent returning group when he states that "O'Beirne implied that Eagle Horn, White Horse, Bear Pipe, Kills Weasel, and Kills Plenty had sailed from Europe without an interpreter 'or anyone to conduct them.' In fact, Fred Matthews, a veteran stage driver, accompanied the showmen" (ibid., 95). Fred Matthews only accompanied the second group, which included White Horse, Bear Pipe, and Kills White Weasel, who arrived in New York on 19 July 1890.

26. Moses, *Wild West Shows and the Images of American Indians, 1883–1933*, 95.

27. *New York World*, 20 July 1890, and *New York Herald*, 22 July 1890, CS, MS6.IX, Box 2, McCracken Research Library, BBHC. Matthews had been the stagecoach driver in Buffalo Bill's Wild West for some years; see Russell, *Lives and Legends*, 294.

28. *New York Herald*, 22 July 1890, CS, MS6.IX, Box 2, McCracken Research Library, BBHC.

29. Unidentified newspaper clipping, n.d., CS, MS6.IX, Box 2, McCracken Research Library, BBHC. See also Moses, *Wild West Shows and the Images of American Indians, 1883–1933*, 97.

30. Gallagher to CIA, 28 July 1890, LR 23464–1890, Box 646, RG 75, NARA. See also Moses, *Wild West Shows and the Images of American Indians, 1883–1933*, 97.

31. *New York Herald*, 22 July 1890, CS, MS6.IX, Box 2, McCracken Research Library, BBHC.

32. William F. Cody to "My Dear Doctor," 15 February 1890, MS6, Series I:B Correspondence from William F. Cody, Box 1, folder 11, 1890–92, Cody Archive, BBHC.

33. Russell, *Lives and Legends*, 351; Reddin, *Wild West Shows*, 115.

34. Burke to Crager, telegram, 25 July 1890, and John W. Hamilton to City Editor, unidentified newspaper, telegram, 26 July 1890, CS, MS6.IX, Box 2, McCracken Research Library, BBHC.

35. *New York World*, 30 July 1890, and *New York News*, 29 July 1890, CS, MS6.IX, Box 2, McCracken Research Library, BBHC.

36. *New York Herald*, 30 July 1890, CS, MS6.IX, Box 2, McCracken Research Library, BBHC.

37. *New York Press*, 24 August 1890, CS, MS6.IX, Box 2, McCracken Research Library, BBHC.

38. *New York World*, 30 July 1890, CS, MS6.IX, Box 2, McCracken Research Library, BBHC.

39. *New York Herald*, 30 July 1890, CS, MS6.IX, Box 2, McCracken Research Library, BBHC.

40. *New York World*, 30 July 1890; *New York Journal*, 30 July 1890; and *New York Herald*, 30 July 1890; all in CS, MS6.IX, Box 2, McCracken Research Library, BBHC.

41. Ibid.

42. *New York Herald*, 30 July 1890, CS, MS6.IX, Box 2, McCracken Research Library, BBHC.

43. *New York Journal*, 30 July 1890, CS, MS6.IX, Box 2, McCracken Research Library, BBHC.

44. Ibid. The term "seeing the elephant" means "to see or experience a great deal," or "a loss of innocence," the elephant being seen as something exotic, while "mashing" can be translated as "seducing" or "making advances to" the opposite sex. See *Cassell Dictionary of Slang*, s.v.

45. *New York Journal*, 30 July 1890, CS, MS6.IX, Box 2, McCracken Research Library, BBHC.

46. Ibid.

47. Gallagher to CIA, 13 August 1890, LR 25179–1890, Box 651, RG 75, NARA. See also Moses, *Wild West Shows and the Images of American Indians, 1883–1933*, 97.

48. O'Beirne to CIA, 3 August 1890, LR 23831–1890, Box 647, RG 75, NARA.

49. Noble to CIA, 4 August 1890, LR 23943–1890, Box 647, RG 75, NARA. See also Moses, *Wild West Shows and the Images of American Indians, 1883–1933*, 97.

50. Hagan, *Indian Rights Association*, 103.

51. Moses, *Wild West Shows and the Images of American Indians, 1883–1933*, 97. It was not only Cody's show that concerned the Indian Office, but also the Carver & Whitney and the Adam Forepaugh shows, which had Indians traveling with them. See Moses, *Wild West Shows and the Images of American Indians, 1883–1933*, 104.

52. CIA to Cody and Salsbury, 22 August 1890, LB 203, 85–87, RG 75, NARA.

53. CIA to Gallagher, 22 August 1890, LB 203, 93–94, RG 75, NARA.

54. CIA to O'Beirne, 22 August 1890, LB 203, 100–102, RG 75, NARA.

55. Loose document from PR Agency, dated 28 August 1890, presumably written by Agent Gallagher (handwritten), 8–10, "Show Business," PR General Records, Misc. LS 1887–1891, Box 54, RG 75, FARC.

56. *New York Press*, 28 August 1890; *New York Sun*, 28 August 1890; and *New York World*, 28 August 1890; all in CS, MS6.IX, Box 2, McCracken Research Library, BBHC.

57. Nate Salsbury, Cologne, to W. D. Stamur, U.S. Consul, 18 September 1890, LR 33697–1890, Box 674, RG 75, NARA. See also Moses, *Wild West Shows and the Images of American Indians, 1883–1933*, 98.

58. Uses the Sword was reportedly also known as "Moskito." Hugo M. Starkloft, U.S. Consul, Bremen, to Wharton, 26 September 1890, LR 33015–1890, Box 674, RG 75, NARA.

59. Ibid.; Moses, *Wild West Shows and the Images of American Indians, 1883–1933,* 98.

60. Burke, Strasburg, to CIA, telegram, 26 October 1890, LR 33009–1890, Box 673, RG 75, NARA; Moses, "Wild West Shows," 206.

61. *Philadelphia Press,* 14 November 1890, and *New York Sun,* 13 November 1890, CS, MS6.IX, Box 2, McCracken Research Library, BBHC.

62. *Philadelphia Press,* 14 November 1890, CS, MS6.IX, Box 2, McCracken Research Library, BBHC. This appears to be a reference to Cody's former partner, Doc Carver, who had also been touring Europe with a competing Wild West show.

63. See Moses, *Wild West Shows and the Images of American Indians, 1883–1933,* 100n.79.

64. *Philadelphia Press,* 14 November 1890, CS, MS6.IX, Box 2, McCracken Research Library, BBHC. See also Moses, *Wild West Shows and the Images of American Indians, 1883–1933,* 100–101; and Hagan, *Indian Rights Association,* 144.

65. Welsh to George Chandler, Acting Secretary of the Interior, 13 November 1890, LR 35081–1890, Box 678, RG 75, NARA.

66. Ibid. Crager had been dispatched to deliver a second letter to Burke, reiterating Welsh's authority. *Philadelphia Times,* 14 November 1890, CS, MS6.IX, Box 2, McCracken Research Library, BBHC.

67. Welsh to Chandler, 13 November 1890, LR 35080–1890, Box 678, RG 75, NARA. See also Moses, *Wild West Shows and the Images of American Indians, 1883–1933,* 101.

68. Moses, *Wild West Shows and the Images of American Indians, 1883–1933,* 100.

69. R. V. Belt, Acting CIA, to Noble, 18 November 1890, LB 207, 191–204, RG 75, NARA.

70. Ibid. See also Moses, *Wild West Shows and the Images of American Indians, 1883–1933,* 101; Belt to Cody and Salsbury, 15 November 1890, LB 207, 113, RG 75, NARA.

71. Belt to Noble, 18 November 1890, LB 207, 191–204, RG 75, NARA; Moses, *Wild West Shows and the Images of American Indians, 1883–1933,* 101.

72. Belt to Noble, 18 November 1890, LB 207, 191–204, RG 75, NARA.

73. Ibid.

74. For note on Indians explaining away deaths, see Moses, "Wild West Shows," 206.

75. Belt to Noble, 18 November 1890, LB 207, 191–204, RG 75, NARA.

76. Ibid.

77. Ibid.

78. Reddin, *Wild West Shows,* 114.

79. Belt to Noble, 18 November 1890, LB 207, 191–204, RG 75, NARA.

80. Moses, *Wild West Shows and the Images of American Indians, 1883–1933,* 103.

81. Belt to Noble, 18 November 1890, LB 207, 191–204, RG 75, NARA.

82. Ibid.

83. Ibid.

84. Moses, *Wild West Shows and the Images of American Indians, 1883–1933*, 103.

85. Belt to Noble, 18 November 1890, LB 207, 191–204, RG 75, NARA.

86. Ibid.

87. Ibid. See also Moses, *Wild West Shows and the Images of American Indians, 1883–1933*, 103.

88. O'Beirne to Belt, 17 November 1890, LR 35577–1890, Box 679, RG 75, NARA. See also Moses, *Wild West Shows and the Images of American Indians, 1883–1933*, 103.

89. *New York Press*, 17 November 1890, CS, MS6.IX, Box 2, McCracken Research Library, BBHC. O'Beirne also wrote to Welsh, urging him to pursue the matter, but Welsh declined, stating, "I think it a more dignified position to remain silent since it is not likely that good could be accomplished by the opposite course." See Welsh to Father Craft, 17 November 1890, Series I-C Letterpress Copy Books, Reel 70, vol. 6, p. 478, IRA; O'Beirne to Welsh, 18 November 1890, Incoming Correspondence, Reel 6, IRA; and Welsh to CIA, 23 November 1892, Series I-C Letterpress Copy Books, Reel 71, vol. 8, p. 979, IRA.

90. Belt to Agent D. F. Royer, PR, 24 November 1890, PR General Records, Box 9, RG 75, FARC. See also Moses, *Wild West Shows and the Images of American Indians, 1883–1933*, 103–4.

91. *New York World*, 19 November 1890, CS, MS6.IX, Box 2, McCracken Research Library, BBHC.

92. *New York Herald*, 19 November 1890, CS, MS6.IX, Box 2, McCracken Research Library, BBHC.

93. Unidentified newspaper clipping, 30 November 1890, CS, MS6.IX, Box 2, McCracken Research Library, BBHC.

94. Belt to Noble, 1 December 1890, LB 207, 484–89, RG 75, NARA. See also Moses, *Wild West Shows and the Images of American Indians, 1883–1933*, 104.

95. Hyde, *Sioux Chronicle*, 238.

96. Mooney, *Ghost Dance*, 202–3.

97. Moses, *Wild West Shows and the Images of American Indians, 1883–1933*, 104.

98. Yost, *Buffalo Bill*, 225.

99. "He [Cody] came at great expense from Europe to reach the field in the Ghost Dance Campaign" (Yost, *Buffalo Bill*, 488n.11).

100. *New York Herald*, 1 July 1894, Scrapbook 1894, MS6, Series IX, Box 10, 83, Cody Archives, McCracken Research Library, BBHC. This rewriting of the facts began as early as 1891, while the Wild West toured Britain; see *Leicester Daily Post*, 31 August 1891, 5 ("Buffalo Bill's Show in Leicester").

101. Kasson, *Buffalo Bill's Wild West*, 161–62.

102. Ibid., 62.

103. Ibid., 221.

104. Ibid., 85.

105. Ibid., 162.

106. Moses, *Wild West Shows and the Images of American Indians, 1883–1933*, 5.

CHAPTER FIVE: SUPPRESSING THE GHOST DANCE
AND SAVING BUFFALO BILL'S WILD WEST

1. Moses, *Wild West Shows and the Images of American Indians, 1883–1933*, 104.

2. Jensen et al., *Eyewitness at Wounded Knee*, 28.

3. Ibid., 44.

4. Quoted in ibid., 28–29.

5. Ibid., 29; Klein, "'Everything of Interest in the Late Pine Ridge War Are Held by Us for Sale,'" 49; Russell, *Lives and Legends*, 367.

6. Jensen et al., *Eyewitness at Wounded Knee*, 31.

7. Allen, *From Fort Laramie to Wounded Knee*, ed. Jensen, 168–69. Burke later recounted to a journalist that "Black Heart, while unwilling to take up arms against his own people, was nevertheless willing to aid me in a semi-neutral way in whatever manner I might direct" (*New York Herald*, 1 July 1894, Scrapbook 1894, MS6, Series IX, Box 10, 83, Cody Archives, McCracken Research Library, BBHC).

8. Welsh to O'Beirne, 16 December 1890, Letterpress Copy Books, Reel 70, 593, IRA.

9. Secretary of War, *Annual Report, 1891*, 145–46. In his autobiography *Serving the Republic*, Miles simplified the event to "my first effort in that direction [arresting Sitting Bull] proved a failure, owing to diverse influence that was used to defeat my purpose" (238).

10. Alvin M. Josephy Jr., "Wounded Knee," in Josephy et al., *Wounded Knee*, 17.

11. Cody, *Buffalo Bill's Life Story*, 305–6, quoted in Russell, *Lives and Legends*, 359.

12. Hyde, *Sioux Chronicle*, 286.

13. Utley, *Last Days of the Sioux Nation*, 123.

14. Unidentified newspaper clipping, 29 May 1891, CS, MS6.IX, Box 2, McCracken Research Library, BBHC.

15. Russell, *Lives and Legends*, 358.

16. *Chicago Herald*, n.d., Buffalo Bill Scrapbook, Microfilm FF18, Cody Papers, SHSC.

17. Russell, *Lives and Legends*, 359.

18. *Daily Telegraph* (London), 25 November 1890, 5.

19. *Daily Telegraph* (London), 29 November 1890, 3.

20. Vestal [Campbell], *Sitting Bull*, 280.

21. Cody quoted in an unidentified newspaper clipping, 29 May 1891, CS, MS6.IX, Box 2, McCracken Research Library, BBHC. Pfaller mentions that it was G. W. Chadwick, and makes no reference to John Keith; see Pfaller, "'Enemies in '76, Friends in '85,'" 28. See also Utley, *Last Days of the Sioux Nation*, 124; and Reddin, *Wild West Shows*, 116. Russell makes no reference to either Chadwick or Keith, but instead names Steve Burke and Bully White; see Russell, *Lives and Legends*, 361. In a clipping from the *Chicago Herald*, 13 December 1890, which was reproduced in the 1893 program for Buffalo Bill's Wild West, Lt. G. W. Chadwick was quoted as saying that he "was not detailed to accompany Colonel Cody . . . and that he never saw him

till several days after Cody's return" (*Buffalo Bill's Wild West* 1893 program, 50, MS6, Series VI:A, Box 1, folder 10, Cody Archives, McCracken Research Library, BBHC). Both Utley and Wooster state that the party also included five journalists, but Russell argues against that on the grounds of the poor coverage the whole episode received. See Utley, *Last Days of the Sioux Nation*, 124; Wooster, *Nelson A. Miles and the Twilight of the Frontier Army*, 181; Russell, *Lives and Legends*, 361.

22. Pfaller, "'Enemies in '76, Friends in '85,'" 28.

23. Russell, *Lives and Legends*, 360.

24. McLaughlin, *My Friend the Indian*, 209.

25. Vestal [Campbell], *New Sources of Indian History*, 8–9.

26. Ibid., 10. Despite issuing this warning, on the day that Cody arrived at Standing Rock, Carignan himself escorted a Chicago newspaperman, Sam Clover, to Sitting Bull's camp, where Clover proceeded to photograph a Ghost Dance from the seat of a wagon. See Vestal [Campbell], *Sitting Bull*, 281.

27. Pfaller, "'Enemies in '76, Friends in '85,'" 28.

28. Ibid., 28, 30.

29. W. H. Hare to Welsh, 12 December 1890, Incoming Correspondence, Reel 6, IRA.

30. Russell, *Lives and Legends*, 360.

31. Pfaller, "'Enemies in '76, Friends in '85,'" 30. Miles wrote to Drum, "Cody's orders were to quietly carry out the letter of his instructions if he or you secure the person of S. B. hold him. This will comply with the Secretary's wishes, and he authorizes this construction" (Miles to Commanding Officer, Fort Yates, 30 November 1890, SC 188, 350, RG 75, NARA).

32. Vestal [Campbell], *Sitting Bull*, 280–81; Russell, *Lives and Legends*, 361. In his autobiography Cody states, "I had never served with the Eighth Cavalry to which the companies at the Post belonged, but I had many friends among the officers, and spent a very pleasant afternoon and evening talking over old times, and getting information about the present situation" (Cody, *Buffalo Bill's Life Story*, 309).

33. Wooster stated that "great indeed was everybody's surprise to see the latter [Cody] emerge from his temporary quarters sweet, smiling and happy, ready for the start to Sitting Bull's camp and asking for transportation and an escort" (Wooster, *Nelson A. Miles*, 181).

34. Pfaller, "'Enemies in '76, Friends in '85,'" 30; Vestal [Campbell], *Sitting Bull*, 281; Russell, *Lives and Legends*, 361.

35. *Daily Telegraph* (London), 1 December 1890, 3.

36. Cody, *Buffalo Bill's Life Story*, 311; McLaughlin, *My Friend the Indian*, 211.

37. Pfaller, "'Enemies in '76, Friends in '85,'" 31.

38. Unidentified newspaper clipping, 29 May 1891, CS, MS6.IX, Box 2, McCracken Research Library, BBHC.

39. McLaughlin, *My Friend the Indian*, 211.

40. Russell, *Lives and Legends*, 364.

41. Ibid.

42. Utley, *Last Days of the Sioux Nation*, 126.

43. Wooster, *Nelson A. Miles*, 181; Eastman, *Sister to the Sioux*, 142.

44. Russell, *Lives and Legends*, 358.

45. Ibid., 364.

46. Hare to Welsh, 12 December 1890, Incoming Correspondence, Reel 6, IRA.

47. Wooster, *Nelson A. Miles*, 181–82.

48. Utley, *Last Days of the Sioux Nation*, 146–66; Jensen et al., *Eyewitness at Wounded Knee*, 32. One oft-repeated story of Sitting Bull's death is that a horse given to Sitting Bull by Cody when the former left the Wild West exhibition started performing tricks during the gun battle. For a very interesting reexamination of the myth, see Lemons, "History by Unreliable Narrators," 64–74.

49. Blackstone, *Business of Being Buffalo Bill*, 8–9.

50. John Shangrau interview, 1906, Series Two "Ricker Tablets," Tablet No. 27, Box 6, Reel 5, 105, Eli Ricker Collection, NSHS; Maddra, "Wounded Knee Ghost Dance Shirt," 50.

51. DeMallie, *Sixth Grandfather*, 270, 272–74, 276. DeMallie noted that another Oglala with the same name, possibly his brother, did enlist as a scout (270n.21).

52. Russell, *Lives and Legends*, 366; Yost, *Buffalo Bill*, 226.

53. Russell, *Lives and Legends*, 378.

54. Hagan, *Indian Rights Association*, 144.

55. Royer to CIA, 10 January 1891, LR 3186–1891, Box 699, RG 75, NARA. Royer included fifty-nine affidavits, and commented that "in fact their statements go to prove that Messrs. Cody & Salsbury have if anything more than complied with the strict provisions of their contracts with these people." He also noted that three Indians, Standing Bear, Kills Enemy Alone, and William Garnett, had remained in Europe, and he listed those who had died, with the addition of Shade who had returned and died at the agency.

56. Moses, *Wild West Shows and the Images of American Indians, 1883–1933*, 109.

57. Tibbles recounted, "There is not a fairer man to be found anywhere than Major Swords, who is in command of the two companies of Indian police. Serving under him are Little Chief, Cheyenne Butcher, Plenty Horses, Gun-on-the Middle, Knife, Lone Elk, Little Wolf, Red Owl, Strikes Plenty, Frank White, Yellow Boy, White Horse. Among the leading men, whom every one knows and who have done excellent service, are American Horse, Rocky Bear, Long Wolf, Lone Wolf, Black Heart, Spotted Elk, Lone Bear, and Plenty Bear. Over 200 others have taken part in the peace commissions and other duties. With Taylor's command of guards, scouts and the Ninth cavalry are: Yankton Charlie, No Neck, Stands First, Red Shirt, Walking Bull, Picket Pin, Prairie Chicken, Ribs, Bad Corn, Little Bull, Eagle Chief, Eagle Shield, Runs-Close-to-Lodge and Jim Chinchy" (*Omaha Morning World-Herald*, 15 January 1891).

58. Cody and Salsbury to CIA (enclosure 3), 26 February 1891, LR 7678–1891, Box 708, RG 75, NARA.

59. Cody and Salsbury to CIA (enclosure 2), 26 February 1891, LR 7678–1891, Box 708, RG 75, NARA.

60. Cody and Salsbury to CIA (enclosure 6), 26 February 1891, LR 7678–1891, Box 708, RG 75, NARA.

61. Cody and Salsbury to CIA (enclosure 1), 26 February 1891, LR 7678–1891, Box 708, RG 75, NARA.

62. Cody and Salsbury to CIA (enclosure 4), 26 February 1891, LR 7678–1891, Box 708, RG 75, NARA.The document was "signed" by American Horse, Spotted Horse, Hump, Spotted Elk, Little Wound, Big Road, Young Man Afraid of His Horses, Fire Lightening, High Hawk, He Dog, Fast Thunder, High Pipe, Two Strike, Grass, White Bird, and Maj. George Sword, and witnessed by Amos F. Towne and George C. Crager. The last-named was the very same man who had seemingly been involved in the campaign against Cody and the Wild West the previous summer.

63. Cody and Salsbury to CIA, (enclosure 4), 26 February 1891, LR 7678–1891, Box 708, RG 75, NARA.

64. Ibid.

65. Moses, *Wild West Shows and the Images of American Indians, 1883–1933*, 109.

66. Cody and Salsbury to CIA, 26 February 1891, LR 7678–1891, Box 708, RG 75, NARA.

67. Moses noted that the four were "members of the Nebraska delegation to Congress," Republican senator Manderson being "president *pro tem.*" Moses, *Wild West Shows and the Images of American Indians, 1883–1933*, 109.

68. Charles F. Manderson et al. to CIA, 26 February 1891, LR 7679–1891, RG 75, NARA.

69. CIA to Manderson, 2 March 1891, LB 212, 140–45, RG 75, NARA.

70. Prucha, *American Indian Policy in Crisis,* 321.

71. CIA to Manderson, 2 March 1891, LB 212, 140–45, RG 75, NARA.

72. Ibid.

73. Chandler to CIA, 6 March 1891, M1282 LS, 175, RG 75, FARC.

74. *New York Times,* 7 March 1891, 4.

75. CIA to Penny, 9 March 1891, LB 212, 197–98, RG 75, NARA; CIA to Agent James McLaughlin, Standing Rock, 9 March 1891, Standing Rock General Records, Misc. Correspondence 1891, File 517204/3, Box 392, RG 75, FARC.

76. Moses, *Wild West Shows and the Images of American Indians, 1883–1933,* 118; Russell, *Lives and Legends,* 370.

77. Slotkin, *Gunfighter Nation,* 67–68, 74.

78. Unidentified newspaper clipping, n.d., Buffalo Bill Scrapbook, 13, Microfilm FF18, Cody Papers, SHSC.

79. Ibid.

80. Ibid.

81. "Statement of Mary Collins," 2, Collins Papers, SDSHS.

82. Crofton to Adjutant General, 31 March (4 April) 1891, M983, 1338, RG 94, NARA.

83. Miles to Adjutant General, telegram, 14 March 1891, M983, 1220–21, RG 94, NARA.

84. Utley, *Last Days of the Sioux Nation*, 271.

85. Miles to Adjutant General, telegram, 14 March 1891, M983, 1220–21, RG 94, NARA.

86. Miles to Penny, 17 March 1891, PR General Records, Misc. Correspondence Received (1891–95), Box 30, RG 75, FARC.

87. Welsh to Mary C. Collins, 16 March 1891, Folder 48, Collins Papers, SDSHS; Welsh to CIA, 7 March 1891, Letterpress Copy Books, Reel 71, 86, IRA; Welsh to Rev. Wm. J. Cleveland, 9 March 1891, Letterpress Copy Books, Reel 71, 90, IRA.

88. Welsh to Collins, 16 March 1891, Folder 48, Collins Papers, SDSHS.

89. Welsh to CIA, 11 March 1891, Letterpress Copy Books, Reel 71, 105, IRA.

90. Miles to Adjutant General, telegram, 17 March 1891, M983, 1223, RG 94, NARA.

91. C. McKeever, Assistant Adjutant General, Chicago, to Cody and Salsbury, 18 March 1891, PR, M1282, 156, RG 75, FARC.

92. Nathan H. Whittlesey, Chicago Congregational Club, to "Whom Those Present May Come," letter of introduction, 18 March 1891, Folder 48, Collins Papers, SDSHS.

93. "Statement of Mary Collins," 1, Collins Papers, SDSHS.

94. Moses, *Wild West Shows and the Images of American Indians, 1883–1933*, 111. See also "Statement of Mary Collins," 1, Collins Papers, SDSHS, in which Collins stated that Sitting Bull had "said when they were off of exhibition they were allowed to have all the whisky they wanted, [and] described the places of entertainment to which they were taken, which were very low vile places."

95. "Statement of Mary Collins," 2, Collins Papers, SDSHS.

96. Ibid., 2–3.

97. Miles to Adjutant General, 19 March 1891, M983, 1225, RG 94, NARA.

98. "Statement of Mary Collins," 3, Collins Papers, SDSHS.

99. Whittlesey, letter of introduction, 18 March 1891, Folder 48, Collins Papers, SDSHS; "Statement of Mary Collins," 3, Collins Papers, SDSHS. See also Moses, *Wild West Shows and the Images of American Indians, 1883–1933*, 112–13.

100. "Statement of Mary Collins," 4–5, Collins Papers, SDSHS. Secretary of State James G. Blaine wrote to Noble on 5 March 1891: "When I was in London in 1887, I spent a day in Col. Cody's camp and in witnessing the Wild West Show. I carefully went through the Indian camp; it was thoroughly clean, nice, well kept, and well policed. . . . I have no doubt the Indians engaged by him came back to America improved in their morals, in their sense of individual responsibility, in the art of decent living and of clothing, and in general highly advanced in respectable manhood" ("Correspondence in Relation to the Employment of Indians with the Wild West Exhibitions," Noble to Hon. Philip C. Garrett, President, and Others, Indian Rights Association, 2 May 1892, Incoming Correspondence, Reel 9, IRA).

101. "Statement of Mary Collins," 5, Collins Papers, SDSHS.

102. Ibid., 6.

103. Ibid., 6–7.

104. Collins to Members of Congregational Club, Chicago, 7 April 1891, Folder 48, Collins Papers, SDSHS.

105. Grant to E. W. Halford, Private Secretary, Executive Mansion, 21 March 1891, M983, 1226, RG 94, NARA.

106. Such a move had been tried and tested by Captain Pratt, who had been inspired to set up Carlisle Indian School after his experience with the Fort Marion prisoners, believing that education was the most practical way to assimilate the Indians. See Adams, *Education for Extinction*, 36–49.

107. Collins to Members of Congregational Club, Chicago, 7 April 1891, Folder 48, Collins Papers, SDSHS.

108. Penny to CIA, 28 March 1891, PR, M1282, 179–81, RG 75, FARC.

109. Penny to CIA, 21 March 1891, LR E91, Box 717, RG 75, NARA.

110. Crofton to, Adjutant General, 31 March 1891, M983, 1338, RG 94, NARA.

111. J. M. Schofield, Major General Commanding, to Adjutant General, 6 April 1891, M983, 1339, RG 94, NARA; Grant to Cody, 17 April 1891, M983, 1340, RG 94, NARA.

112. Crofton to Assistant Adjutant General, 6 April 1891, M983, 1385, RG 94, NARA.

113. L. W. Crampton, Assistant Surgeon, Fort Sheridan, to Post Adjutant, 6 April 1891, M983, 1383, RG 94, NARA. The commanding officer at Fort Sheridan, Colonel Crofton, felt that the Indians' ailments were due more to homesickness than to any disease, but he too recommended that they be sent home. Crofton to Penny, telegram, 10 April 1891, PR, General Records, Misc. Correspondence Received (1891–95), Box 28, RG 75, FARC; Crofton to Assistant Adjutant General, 6 April 1891, M983, 1385, RG 94, NARA.

114. Schofield to McKeever, telegram, 9 April 1891 M983, 1388, RG 94, NARA; McKeever to Schofield, telegram, 10 April 1891, M983, 1389, RG 94 NARA.

115. Thomas M. Vincent, Assistant Adjutant General, Washington, D.C., to Grant, 11 April 1891, M983, 1386, RG 94, NARA; Samuel Breck, Assistant Adjutant General, Washington, D.C., to McKeever, telegram, 11 April 1891, M983, 1387, RG 94, NARA; Crofton to Assistant Adjutant General, Chicago, 1 May 1891, M983, 1476, RG 94, NARA.

116. M. K. Sniffen, Clerk, Indian Rights Association, to CIA, 17 April 1891, SC 188, 11–40/41, RG 75, NARA.

117. Sniffen to CIA, 17 April 1891, SC 188, 11–40/41, RG 75, NARA.

118. Noble to CIA, 20 April 1891, SC 188, 11–42, RG 75, NARA.

119. Crofton to Assistant Adjutant General, Chicago, 1 May 1891, M983, 1476, RG 94, NARA.

120. Isabel C. Barrows, wife of the editor of the *Register*, forwarded a copy of the clipping to Morgan; see Barrows to CIA, 31 March 1891, LR 12090–1891, Box 719, RG 75, NARA.

121. Welsh to Rev. T. L. Elliot, 18 May 1891, Letterpress Copy Books, Reel 71, vol. 7, p. 522, IRA.

122. Welsh to John Nicholas Brown, 12 May 1891, Letterpress Copy Books, Reel 71, vol. 7, p. 527, IRA; Welsh to O. J. Hiles, 27 May 1891, Letterpress Copy Books, Reel 71, vol. 7, p. 622, IRA.

123. Welsh to CIA, 3 April 1891, SC 188, 11–1, RG 75, NARA.

124. *New York Evening Post*, 27 April 1891, Folder 48, Collins Papers, SDSHS.

125. Indian Rights Association to Noble, 3 June 1891, Incoming Correspondence, Reel 7, IRA.

126. Salsbury to Editor, *New York Evening Post*, 18 May 1891, Folder 48, Collins Papers, SDSHS.

127. Salsbury to Welsh, 18 May 1891, Folder 48, Collins Papers, SDSHS.

128. Ibid.

129. Salsbury wrote, "Bigoted abuse of honorable men is distasteful to the great majority of Americans, and in your character of a pestiferous meddler you would do well to subside, for be assured I will impeach your veracity with the testimony of men in high places in public esteem,—an attitude you can never hope to attain unless you overhaul your liver and get your spleen regulated, so that you can employ your abilities (if you have any) in legitimate fashion" (ibid.).

130. Hagan noted that at the time the IRA was at the height of its power and influence. See Hagan, *Indian Rights Association*, 143.

131. Welsh to Joshua W. Davies, 3 June 1891, Letterpress Copy Books, Reel 71, vol. 7, p. 644, IRA; Welsh to M. E. Strieby, 3 June 1891, Letterpress Copy Books, Reel 71, vol. 7, p. 645, IRA; Welsh to McLaughlin, 3 June 1891, Letterpress Copy Books, Reel 71, vol. 7, p. 647, IRA.

132. Welsh to Collins, 4 June 1891, Letterpress Copy Books, Reel 71, vol. 7, p. 652, IRA.

133. Welsh to J. E. Learned, Managing Editor, *New York Evening Post*, 4 June 1891, Letterpress Copy Books, Reel 71, vol. 7, p. 653, IRA; Learned to Welsh, 5 June 1891, Incoming Correspondence, Reel 7, IRA.

134. McLaughlin to Welsh, 12 June 1891, Incoming Correspondence, Reel 7, IRA.

135. Collins to Welsh, 12 June 1891, Incoming Correspondence, Reel 7, IRA.

136. Welsh to Collins, 26 June 1891, Folder 48, Collins Papers, SDSHS.

137. See Moses, *Wild West Shows and the Images of American Indians, 1883–1933*.

CHAPTER SIX: THE WILD WEST SHOW'S
1891–1892 TOUR OF BRITAIN

1. Passenger List of SS *Switzerland*, CS, MS6.IX, Box 2, McCracken Research Library, BBHC; Russell, *Lives and Legends*, 369; Moses, *Wild West Shows and the Images of American Indians, 1883–1933*, 111. The tour had opened in Paris at the Exposition Universelle, 19 May 1889, and had extensively toured Continental Europe. For details of this tour see Russell, *Lives and Legends*, 350–53; Moses, *Wild West Shows and the Images of American Indians, 1883–1933*, 80–92; Rosa and May, *Buffalo Bill and His Wild West*,

143–47; Reddin, *Wild West Shows*, 96–114; and Kasson, *Buffalo Bill's Wild West*, 83–91. Cody himself sailed on the SS *Noordlund*, with other personnel, on the same day.

2. CIA to Agent Penny, Pine Ridge, 9 March 1891, LB 212, 197–98, RG 75, NARA; George Chandler, Acting Secretary of the Interior, to CIA, 6 March 1891, M1282 LS, 175, RG 75, FARC; Penny to CIA, 28 March 1891, M1282 LS, 179–81, RG 75, FARC; Moses, *Wild West Shows and the Images of American Indians, 1883–1933*, 111. Russell, and Rosa and May, give the figure erroneously as 100, the latter citing the 1893 Buffalo Bill's Wild West program; see Russell, *Lives and Legends*, 371, and Rosa and May, *Buffalo Bill and His Wild West*, 154.

3. Penny to CIA, 28 March 1891, M1282 LS, 179–81, RG 75, FARC; R. E. A. Crofton to Adjutant General, 31 March 1891, M983, 1338, RG 94, NARA; Moses, *Wild West Shows and the Images of American Indians, 1883–1933*, 111; Russell, *Lives and Legends*, 369; Utley, *Last Days of the Sioux Nation*, 271.

4. Buffalo Bill's Wild West, 1891 program, 64, Glasgow Room, Mitchell Library, Glasgow; Russell, *Lives and Legends*, 372; Moses, *Wild West Shows and the Images of American Indians, 1883–1933*, 119; Rosa and May, *Buffalo Bill and His Wild West*, 154.

5. Rosa and May, *Buffalo Bill and His Wild West*, 106, 130. See also Russell, *Lives and Legends*; Moses, *Wild West Shows and the Images of American Indians, 1883–1933*.

6. Slotkin, *Gunfighter Nation*, 67.

7. *North British Daily Mail*, 6 November 1891, 4 ("Buffalo Bill's Wild West").

8. *Argus* (Brighton), 12 October 1891, 3 ("'Buffalo Bill' at Brighton—Crowds Watch the Cavalcade—An Imposing Sight").

9. *Evening Express* (Cardiff), 26 September 1891, 4.

10. Hyde, *Sioux Chronicle*, 318.

11. Cunninghame Graham's letter was published in the *Daily Graphic* on 5 January 1891. Walker, ed., *North American Sketches of R. B. Cunninghame Graham*, 32.

12. *Liverpool Mercury*, 6 July 1891, 5 ("The Wild West Show").

13. *Argus* (Brighton), 12 October 1891, 3 ("'Buffalo Bill' at Brighton"); *Leicester Daily Post*, 1 September 1891, 5 ("The 'Wild West' in Leicester—The Opening Day"); *Bristol Evening News*, 28 September 1891, 3 ("The Wild West at Horfield. A Visit to the Camp. The Procession"); *Evening News* (Portsmouth), 5 October 1891, 3 ("The Wild West at Portsmouth").

14. *Argus* (Brighton), 12 October 1891, 3 ("'Buffalo Bill' at Brighton").

15. *Birmingham Daily Post*, 8 September 1891, 5 ("The Wild West Show").

16. *Leicester Daily Post*, 31 August 1891, 5 ("'Buffalo Bill's' Show in Leicester—A Preliminary Inspection").

17. *Argus* (Brighton), 12 October 1891, 3 ("'Buffalo Bill' at Brighton"). The *Sheffield and Rotherham Independent* observed that the gathering was very representative "of [all] the classes and masses of this big industrial centre" (*Sheffield and Rotherham Independent*, 11 August 1891, 6, "The Wild West in Sheffield—Opening Day"). *Croydon Times*, 17 October 1892, 4. The figure of 4 million is roughly based on the total number of tickets available for sale.

18. *Bristol Evening News*, 5 October 1891, 3 ("Local News and Jottings, the Wild West Show").

19. *Nottingham Daily Express*, 27 August 1891, 8.

20. *Sheffield and Rotherham Independent*, 11 August 1891, 6 ("The Wild West in Sheffield—Opening Day").

21. *Evening News* (Portsmouth), 10 October 1891, 3 ("Round the 'Wild West'—The Inner Life of the Show").

22. *Evening News* (Portsmouth), 14 October 1891, 3 ("Last Night's Gale"); *Argus* (Brighton), 14 October 1891, 3 ("The Wild West at Brighton").

23. *Sheffield and Rotherham Independent*, 13 August 1891, 5 ("Men and Things").

24. *Sheffield and Rotherham Independent*, 12 August 1891, 6 ("In the 'Wild West' Camp"); *Evening Express* (Cardiff), 26 September 1891, 4 ("The 'Wild West' Show at Cardiff—Some of the Celebrities Interviewed"); Crager, "As Narrated by Short Bull," 20, BBMG.

25. Standing Bear, *My People, the Sioux*, 262.

26. *Bristol Evening News*, 5 October 1891, 3 ("Local News and Jottings, the Wild West Show").

27. *Nottingham Daily Express*, 31 August 1891, 8 ("Exciting Scene at the 'Wild West' Show—Collapse of a Stand").

28. *Leicester Daily Post*, 1 September 1891, 5 ("The 'Wild West' in Leicester—The Opening Day").

29. Russell, *Lives and Legends*, 372; *Bristol Evening News*, 5 October 1891, 3 ("Local News and Jottings, the Wild West Show").

30. *Bristol Evening News*, 28 September 1891, 3 ("The Wild West at Horfield—A Visit to the Camp—The Procession").

31. *Sheffield and Rotherham Independent*, 20 August 1891, 5 ("Men and Things"); *Nottingham Daily Express*, 29 August 1891, 5 ("Saturday Notes").

32. *Bristol Evening News*, 29 September 1891, 3 ("The Wild West at Horfield—Successful Opening").

33. *Sheffield and Rotherham Independent*, 15 August 1891, 3 ("The Wild West in Sheffield").

34. *Nottingham Daily Express*, 29 August 1891, 5 ("Saturday Notes").

35. *Manchester Evening Mail*, 23 July 1891, 2 ("The Refreshment Licence of the 'Wild West'"); *Leicester Daily Post*, 29 August 1891, 6 ("'Buffalo Bill's' Wild West in Leicester").

36. White, "Frederick Jackson Turner and Buffalo Bill," in *Frontier in American Culture*, ed. Grossman, 9, 11.

37. *Leeds Daily News*, 25 June 1891.

38. Russell, *Lives and Legends*, 322. "The Drama of Civilization" was also performed in Manchester in 1887. See Gallop, *Buffalo Bill's British Wild West*, 142; and Blackstone, *Buckskins, Bullets, and Business*, 21.

39. Parker, *Odd People I Have Met*, 84.

40. *Glasgow Evening News*, 17 November 1891, 2 ("Buffalo Bill's 'Wild West'"); *Glasgow Herald*, 17 November 1891, 9 ("Buffalo Bill's Wild West").

41. Kasson, *Buffalo Bill's Wild West*, 113, 245.

42. *Lady's Pictorial* (London), 21 May 1892, stated, "Strange to say, I have lived in the crass ignorance of there ever having been any ancient America."

43. *Evening Citizen* (Glasgow), 17 November 1891 ("Buffalo Bill's Wild West Show—Opening Night in Glasgow").

44. *North British Daily Mail*, 23 November 1891, 6 ("Saturday Entertainment").

45. *Birmingham Daily Post*, 8 September 1891, 5 ("The Wild West Show").

46. *Queen* (London), 28 May 1892, Scrapbook 1892, MS6, Series IX, Box 7, Cody Archives, McCracken Research Library, BBHC.

47. *Morning* (London), 3 June 1892, Scrapbook 1892, MS6, Series IX, Box 7, Cody Archives, McCracken Research Library, BBHC.

48. Deloria Jr., "Indians," in *Buffalo Bill and the Wild West*, 51.

49. Publicity poster for Buffalo Bill's Wild West, Leeds, 1891, Leeds City Library Archives.

50. *Leicester Daily Post*, 31 August 1891, 5 ("'Buffalo Bill's' Show in Leicester—A Preliminary Inspection").

51. *Birmingham Daily Post*, 8 September 1891, 5 ("The Wild West Show").

52. *Umpire* (Manchester), 8 May 1892, Scrapbook 1892, MS6, Series IX, Box 7, Cody Archives, McCracken Research Library, BBHC.

53. See *New York Evening Post*, 27 April 1891, Folder 48, Collins Papers, SDSHS; and Salsbury to Welsh, 18 May 1891, Folder 48, Collins Papers, SDSHS.

54. However, in 1913 Cody did reenact the massacre for his film *The Indian Wars*, and he even had Short Bull participate in it. See Paul, "Buffalo Bill and Wounded Knee."

55. The Portsmouth *Evening News* erroneously stated that "Buffalo Bill's Indians have performed the war-like 'ghost dance' under the shadow of Vesuvius." The Wild West Indians had not yet encountered the Ghost Dance when the show toured in Italy, and therefore could not have performed it then. This misinformation was most likely inspired by an illustration in the exhibition's program.

56. Unidentified newspaper clipping, 29 May 1891 ("An Hour with General Cody"), CS, MS6.IX, Box 2, McCracken Research Library, BBHC.

57. Cunningham, *Diamond's Ace*, 114.

58. *Glasgow Evening News*, 1 March 1892, Buffalo Bill Museum, Paul Fees Files—Scotland, BBHC.

59. Flood, *Lost Bird of Wounded Knee*, 70.

60. Ibid., 62. See also *Woman's Tribune*, 10 January 1891; and Huls, *Winter of 1890 (What Happened at Wounded Knee)*, 39, 49.

61. Flood, *Lost Bird of Wounded Knee*, 70–71. Colby's acquisition of the child was not the end of the story, and Cody became involved in Colby's successful attempt to recapture the baby, when it had been taken by Annie Yellow Bird into the encampment of

the Ghost Dancers. For information on the child's subsequent life, see Flood, *Lost Bird of Wounded Knee*.

62. Buffalo Bill's Wild West, 1891 program, 42, Glasgow Room, Mitchell Library, Glasgow.

63. Crager, "As Narrated by Short Bull," 18, BBMG.

64. *Evening Express* (Cardiff), 22 September 1891 ("'Wild West' in Cardiff").

65. Penny to CIA, 28 March 1891, PR, M1282, 179–81, RG 75, FARC.

66. Buffalo Bill's Wild West, 1891 program, 42, Glasgow Room, Mitchell Library, Glasgow.

67. *Sheffield and Rotherham Independent*, 8 August 1891, 6 ("Buffalo Bill at Sheffield"); *Leicester Daily Post*, 31 August 1891, 5 ("'Buffalo Bill's' Show in Leicester—A Preliminary Inspection").

68. *Argus* (Brighton), 12 October 1891, 3 ("'Buffalo Bill' at Brighton").

69. Klein, "'Everything of Interest in the Late Pine Ridge War Are Held by Us for Sale,'" 68; Jensen et al., *Eyewitness at Wounded Knee*, 58.

70. Maddra, *Glasgow's Ghost Shirt*, 12; Acquisition Register, Art Gallery and Museum, Kelvingrove, Glasgow.

71. *Oakland Tribune*, 30 August 1962, RG 3623, series 3, Folder 2, MC 32, WC, Nebraska State Historical Society; and Moses, *Wild West Shows and the Images of American Indians, 1883–1933*, 125.

72. *Oakland Tribune*, 30 August 1962, RG 3623, series 3, Folder 2, MC 32, WC, Nebraska State Historical Society; Moses, *Wild West Shows and the Images of American Indians, 1883–1933*, 125. See also Cody, Stoke on Trent, to Secretary of War, 19 August 1891, LR 32171–1891, RG 75, NARA.

73. See Moses, *Wild West Shows and the Images of American Indians, 1883–1933*, 124–25.

74. *Leicester Daily Post*, 29 August 1891, 4.

75. *Evening News and Post* (London), 14 May 1892, 2 ("'The Wild West' with Special Reference to the Fiery Untamed Wildness of Its Indian Chiefs").

76. *Evening Citizen* (Glasgow), 17 November 1891 ("Buffalo Bill's Wild West Show—Opening Night in Glasgow").

77. *Liverpool Mercury*, 10 July 1891, 1.

78. Standing Bear, *My People, the Sioux*, 252.

79. Deloria Jr., "Indians," 52.

80. DeMallie, *Sixth Grandfather*, 246.

81. Gossett, *Race*, 320; MacKenzie, *Propaganda and Empire*, 2, 6, 253.

CHAPTER SEVEN: PERCEPTIONS
OF "THE OTHER" ON THE BRITISH TOUR

1. *Daily Telegraph* (London), 31 December 1890, 3 ("Indian Treachery").

2. *Standard* (London), 2 January 1891, 3.

3. Walker, *North American Sketches of R. B. Cunninghame Graham*, 25.

4. Ibid., 27.

5. Ibid., 28–30.

6. *Denver Rocky Mountain News,* 22 December 1890, 1 ("Seems to Know All about It").

7. Walker, *North American Sketches of R. B. Cunninghame Graham,* 30–31.

8. Buffalo Bill's Wild West, 1891 program, 47, Glasgow Room, Mitchell Library, Glasgow.

9. Ibid., 48.

10. MacKenzie, *Propaganda and Empire,* 5–6.

11. Ibid., 46.

12. Kasson, *Buffalo Bill's Wild West,* 212–13.

13. *Evening Express* (Cardiff), 23 September 1891, 2 ("The 'Wild West' in Cardiff—Among the Indians").

14. *Land and Water* (London), 14 May 1892; *St James Gazette* (London), 11 August 1891; *Referee* (London), 10 July 1892; all in Scrapbook 1892, MS6, Series IX, Box 7, Cody Archives, McCracken Research Library, BBHC.

15. *Glasgow Evening News,* 2 January 1892.

16. Marriage certificate of John Shangram (*sic*) and Lillie Orr, extract of entry in Register of Marriages, 1861–1921, District of Dennistoun, County of Lanark.

17. John Shangrau interview, 1906, Box 6, Reel 5, 105, Eli Ricker Collection, NSHS.

18. Buffalo Bill's Wild West, 1891 program, 41, Glasgow Room, Mitchell Library, Glasgow. Shangrau had previously worked for Cody's Wild West at least once, in 1884; see Blackstone, *Business of Being Buffalo Bill,* 8.

19. Marriage certificate of John Shangram (*sic*) and Lillie Orr, County of Lanark.

20. George C. Crager, Buffalo Bill's Wild West Co., to Penny, 2 May 1891, PR, General Records, Box 28, RG 75, FARC; Cody to Secretary of War, 19 August 1891, LR 32171–1891, RG 75, NARA; Penny to Cody, 30 July 1891, PR, General Records, Copies of Misc. LS (1891–95), vol. 8, p. 126, Box 55, RG 75, FARC; Penny to Cody, 4 August 1891, PR, General Records, Copies of Misc. LS (1891–95), vol. 8, p. 148, RG 75, FARC.

21. *New York Herald,* 22 July 1894 ("Glimpses of Squaw Life—Habits and Occupations of the Indian Women in the Tepees at the Wild West Show"), Scrapbook 1894, MS6, Series IX, Box 10, Cody Archives, McCracken Research Library, BBHC.

22. *Glasgow Weekly News,* 9 January 1892, 2 ("Marriage of Buffalo Bill's Interpreter").

23. *Morning* (London), 18 August 1892 ("Wild West Ladies, by Our Lady Representative"). Lillie accompanied her husband back to South Dakota at the end of the tour "where her child . . . was born." John and Lillie toured with Cody's Wild West until 1897, and "over time, the couple added nine more children to their family." *Casper Star-Tribune,* 7 September 1997 ("Shangrau Collection Honors American Indians").

24. Unidentified newspaper clipping, CS, MS6.IX, Box 2, McCracken Research Library, BBHC.

25. *Glasgow Evening News*, 15 February 1892.

26. In America interracial marriages between whites and Indians were not such an anathema as those involving whites and blacks, even when white women were involved. Indian women had historically been seen as cultural mediators, and therefore such interracial marriages offered obvious benefits to whites. See Pierson and Chaudhuri, eds., *Nation, Empire, Colony*, 58.

27. *Pall Mall Gazette* (London), 27 May 1892, Scrapbook 1892, MS6, Series IX, Box 7, Cody Archives, McCracken Research Library, BBHC.

28. *World* (London), 29 June 1892, Scrapbook 1892, MS6, Series IX, Box 7, Cody Archives, McCracken Research Library, BBHC.

29. *Lady Pictorial* (London), 24 September 1892, Scrapbook 1892, MS6, Series IX, Box 7, Cody Archives, McCracken Research Library, BBHC.

30. *Oracle* (London), 28 May 1892, Scrapbook 1892, MS6, Series IX, Box 7, Cody Archives, McCracken Research Library, BBHC.

31. *Evening Telegraph and Star* (Sheffield), 15 August 1891, 3 ("An Indian Festival at the 'Wild West'").

32. Ibid.

33. Ibid. In James R. Walker's *Lakota Society*, there is a reference to a similar "buffalo dance," where the dancers both "dance in their tents" and "act like bunting buffalo hooking each other, etc." The dance was associated with the Big Bellies Society or Chiefs Society, which was originally known as Buffalo Headdress (Tatanka Wapahun). See Walker, *Lakota Society*, ed. DeMallie, 35–36.

34. *Million* (London), 3 September 1892, 245 ("The Mild Wild West").

35. *Bailie* (Glasgow), 20 January 1892, 5.

36. *New York Times*, 15 July 1894, Scrapbook 1894, MS6, Series IX, Box 10, 83, Cody Archives, McCracken Research Library, BBHC.

37. DeMallie, *Sixth Grandfather*, 8.

38. *Sheffield and Rotherham Independent*, 10 August 1891, 5 ("The Wild West in Sheffield—A Visit to the Camp").

39. *Evening Express* (Cardiff), n.d. ("'Wild West' in Cardiff—Opening Day").

40. Porter, *Lion's Share*, 71–72.

41. Reddin, *Wild West Shows*, 93–94.

42. Such perceptions were both informed and reinforced by the popular culture of the day, and as MacKenzie has noted, contemporary Victorian theater shared many themes with Buffalo Bill's Wild West. MacKenzie, *Propaganda and Empire*, 45.

43. Kasson, *Buffalo Bill's Wild West*, 219.

44. Unidentified newspaper clipping, 11 May 1892, Scrapbook 1892, MS6, Series IX, Box 7, Cody Archives, McCracken Research Library, BBHC.

45. *Evening Express* (Leeds), 20 June 1891, 5 ("In The Wild West Camp").

46. *Sheffield and Rotherham Independent*, 10 August 1891, 5 ("The Wild West in Sheffield—A Visit to the Camp").

47. *Chronicle* (Manchester), 3 July 1892, Scrapbook 1892, MS6, Series IX, Box 7, Cody Archives, McCracken Research Library, BBHC.

48. *Science Siftings* (London), 30 July 1892, Scrapbook 1892, MS6, Series IX, Box 7, Cody Archives, McCracken Research Library, BBHC.

49. *Leicester Daily Post*, 31 August 1891, 5 ("'Buffalo Bill's' Show in Leicester—A Preliminary Inspection").

50. *Evening Citizen* (Glasgow), 7 November 1891 ("Buffalo Bills Wild West Show in Glasgow").

51. For a further discussion of this point, see Deverell, "Fighting Words," in *New Significance*, ed. Milner, 44.

52. Foote, *Letters from "Buffalo Bill,"* 71.

53. Parker, *Odd People I Have Met*, 84–85.

54. Ibid., 85; *Evening Times* (Glasgow), 16 January 1892 ("Buffalo Bill's Wild West Show"); *Glasgow Evening News*, 16 January 1892, 3 ("The 'Wild West' Improved—A Unique Ceremony"). The Africans were from Schuli, a district to the northeast of Lake Albert Nyanza.

55. Parker, *Odd People I Have Met*, 85. In Parker's anecdote he refers to the interpreter as being Bronco Bill and the Cheyenne (Lakota) chief as Rocky Bear; this is repeated in Russell, *Lives and Legends*, 373; Rosa and May, *Buffalo Bill and His Wild West*, 155; and Moses, *Wild West Shows and the Images of American Indians, 1883–1933*, 119. Writing some years after the fact, Parker got the identity of these two people wrong. Neither Bronco Bill nor Rocky Bear was on this tour of Britain; the interpreter would have either been George Crager or John Shangrau, and it seems likely from newspaper coverage of the episode that the Lakota chief would have been No Neck, Kicking Bear, or Short Bull.

56. *Glasgow Evening News*, 16 January 1892, 3 ("The 'Wild West' Improved—A Unique Ceremony").

57. *Evening Times* (Glasgow), 16 January 1892.

58. *Evening Citizen* (Glasgow), 16 January 1892 ("The Wild West").

59. *Birmingham Daily Post*, 5 September 1891, 5 ("Buffalo Bill's Show").

60. *Sheffield and Rotherham Independent*, 8 August 1891, 6 ("Buffalo Bill at Sheffield").

61. *Nottingham Daily Express*, 25 August 1891, 6 ("The Wild West in Nottingham—The Opening Day").

62. *Manchester Weekly Times*, 24 July 1891 ("Buffalo Bill in Manchester").

63. *Sheffield and Rotherham Independent*, 13 August 1891, 5 ("Men and Things").

64. Paul Eagle Star, Long Wolf, and Charging Thunder were all mistakenly identified as such. The first two died on the tour, and the latter was jailed briefly in Glasgow (see chapter 8).

65. *Glasgow Herald*, 6 November 1891, 4 ("Buffalo Bill's Wild West"). The paper was mistaken in stating that Scatter was in Glasgow; he had returned to America some months earlier.

66. *Quiz* (Glasgow), 30 October 1891, 65.

67. *Nottingham Evening Express*, 24 August 1891, 4 ("Buffalo Bill in Nottingham—The New Town at Trent Bridge").

68. *Leeds Daily News,* 20 June 1891 ("The Indian Camp in Leeds").

69. *Evening Express* (Cardiff), 26 September 1891, 4 ("The 'Wild West' Show at Cardiff—Some of the Celebrities Interviewed—By Our Special Correspondent").

70. *Leeds Evening Express,* 20 June 1891, 5 ("In the Wild West Camp").

71. *Leicester Daily Post,* 31 August 1891, 5 ("'Buffalo Bill's' Show in Leicester—A Preliminary Inspection").

72. *Nottingham Evening Express,* 24 August 1891, 4 ("Buffalo Bill in Nottingham—The New Town at Trent Bridge").

73. Salsbury to Miles, 29 February 1892, 27617 PRD 1892, Box 56, RG 94, NARA.

74. It was not until a month and a half before arriving in Glasgow that the managers of the Wild West knew for sure where the show would be that winter. Some of the earliest histories of Buffalo Bill and his Wild West make no mention of a visit to Scotland in the early 1890s; see Foote, *Letters from "Buffalo Bill,"* 73; Yost, *Buffalo Bill,* 231.

75. *Bailie* (Glasgow), 13 January 1892, 4; *Manchester Weekly Times,* 31 July 1891, 6 ("The Children's Hour—By Uncle Oldman"); *Manchester Weekly Times,* 14 August 1891, 6 ("The Children's Hour—By Uncle Oldman").

76. Accession Register, 226–28, Art Gallery and Museum, Kelvingrove, Glasgow Museums.

77. Maddra, *Glasgow's Ghost Shirt,* 12–21.

78. *Sheffield and Rotherham Independent,* 10 August 1891, 5 ("The Wild West in Sheffield—A Visit to Camp"); *Staffordshire Sentinel* (Stoke on Trent), 20 August 1891.

79. *Music Hall* (London), 22 July 1892, Scrapbook 1892, MS6, Series IX, Box 7, Cody Archives, McCracken Research Library, BBHC. Gallop suggested that "Indians in the company would have been alarmed if they had ever learned that their interpreter had sold native artefacts without consulting them, particularly the 'ghost dance' shirt. . . . It was never clear who the rightful owners of the property might have been. . . . Had some of the artefacts once been the property of Paul Eagle Star, who had died in the Sheffield Infirmary while holding on to Crager's hand?" But this is speculation; the evidence suggests that there was never any doubt about Crager's rightful ownership of the items. It also does not take into account the Lakota tradition of gift giving. See Gallop, *Buffalo Bill's British Wild West,*188–89.

80. Deloria Jr., "Indians," 54–55.

81. Reddin contends that the French had a much more sympathetic response to the Lakota performers than the British; Reddin, *Wild West Shows,* 100.

82. Prucha, *Indians in American Society,* ix.

83. Dippie, "American Wests," in *Trails,* ed. Limerick et al., 130.

84. Kasson, *Buffalo Bill's Wild West,* 219.

CHAPTER EIGHT: THE INDIANS' EXPERIENCES ON THE BRITISH TOUR

1. DeMallie, *Sixth Grandfather,* 246.

2. Crager, "As Narrated by Short Bull," 20, BBMG.

3. Starita, *Dull Knifes of Pine Ridge*, 145–46.

4. DeMallie, *Sixth Grandfather*, 247–48.

5. Standing Bear, *My People, the Sioux*, 250.

6. Unidentified newspaper clipping, 29 May 1891 ("An Hour with General Cody"), CS, MS6.IX, Box 2, McCracken Research Library, BBHC.

7. *Galignani Messenger*, 7 June 1891 ("Brussels Gossip—From Wounded Knee to Waterloo—Buffalo Bill and His Indians on the Famous Field"), CS, MS6.IX, Box 2, McCracken Research Library, BBHC.

8. *Liverpool Echo*, 17 July 1891 ("Alarming Accident at the 'Wild West'"); *Nottingham Daily Express*, 25 August 1891, 6 ("The Wild West in Nottingham—The Opening Day").

9. *Birmingham Daily Post*, 8 September 1891, 5 ("The Wild West Show").

10. *Sheffield and Rotherham Independent*, 26 August 1891, 6 ("The Death of 'Eagle Star' in Sheffield—Inquest at the Infirmary").

11. *Sheffield and Rotherham Independent*, 25 August 1891, 6 ("Death of One of Buffalo Bill's Indians in Sheffield"); *Sheffield and Rotherham Independent*, 26 August 1891, 6 ("The Death of 'Eagle Star' in Sheffield—Inquest at the Infirmary").

12. *Nottingham Daily Express*, 26 August 1891, 6 ("The Wild West Show").

13. *Sheffield and Rotherham Independent*, 25 August 1891, 6 ("Death of One of Buffalo Bill's Indians in Sheffield"); *Sheffield and Rotherham Independent*, 26 August 1891, 6 ("The Death of 'Eagle Star' in Sheffield—Inquest at the Infirmary").

14. Ibid.; *Nottingham Daily Express*, 26 August 1891, 6 ("The Wild West Show").

15. Ibid.

16. Philip James, who is compiling a biography of Eagle Star, has stated in a personal communication that Eagle Star had been a member of the Indian police at Rosebud. Although he is not listed as such on the payrolls, he appears in a photograph with a police badge, received the same remuneration as the police, but was listed simply as a labourer. This was not uncommon, especially in times of need; when the agent was unable to secure any more funding for the tribal police, he would hire them under the auspices of another job. See Hagan, *Indian Police and Judges*, 88, 90.

17. John Shangrau, Nottingham, to "Dear Friend Louis," Rosebud, 26 August 1891, Rosebud Agency, Gen. Correspondence 1889–1892, Box A-358, RG 75, FARC.

18. Unidentified Chicago newspaper clipping, c. March 1892 ("Big Red Men in the City.—On Their Return from an Extended European Trip"), Buffalo Bill Scrapbook, 13, Microfilm FF18, Cody Papers, SHSC.

19. Moses, *Wild West Shows and the Images of American Indians, 1883–1933*, 122; Cody to Secretary of War, 6 June 1891, M983, 1535, RG 94, NARA; Cody to Grant, 22 June 1891, M983, 1552, RG 94, NARA; Salsbury to Penny, 23 June 1891, PR, General Records, Misc. Correspondence Received (1891–95), Box 31, RG 75, FARC; affidavits of Horn Point Eagle and Sorrel Horse, sworn at U.S. Consulate, Bradford, England, 23 June 1891, LR 28591–1891, RG 75, NARA; Cody, Liverpool, to Secretary of War, 17 July, LR 28591–1891, RG 75, NARA; Penny to Cody, 4 August 1891, PR, General

Records, Copies of Misc. LS (1891–92), Box 55, vol. 8, p. 148, RG 75, FARC; Cody, Stoke on Trent, to Secretary of War, 19 August 1891, LR 32171–1891, RG 75, NARA.

20. *Sheffield and Rotherham Independent*, 12 August 1891, 6 ("In the 'Wild West' Camp")

21. *Leeds Daily News*, 20 June 1891 ("The Indian Camp in Leeds").

22. *Birmingham Daily Post*, 5 September 1891, 5 ("Buffalo Bill's Show").

23. Cody to Secretary of War, 6 June 1891, M983, 1535, RG 94, NARA.

24. Affidavits of Horn Point Eagle and Sorrel Horse, sworn at U.S. Consulate, Bradford, England, 23 June 1891, LR 28591–1891, RG 75, NARA.

25. Salsbury to Penny, 23 June 1891, PR, General Records, Misc. Correspondence Received (1891–95), Box 31, RG 75, FARC.

26. Cody, Liverpool, to Secretary of War, 17 July 1891, LR 28591–1891, RG 75, NARA.

27. Penny to Cody, 4 August 1891, PR, General Records, Copies of Misc. LS (1891–92), Box 55, vol. 8, p. 148, RG 75, FARC.

28. Cody, Stoke on Trent, to Secretary of War, 19 August 1891, LR 32171–1891, RG 75, NARA.

29. *Star* (London), 12 July 1892, Scrapbook 1892, MS6, Series IX, Box 7, Cody Archives, McCracken Research Library, BBHC. Long Wolf's Lakota name should be written as "wuZgmánitu háZska."

30. *Pall Mall Gazette* (London), 18 June 1892, Letter to the Editor, from Mr. R. J. Gilbert, Secretary-Superintendent of West London Hospital, Scrapbook 1892, MS6, Series IX, Box 7, Cody Archives, McCracken Research Library, BBHC.

31. *Daily Graphic* (London), 14 June 1892 ("A Red Indian Warrior Buried in London").

32. Gallop, *Buffalo Bill's British Wild West*, 163.

33. Buffalo Bill's Wild West, 1891 program, 41, Glasgow Room, Mitchell Library, Glasgow.

34. *Birmingham Daily Post*, 8 September 1891, 5 ("The Wild West Show"). The "rebels" referred to here are the Ghost Dancers. Many of the reports of Long Wolf's death erroneously suggested that he had been a Ghost Dancer, stating "he was the first to surrender his rifle to General Miles in the last war at Pine Ridge."

35. *Evening News and Post* (London), 15 June 1892, 1 ("Death of a 'Wild West' Indian").

36. *Daily Graphic* (London), 14 June 1892 ("A Red Indian Warrior Buried in London"); Royal Parks press release (London), 25 September 1997 ("Long Wolf Goes Home") A reporter for the *Magazine Journal* bemoaned the fact that no journalists were present to record the event, but an illustration, whether real or imagined, did appear on the front page of the *Illustrated Police News*, under the heading of "Tragic Occurrences of the Week." *Magazine Journal* (London), 25 June 1892, Scrapbook 1892, MS6, Series IX, Box 7, Cody Archives, McCracken Research Library, BBHC; *Illustrated Police News* (London), 25 June 1892, 1 ("Funeral of an Indian Chief at West Brompton").

37. Gallop, *Buffalo Bill's British Wild West*, 200.

38. Foreman, *Indians Abroad, 1493–1938*, 204.

39. Jessie Black Feather (Lizzie Long Wolf's daughter) quoted in *Observer* (London), 12 February 1995 ("Long Wolf to Be Freed from London Lair"). This is also referred to in Swartwout, *Annie Oakley*, 131. The remains of both Long Wolf and Star were repatriated to South Dakota in 1999, as were those of Paul Eagle Star, in a separate and private ceremony.

40. Nate Salsbury to Rebecca Salsbury, 21 December 1891, Nathan Salsbury Papers, Series I: Correspondence, Box 1, Folder 7, 1890–93, Beinecke Rare Book and Manuscript Library, Yale University Library; *Quiz* (Glasgow), 12 February 1892, 214.

41. Marriage certificate of Black Heart and Calls the Name, 8 August 1891, at the parish church in the Parish of St. Brides, Stafford, County of Lancaster, in Buffalo Bill Museum, Paul Fees Files—Indians, BBHC.

42. *Manchester Weekly Times*, 14 August 1891, 7 ("Marriage of Indians at Old Trafford"); *Sheffield and Rotherham Independent*, 10 August 1891, 5 ("The Wild West in Sheffield—A Visit to Camp"); *Argus* (Brighton), 14 October 1891, 3 ("The Wild West at Brighton").

43. Moses, *Wild West Shows and the Images of American Indians, 1883–1933*, 85.

44. Brown to Cody, 22 April 1892, PR, General Records, Misc. LS 1892, vol. 12, p. 102, Box 56, RG 75, FARC; marriage certificate of Black Heart and Calls the Name, 8 August 1891, Buffalo Bill Museum, Paul Fees Files—Indians, BBHC; Pine Ridge Census Rolls 1893–1924, Microfilm M595, Western History and Genealogy Department, DPL; *Morning* (London), 18 August 1892, 2 ("Wild West Ladies").

45. *New York Tribune*, 19 March 1892 ("Arrival of 'the Wild West' Indians in America"). The Paris edition of the *New York Herald*, 16 April 1891, listed her as "Mrs. Crow Cane," but also had "Mrs Calls the Name."

46. *Evening Express* (Leeds), 24 June 1891, 2 ("Local Gossip").

47. *Evening News* (Portsmouth), 10 October 1891, 3 ("Round the 'Wild West'—The Inner Life of the Show").

48. *Evening Express* (Leeds), n.d., 5 ("In the Wild West Camp").

49. Standing Bear, *My People, the Sioux*, 261.

50. *Leicester Daily Post*, 31 August 1891, 5 ("'Buffalo Bill's' Show in Leicester—A Preliminary Inspection").

51. *Evening News* (Portsmouth), 10 October 1891, 3 ("Round the 'Wild West'—The Inner Life of the Show").

52. *Leeds Daily News*, 20 June 1891. The only complaint the Pine Ridge agent received from one of the Wild West's returning Indians in the spring of 1892 was that they were fined "when they refused to take part in the dances, or to wear the regalia pertaining to their duties." See "Correspondence in Relation to the Employment of Indians with the Wild West Exhibitions," Noble to Garrett, 2 May 1892, Incoming Correspondence, Reel 9, IRA.

53. Standing Bear, *My People, the Sioux*, 249.

54. *Evening Times* (Glasgow), 12 February 1892.

55. *Glasgow Evening News,* 12 March 1892.

56. *Evening Citizen* (Glasgow), 4 January 1892 ("Charging Thunder Remitted").

57. *Evening Citizen* (Glasgow), 1 January 1892 ("Buffalo Bill's Interpreter Attacked, Charging Thunder in Custody"); *Evening Times* (Glasgow), 2 January 1892 ("Alleged Assault by Wild West Indian"); *Glasgow Evening News,* 4 January 1892 ("The Assault on Buffalo Bill's Interpreter").

58. *Evening Times* (Glasgow), 5 January 1892.

59. *North British Daily Mail,* 5 January 1892, 4.

60. *Evening Times* (Glasgow), 12 January 1892 ("Charging Thunder Sent to Prison"); *Evening Citizen* (Glasgow), 12 January 1892 ("Charging Thunder Gets 30 Days Imprisonment"); *Glasgow Evening News,* 12 January 1892, 2 ("Charging Thunder Gets 30 Days—His Lemonade Was Mixed").

61. Cameron, *Prisons and Punishment in Scotland,* 150–51, 155.

62. Forbes and Meehan, *Such Bad Company,* 151.

63. The author of the story that refers to Charging Thunder's incarceration was Paddy Meehan, a former inmate himself. Unfortunately, he has since passed away, and his coauthor was unable to say what Meehan's sources were.

64. *Evening Times* (Glasgow), 11 February 1892.

65. *Evening Times* (Glasgow), 23 December 1891 ("A Chat with Colonel Cody").

66. Rosa and May, *Buffalo Bill and His Wild West,* 140.

67. *Glasgow Herald,* 11 January 1892.

68. *Quiz* (Glasgow), 11 December 1891, 124.

69. Dippie, *Vanishing American,* 36.

70. Charging Thunder had previously been in trouble with the police. The numerous reports of Indians drinking quite freely suggest that it is highly unlikely that one whisky-spiked lemonade would have been enough to render him completely inebriated.

71. *Evening News* (Portsmouth), 10 October 1891, 3 ("Round the 'Wild West'— The Inner Life of the Show"). Crager's statement is intriguing considering that he had been involved with Gen. O'Beirne and Father Craft in the summer of 1890, when O'Beirne had spearheaded the campaign against Cody's Wild West and its treatment of the Indian employees. Conceivably Crager was persuaded that O'Beirne was mistaken, but at the same time, and perhaps more significant, his true role in the summer of 1890 was never clearly apparent. Crager had drawn the attention of the secretary of the interior to the plight of Kills Plenty, and had set the ball rolling with regard to the ban on permits. At the same time he had been in touch with John Burke and appears to have been working in the interests of Buffalo Bill's Wild West.

72. Crager, "As Narrated by Short Bull," 20, BBMG.

73. *Birmingham Daily Post,* 5 September 1891, 5 ("Buffalo Bill's Show"). Such reporting also informed British readers how marvelous the industry and products of their great nation and empire were.

74. *Sheffield and Rotherham Independent,* 14 August 1891, 5 ("Colonel Cody's Indians at Messrs Rodgers' Works").

75. The Eugene Buechel Lakota Museum on the Rosebud Reservation reportedly obtained Short Bull's cane from Little Horn in September 1921. Charles Henckel acquired the notebook of Short Bull's sketches, which is now part of the collection of the Museum für Völkerkunde in Leipzig. See Wildhage, "Material on Short Bull," 38, 42n7.

76. Crager to Penny, 2 May 1891, PR, General Records, Box 28, RG 75, FARC.

77. Penny to Cody, 21 May 1891, PR, General Records, Misc. LS (1890–91), Box 54, vol. 7, p. 342, RG 75, FARC; Penny to Cody, 6 August 1891, PR, General Records, Misc. LS (1891–92), Box 55, vol. 8, p. 151, RG 75, FARC.

78. Penny to Cody, 2 November 1891, PR, General Records, Misc. LS (1891–92), Box 55, vol. 9, p. 38, RG 75, FARC.

79. Penny to Cody, 22 August 1891, PR, General Records, Misc. LS (1891–92), Box 55, vol. 8, p. 230, RG 75, FARC.

80. Cody to Acting Indian Agent, Pine Ridge, 1 December 1891, PR, General Records, Box 28, RG 75, FARC; Agent Brown, Pine Ridge, to Cody, 26 December 1891, PR, General Records, Box 55, vol. 10, p. 139, RG 75, FARC.

81. Cody to Penny, 29 May1891, PR, General Records, Box 55, vol.10, RG 75, FARC.

82. Penny to Additional Farmer, Wounded Knee District, 3 July 1891, PR, General Records, Box 55, vol. 8, RG 75, FARC.

83. Penny to Cody, 22 August 1891, PR, General Records, Box 55, vol. 8, p. 229, RG 75, FARC; James Cooper, Special Agent, Pine Ridge, to CIA, 22 August 1891, LR 31274–1891, Box 771, RG 75, NARA.

84. Cooper to CIA, 22 August 1891, LR 31274–1891, Box 771, RG 75, NARA.

85. Brown to Cody, 22 April 1892, PR, General Records, Misc. LS 1892, Box 56, vol. 12, p. 102, RG 75, FARC.

86. No Neck's affidavit, sworn at U.S. Consulate, Brussels, Belgium, 5 June 1891, PR, General Records, Misc. Correspondence Received (1891–95), Box 31, RG 75, FARC.

87. Cody to Penny, 8 June 1891, PR, General Records, Misc. Correspondence Received (1891–95), Box 28, RG 75, FARC.

88. Penny to Cody, 30 July 1891, PR, General Records, Box 55, vol. 8, p. 126, RG 75, FARC.

89. Penny to Cody, 6 August 1891, PR, General Records, Box 55, vol. 8, p. 151, RG 75, FARC.

90. Penny to Cody, 4 September 1891, PR, General Records, Box 55, vol. 8, p. 294, RG 75, FARC; Cody to Penny, 17 August 1891, PR, General Records, Box 28, RG 75, FARC.

91. Penny to Cody, 4 September 1891, PR, General Records, Box 55, vol. 8, p. 294, RG 75, FARC.

92. Penny to Cody, 4 August 1891, PR, General Records, Box 55, vol. 8, p. 148, RG 75, FARC.

93. Penny to Cody, 6 August 1891, PR, General Records, Box 55, vol. 8, p. 151, RG 75, FARC.

94. The "boss farmer" was the agency farmer employed by the government to advise and counsel the Indians about farming operations. See Washburn, *American Indian and the United States*, 393–94.

95. Cody to Penny, 30 September 1891, PR, General Records, Box 28, RG 75, FARC.

96. Penny to Cody, 2 November 1891, PR, General Records, Box 55, vol. 9, p. 38, RG 75, FARC.

97. Cody to Miles, 12 November 1891, PR, General Records, Box 28, RG 75, FARC.

98. Ibid.; Cody to Penny, 13 November 1891, PR, General Records, Box 28, RG 75, FARC.

99. Cody to Penny, 18 December 1891, PR, General Records, Box 28, RG 75, FARC.

100. Brown to Cody, 4 January 1892, PR, General Records, Box 55, vol. 10, p.175, RG 75, FARC.

101. W. H. Hart, Auditor, Treasury Department, to No Neck, 10 September 1892, PR, General Records, Misc. Correspondence Received (1891–95), Box 29, RG 75, FARC.

102. *Evening News* (Portsmouth), 10 October 1891, 3 ("Round the 'Wild West'— The Inner Life of the Show").

103. Standing Bear, *My People, the Sioux*, 258.

104. Deloria Jr., "Indians," 52.

105. Ibid., 53.

106. Kasson, *Buffalo Bill's Wild West*, 211.

107. Hoxie, "Exploring a Cultural Borderland," in *American Nations*, ed. Hoxie et al., 275.

CHAPTER NINE: RETURN TO AMERICA AND THEREAFTER

1. "Counting coup" meant touching an opposing warrior in battle, a very dangerous act of courage; it also referred to a warrior recounting his war deeds. "He took every opportunity to count his coups—at dances and at ceremonies he proclaimed his worth." See Hassrick, *Sioux*, 99.

2. Unidentified Chicago newspaper, n.d. ("Big Red Men in the City. On Their Return from an Extended European Trip"), Buffalo Bill Scrapbook, 13, Microfilm FF18, Cody Papers, SHSC.

3. Salsbury to Miles, 29 February 1892, 27617 PRD 1892, Box 56, RG 94, NARA.

4. Ibid.

5. Ibid.

6. Salsbury to S. B. Elkins, Secretary of War, 19 February 1892, 27240 PRD 1892, Box 56, RG 94, NARA.

7. Elkins to Crager, 5 March 1892, 27240 PRD 1892, Box 56, RG 94, NARA.

8. Crager to Elkins, 12 March 1892, 27240 PRD 1892, Box 56, RG 94, NARA.

9. J. L. Kelton, Adjutant General, Washington, D.C., to Commanding General, Department of the East, Governor's Island, New York, 12 March 1892, 27240 PRD 1892, Box 56, RG 94, NARA.

10. Ruggles, Assistant Adjutant General, Governor's Island, to Kelton, telegram, 27240 PRD 1892, Box 56, RG 94, NARA.

11. Miles to Kelton, 14 March 1892, 27240 PRD 1892, Box 56, RG 94, NARA.

12. *New York Herald,* 19 March 1892, 8 ("Braves Back from Europe—A Large Party of Sioux from Buffalo Bill's Wild West Show on Their Way to Fort Sheridan").

13. Ibid. The *New York Herald* correctly named both the former prisoners and the other performers from Buffalo Bill's Wild West who had returned from Glasgow. "Besides the three chiefs, the Fort Sheridan Indians are Standing Bear, Wounded with Many Arrows, Revenge, One Star, Brings the White, High Eagle, Brave, Know His Voice and his squaw Medicine Horse. The other Indians who will go on to Rushville, Pine Ridge agency, with Mr. Crager are Kills Crow, Both Sides White, Holy Bird, Charging Thunder, Has No Horses, Pull Him Out, Bears Lay Down, White Horse, Shooting and his squaw, Her Blankets, Short Man and his squaw, Plenty Blankets." Medicine Horse was also reported as being the wife of Brings the White. Several publications mistakenly identified Plenty Blankets as being Short Bull's wife; she was instead married to Short Man, who had also returned from Glasgow. Short Bull is later recorded on the Pine Ridge Census Rolls as having two wives, one called Plenty Shell and the other, Comes Out. Neither of Short Bull's wives had accompanied him; for confirmation of this, see Penny to CIA, 28 March 1891, PR, M1282, 179–81, RG 75, FARC.

14. *New York Herald,* 19 March 1892, 8 ("Braves Back from Europe").

15. *New York Tribune,* 19 March 1892 ("Arrival of 'the Wild West' Indians in America—The Ghost Dancers Arrested").

16. *New York Herald,* 19 March 1892, 8 ("Braves Back from Europe"); *Chicago Daily Tribune,* 21 March 1892, 3 ("Indians Come to Town—Kicking Bear and His Friends Arrive under Escort").

17. *New York Tribune,* 19 March 1892 ("Arrival of 'the Wild West' Indians in America").

18. *New York Herald,* 19 March 1892, 8 ("Braves Back from Europe").

19. Unidentified Chicago newspaper, n.d. ("Big Red Men in the City"), Buffalo Bill Scrapbook, 13, Microfilm FF18, Cody Papers, SHSC.

20. Ibid.

21. *Chicago Daily Tribune,* 21 March 1892, 3 ("Indians Come to Town").

22. Unidentified Chicago newspaper, n.d. ("Big Red Men in the City"), Buffalo Bill Scrapbook, 13, Microfilm FF18, Cody Papers, SHSC.

23. *Chicago Daily Tribune,* 23 March 1892, 7 ("Soldiers for the World's Fair").

24. Miles to Kelton, telegram, 23 April 1892, 30329 PRD 1892, Box 56, RG 94, NARA.

25. CIA to Noble, 29 April 1892, 30329 PRD 1892, Box 56, RG 94, NARA.

26. "Correspondence in Relation to the Employment of Indians with the Wild West Exhibitions," Noble to Garrett, 2 May 1892, Incoming Correspondence, Reel 9, IRA.

27. Noble to Elkins, 4 May 1892, 30329 PRD 1892, Box 56, RG 94, NARA.

28. Miles to Kelton, 6 May 1892, 30329 PRD 1892, Box 56, RG 94, NARA.

29. Miles to Brown, 9 May 1892, PR, General Records, Misc. Correspondence Received (1891–95), Box 30, RG 75, FARC.

30. Miles to Young Man Afraid of His Horses et al., PR, General Records, Misc. Correspondence Received (1891–95), Box 30, RG 75, FARC.

31. John R. Brooke, Brigadier General, Commanding, Headquarters Department of the Platte, Omaha, Neb., to Kelton, 2 April 1892, 30329 PRD 1892, Box 56, RG 94, NARA.

32. Miles to Young Man Afraid Of His Horses et al., PR, General Records, Misc. Correspondence Received (1891–95), Box 30, RG 75, FARC.

33. Miles to Kelton, 7 June 1892, 30329 PRD 1892, Box 56, RG 94, NARA.

34. This sentiment was echoed by Secretary Noble. See Noble to Elkins, 30 June 1892, 30329 PRD 1892, Box 56, RG 94, NARA.

35. Captain Huggins to Pine Ridge Agent, telegram, 17 July 1892, PR, General Records, Box 29, RG 75, FARC.

36. Miles to Kelton, 19 July 1892, 30329 PRD 1892, Box 56, RG 94, NARA.

37. CIA to Noble, 1 August 1892, 36342 PRD 1892, Box 56, RG 94, NARA.

38. Chandler, Acting Secretary of Interior, to Elkins, 2 August 1892, 36342 PRD 1892, Box 56, RG 94, NARA.

39. Calling card signed by Miles, upon which he had written, "Mr. Salsbury has permission to visit the Indians at Fort Sheridan," 20 August 1892, Box 1, Folder 7, Salsbury Papers, Beinecke Rare Book and Manuscript Library, Yale University; *Evening News and Post* (London), 6 September 1892, Scrapbook 1892, MS6, Series IX, Box 7, Cody Archives, McCracken Research Library, BBHC.

40. Kicking Bear was also chosen as a model for the Indian face that appears on the Q Street Bridge spanning Rock Creek in Washington, D.C. See Ahrens, "Bridge Too Far," *Washington Post Magazine*, 16 July 2000, 34; available online at: <http://www.rcpub.com/rcp_about/kicking_bear.html>

41. Brown to Kicking Bear, Fort Sheridan, 23 March 1892, PR, General Records, Misc. LS 1892, Box 56, vol. 11, p. 384, RG 75, FARC.

42. Brown to Kicking Bear, Fort Sheridan, 13 May 1892, PR, General Records, Misc. LS 1892, Box 56, vol. 12, p. 325, RG 75, FARC.

43. Brooke to Kelton, 12 October 1892, 39726 PRD 1892, Box 56, RG 94, NARA.

44. Noble to Brown, 29 March 1892, PR, General Records, Misc. Correspondence Received (1891–95), Box 30, RG 75, FARC; Noble to Elkins, 29 March 1892, 29022

PRD 1892, Box 56, RG 94, NARA; Noble to CIA, 14 April 1892, Standing Rock Agency, General Records, Commissioner's Correspondence 1892, 517204/4, Box 393, RG 75, FARC. See also Brown to Noble, 9 April 1892, RG 48, LR (1892) 1222, National Archives II.

45. Noble to Brown, 14 April 1892, LR 13917–1892, Box 847, RG 75, NARA.

46. Brown to Cody, 18 April 1892, PR, General Records, Misc. LS 1892, Box 56, vol. 12, p. 57, RG 75, FARC.

47. Ibid.

48. Cody, New York, to Brown, 22 April 1892, PR, General Records, Box 28, RG 75, FARC.

49. Ibid.

50. Brown to Cody, 3 May 1892, PR, General Records, Misc. LS 1892, Box 56, vol. 12, p. 216, RG 75, FARC.

51. Cody to Elkins, 28 September 1892, 39592 PRD 1892, Box 56, RG 94, NARA. Cody lists the returning prisoners as being Hard to Hit, One Star, Good Eagle, Brave, and Calls the Name. One Star and Brave were also listed in the group that had returned with Kicking Bear and Short Bull, and the two prisoners whose return home does not appear to have been covered are Coming Grunt and Crow Cane.

52. Moses, *Wild West Shows and the Images of American Indians, 1883–1933*, 128.

53. Wissler, *Indians of the United States*, 175.

54. Danberg, "Letters to Jack Wilson, the Paiute Prophet, Written between 1908 and 1911," 286.

55. Hittman, *Wovoka*, 265. Cloud Horse had been identified by George Sword as being in the 1890 Lakota delegation; see Mooney, *Ghost Dance*, 159. He was not mentioned in Short Bull's list.

56. *Lyon County Times*, 4 August 1906, quoted in Hittman, *Wovoka*, 265.

57. Danberg, "Letters to Jack Wilson, the Paiute Prophet, Written between 1908 and 1911," 285, 294.

58. Pine Ridge Census Rolls, 1893–1924, Microfilm M595, Western History and Genealogy Department, DPL. It appears that along with the whole family (barring his mother) John acquired his Christian name sometime between 1896 and 1898. The English translation of his Lakota name was Shot to Pieces. His father was thereafter referred to as Arnold Short Bull, and all his children took Short Bull as their surname.

59. Danberg, "Letters to Jack Wilson, the Paiute Prophet, Written between 1908 and 1911," 288.

60. Clow, "Lakota Ghost Dance after 1890," 331–32. Clow cites both Danberg ("Letters to Jack Wilson," 286) and Kehoe (*Ghost Dance*, 46–48) as his sources.

61. McCoy, "Short Bull," 57.

62. Haberland, "Die Oglala-Sammlung Weygold . . . (Teil 4)," 21.

63. Flood, *Lost Bird of Wounded Knee*, 133–34.

64. See Kehoe, *Ghost Dance*, 46–47.

65. McCoy, "Short Bull," 61.

66. Pine Ridge Census Rolls, 1893–1924, Microfilm M595, Western History and Genealogy Department, DPL. Although dismissed by Wildhage, Jeanne O. Snodgrass's suggested date of 6 July 1923 seems to concur with the Pine Ridge Census Rolls. See Wilhage, "Material on Short Bull," 35. However, the reliability of census data remains questionable. See Shoemaker, "Overview of American Indian Demographic History," in *American Indian Population Recovery in the Twentieth Century*.

67. *New York Daily News*, 5 June 1894, Scrapbook 1894, MS6, Series IX, Box 10, Cody Archives, McCracken Research Library, BBHC.

BIBLIOGRAPHY

ARCHIVAL DEPOSITORIES

Cheyenne, Wyoming. Wyoming State Archives Museums and Historical Department. John Shangrau Papers.

Cody, Wyoming. Buffalo Bill Historical Center. Buffalo Bill Museum files. Harold McCracken Research Library, William F. Cody Collection.

College Park, Maryland. National Archives II. Record Group 48, Records of the Department of the Interior.

Denver, Colorado. Denver Public Library. Western History and Genealogy Department. Pine Ridge Census Rolls, 1893–1924 (microfilm M595) and William F. Cody Collection.

Denver, Colorado. State Historical Society of Colorado. William Frederick Cody Papers.

Glasgow, Scotland, U.K. Art Gallery and Museum, Kelvingrove. Museum Archives.

Glasgow, Scotland, U.K. Mitchell Library, Glasgow Room and Glasgow City Archives.

Golden, Colorado. Buffalo Bill Museum and Grave, William F. Cody Collection.

Kansas City, Missouri. Federal Archives and Records Center. Record Group 75, Records of the Bureau of Indian Affairs: Pine Ridge Agency, Rosebud Agency, and Standing Rock Agency.

Lincoln, Nebraska. Nebraska State Historical Society. Judge Eli S. Ricker Collection, and William Carver Papers.

London, England. British Library. Newspaper Library, Various British and American publications, 1890–92.

New Haven, Connecticut. Yale University, Beinecke Rare Book and Manuscript Library. Nathan Salsbury Papers.

Norman, Oklahoma. University of Oklahoma Library. Western History Collections, Indian Rights Association Papers, 1864–1973.

Pierre, South Dakota. South Dakota State Historical Society, Mary Clementine Collins Family Papers.

Washington, D.C. National Archives and Records Administration. Record Group 75, Records of the Bureau of Indian Affairs. Record Group 94, Records of the Adjutant General's Office, 1780–1917.

GOVERNMENT PUBLICATIONS

U.S. Secretary of War. *Annual Report, 1891.* Washington, D.C.: Government Printing Office, 1891.

U.S. Commissioner of Indian Affairs. *Annual Report, 1890.* Washington, D.C.: Government Printing Office, 1890.

———. *Annual Report, 1891.* Washington, D.C.: Government Printing Office, 1891.

NEWSPAPERS

Argus (Brighton), October 1891.

Bailie (Glasgow), November 1891–March 1892.

Birmingham Daily Post, September 1891.

Bristol Evening News, September–October 1891.

Casper Star-Tribune, September 1997.

Chicago Daily Tribune, January–April 1891, March–April 1892, September 1998.

Daily Graphic (London), June 1892.

Daily Telegraph (London), October 1890–April 1891.

Denver Rocky Mountain News, December 1890.

Evening Citizen (Glasgow), October 1891–January 1892.

Evening Express (Cardiff), September 1891.

Evening News (Portsmouth), October 1891.

Evening News and Post (London), November 1890–April 1891, June 1892.

Evening Telegraph and Star (Sheffield), August 1891.

Evening Times (Glasgow), October 1891–February 1892.

Glasgow Evening News, October 1891–February 1892.

Glasgow Herald, November 1891–February 1892.

Glasgow Weekly News, November 1891–February 1892.

Leeds Daily News, June–July 1891.

Leeds Evening Express, June–July 1891.

Leicester Daily Post, August–September 1891.

Liverpool Echo, July 1891.

Liverpool Mercury, July 1891.

Manchester Evening Mail, July–August 1891.

Manchester Weekly Times, July–August 1891.

Million (London), September 1892.

Morning (London), August 1892.
New York Herald, March 1892.
New York Times, March 1891, March 1892.
New York World, January 1891–April 1891, March 1892.
North British Daily Mail, October 1891–February 1892.
Nottingham Daily Express, August 1891.
Nottingham Evening Express, August 1891.
Observer (London), February 1995.
Omaha Morning World-Herald, February 1891.
Quiz (Glasgow), October 1891–February 1892.
Sheffield and Rotherham Independent, August 1891.
Standard (London), October 1890–April 1891, June–August 1892.

BOOKS AND ARTICLES

Adams, David Wallace. *Education for Extinction: American Indians and the Boarding School Experience, 1875–1928.* Lawrence: University Press of Kansas, 1995.

Allen, Charles W. *From Fort Laramie to Wounded Knee: In the West That Was.* Edited by Richard E. Jensen. Lincoln: University of Nebraska Press, 1997.

Biolsi, Thomas. "The Birth of the Reservation: Making the Modern Individual among the Lakota." In *American Nations: Encounters in Indian Country, 1850 to Present,* edited by Frederick Hoxie, Peter Mancall, and James Merrell. New York: Routledge, 2001.

Blackstone, Sarah J. *Buckskins, Bullets, and Business: A History of Buffalo Bill's Wild West.* Westport, Conn.: Greenwood Press, 1986.

———. *The Business of Being Buffalo Bill: Selected Letters of William F. Cody, 1879–1917.* New York: Praeger, 1988.

Bland, Thomas A., ed. *A Brief History of the Late Military Invasion of the Home of the Sioux.* Washington, D.C.: National Indian Defence Association, 1891.

Bolt, Christine. *American Indian Policy and American Reform: Case Studies of the Campaign to Assimilate the American Indians.* London: Allen & Unwin, 1987.

Boyd, James P. *Recent Indian Wars.* Philadelphia, 1891.

Buechel, Eugene. *A Grammar of Lakota: The Language of the Teton Sioux Indians.* Saint Francis, S.D., 1939.

———. *Lakota Tales and Texts: Wisdom Stories, Customs, Lives, and Instruction of the Dakota Peoples.* Edited by Paul Manhart. Pine Ridge, S.D.: Red Cloud Lakota Language and Cultural Center, 1978.

———. *Lakota Tales and Texts in Translation.* Edited by Paul Manhart. Chamberlain, S.D.: Tipi Press, 1998.

Cameron, Joy. *Prisons and Punishment in Scotland.* Edinburgh: Canongate, 1983.

Child, Brenda J. *Boarding School Seasons: American Indian Families, 1900–1940.* Lincoln: University of Nebraska Press, 1998.

Clow, Richmond L. "The Lakota Ghost Dance after 1890." *South Dakota History* 20, no. 4 (1990): 323–33.

————. "The Rosebud Sioux: The Federal Government and the Reservation Years, 1878–1940." Ph.D. diss., University of New Mexico, 1977.

Cody, William F. *Buffalo Bill's Life Story: An Autobiography of Buffalo Bill (Colonel W. F. Cody).* New York: Rinehart, 1920.

Coleman, William S. E. *Voices of Wounded Knee.* Lincoln: University of Nebraska Press, 2002.

Cunningham, Tom F. *The Diamond's Ace: Scotland and the Native Americans.* Edinburgh: Mainstream Publishing, 2001.

Curtis, Natalie. *The Indians' Book: Authentic Native American Legends, Lore & Music.* 1907. Reprint, New York: Bonanza Books, 1987.

Danberg, Grace M. "Letters to Jack Wilson, the Paiute Prophet, Written between 1908 and 1911." Smithsonian Institution Bureau of American Ethnology Bulletin 164. *Anthropological Papers* 55 (1957): 279–96.

Deloria, Vine, Jr. "The Indians." In *Buffalo Bill and the Wild West.* New York: Brooklyn Museum, 1981.

DeMallie, Raymond J. "The Lakota Ghost Dance: An Ethnohistorical Account." *Pacific Historical Review* 51, no. 4 (1982): 385–405.

————, ed. *Plains. Handbook of North American Indians,* vol. 13. Series editor, William C. Sturtevant. Washington, D.C.: Smithsonian Institution, 2001.

————. Review of Robert W. Larson, *Red-Cloud: Warrior-Statesman of the Lakota Sioux* (1997). *American Historical Review* (December 2000): 1749–50.

————. *The Sixth Grandfather: Black Elk's Teachings Given to John G. Neihardt.* Lincoln: University of Nebraska Press, 1984.

Deverell, William. "Fighting Words: The Significance of the American West in the History of the United States." In *A New Significance: Re-envisioning the History of the American West,* edited by Clyde A. Milner II. Oxford: Oxford University Press, 1996.

Dippie, Brian W. "American Wests: Historiographical Perspectives." In *Trails: Towards a New Western History,* edited by Patricia Nelson Limerick et al. Lawrence: University Press of Kansas, 1991.

————. *The Vanishing American: White Attitudes and U.S. Indian Policy.* Middletown, Conn.: Wesleyan University Press, 1982.

Draeger, Lothar. "Einige Indianische Darstellungen des Sonnentanzes aus dem Museum für Völkerkunde in Leipzig." *Jahrbuch des Museums für Völkurkunde zu Leipzig* 18 (1961): 59–86.

Eastman, Elaine. "The Ghost Dance War and Wounded Knee Massacre of 1890–91." *Nebraska History* 26 (1945): 26–42.

Eastman, Elaine Goodale. *Sister to the Sioux: The Memoirs of Elaine Goodale Eastman.* Edited by Kay Graber. Lincoln: University of Nebraska Press, 1978.

Flood, Renée Sansom. *Lost Bird of Wounded Knee: Spirit of the Lakota.* New York: Scribner's, 1995.

Foote, Stella Adelyne. *Letters from "Buffalo Bill."* Billings, Mont., 1954.

Forbes, George, and Paddy Meehan. *Such Bad Company: The Story of Glasgow Criminality.* Edinburgh: Paul Harris Publishing, 1982.

Foreman, Carolyn T. *Indians Abroad, 1493–1938*. Norman: University of Oklahoma Press, 1943.

Gallop, Alan. *Buffalo Bill's British Wild West*. Stroud: Sutton Publishing, 2001.

Green, Jerry, ed. *After Wounded Knee: Correspondence of Major and Surgeon John Vance Lauderdale while Serving with the Army Occupying the Pine Ridge Indian Reservation, 1890–1891*. East Lansing: Michigan State University Press, 1996.

Gossett, Thomas F. *Race: The History of an Idea in America*. Dallas: Southern Methodist University Press, 1963.

Green, Jonathan. *The Cassell Dictionary of Slang*. London: Cassell, 1998.

Haberland, Wolfgang. "Adrian Jacobson on Pine Ridge Reservation 1910." *European Review of Native American Studies* 1, no. 1 (1988): 11–15.

———. "Die Oglala-Sammlung Weygold im Hamburgischen Museum für Völkerkunde (Teil 3)." *Mitteilungen aus dem Museum für Völkurkunde zu Hamburg, NF* 6 (1976): 17–35.

———. "Die Oglala-Sammlung Weygold im Hamburgischen Museum für Völkerkunde (Teil 4)." *Mitteilungen aus dem Museum für Völkurkunde zu Hamburg, NF* 7 (1977): 19–52.

Hagan, William T. *Indian Police and Judges: Experiments in Acculturation and Control*. New Haven: Yale University Press, 1966.

———. *The Indian Rights Association: The Herbert Welsh Years, 1882–1904*. Tucson: University of Arizona Press, 1985.

Hassrick, Royal B. *The Sioux: Life and Customs of a Warrior Society*. Norman: University of Oklahoma Press, 1964.

Herman, Daniel Justin. "God Bless Buffalo Bill." *Reviews in American History* 29 (2001): 228–37.

Hittman, Michael. *Wovoka and the Ghost Dance*. Edited by Don Lynch. Lincoln: University of Nebraska Press, 1997.

Horseman, Reginald. *Race and Manifest Destiny: The Origins of American Racial Anglo-Saxonism*. Cambridge, Mass.: Harvard University Press, 1981.

Hoxie, Frederick E. "Exploring a Cultural Borderland: Native American Journeys of Discovery in the Early Twentieth Century." In *American Nations: Encounters in Indian Country, 1850 to Present*, edited by Frederick Hoxie, Peter Mancall, and James Merrell. New York: Routledge, 2001.

———. *A Final Promise: The Campaign to Assimilate the Indians, 1880–1920*. Lincoln: University of Nebraska Press, 1984.

Huls, Don. *The Winter of 1890: What Happened at Wounded Knee*. Chadron, Nebr.: Chadron Record, 1974.

Hyde, George E. *Red Clouds Folk: A History of the Oglala Sioux Indians*. Norman: University of Oklahoma Press, 1937.

———. *A Sioux Chronicle*. Norman: University of Oklahoma Press, 1993.

Jensen, Richard E., et al. *Eyewitness at Wounded Knee*. Lincoln: University of Nebraska Press, 1991.

Josephy, Alvin M., Jr., et al. *Wounded Knee: Lest We Forget*. Cody, Wyo.: Buffalo Bill Historical Center, 1990.

Kasson, Joy S. *Buffalo Bill's Wild West: Celebrity, Memory, and Popular History.* New York: Hill & Wang, 2000.

Kehoe, Alice B. *The Ghost Dance: Ethnohistory and Revitalization.* New York: Holt, Rinehart & Winston, 1989.

Klein, Christina. "'Everything of Interest in the Late Pine Ridge War Are Held by Us for Sale': Popular Culture and Wounded Knee." *Western Historical Quarterly* 25, no. 2 (1994): 45–68.

Lemons, William E. "History by Unreliable Narrators: Sitting Bull's Circus Horse." *Montana: The Magazine of Western History* 2 (1995): 64–75.

Lewis, David Rich. *Neither Wolf nor Dog: American Indians, Environment, and Agrarian Change.* New York: Oxford University Press, 1994.

———. "Reservation Leadership and the Progressive-Traditional Dichotomy: William Wash and the Northern Utes, 1865–1928." In *American Nations: Encounters in Indian Country, 1850 to Present,* edited by Frederick Hoxie, Peter Mancall, and James Merrell. New York: Routledge, 2001.

MacKenzie, John M. *Propaganda and Empire: The Manipulation of British Public Opinion, 1880–1960.* Manchester, England: Manchester University Press, 1984.

Maddra, Sam. *Glasgow's Ghost Shirt.* Glasgow: Glasgow Museums, 1999.

———. "The Wounded Knee Ghost Dance Shirt." *Journal of Museum Ethnography* 8 (1996): 41–58.

McCoy, Ronald. "Short Bull: Lakota Visionary, Historian and Artist." *American Indian Art Magazine* (Summer 1992): 54–65.

McDermott, John D. "Wounded Knee: Centennial Voices." *South Dakota History* 20, no. 4 (1990): 245–93.

McLaughlin, James. *My Friend the Indian.* Boston: Houghton Mifflin, 1910.

Michno, Gregory F. *Lakota Noon: The Indian Narrative of Custer's Defeat.* Missoula, Mont.: Mountain Press Publishing, 1997.

Miles, Nelson A. *Serving the Republic: Memoirs of the Civil and Military Life of Nelson A. Miles Lieutenant-General, United States Army.* New York: Harper & Brothers, 1911.

Mooney, James. *The Ghost Dance.* 1896. Reprint, Massachusetts: J. G. Press, 1996.

———. "The Ghost Dance Religion and the Sioux Outbreak of 1890." *Fourteenth Annual Report of the Bureau of American Ethnology 1892–93.* Part 2. Washington, D.C.: U.S. Government Printing Office, 1896.

Moses, L. G. "'The Father Tells Me So!' Wovoka: The Ghost Dance Prophet." *American Indian Quarterly* 9, no. 3 (1985): 335–51.

———. *The Indian Man: A Biography of James Mooney.* 1984. Reprint, Lincoln: University of Nebraska Press, 2002.

———. "Jack Wilson and the Indian Service: The Response of the BIA to the Ghost Dance Prophet." *American Indian Quarterly* 5, no. 3 (1979): 295–316.

———. *Wild West Shows and the Images of American Indians, 1883–1933.* Albuquerque: University of New Mexico Press, 1996.

———. "Wild West Shows, Reformers, and the Image of the American Indian, 1887–1914." *South Dakota History* 14 (1984): 193–221.

Napier, Rita G. "Across the Big Water: American Indians' Perceptions of Europe and Europeans, 1887–1906." In *Indians and Europe: An Interdisciplinary Collection of Essays*, edited by Christian Feest. Aachen, Netherlands: Radar Verlag, 1987.

Osburn, Katherine M. B. *Southern Ute Women: Autonomy and Assimilation on the Reservation, 1887–1934*. Albuquerque: University of New Mexico Press, 1998.

Osterreich, Shelley Anne. *The American Indian Ghost Dance, 1870 and 1890: An Annotated Bibliography*. New York: Greenwood Press, 1991.

Overholt, Thomas. "The Ghost Dance of 1890 and the Nature of the Prophetic Process." *Ethnohistory* 21, no. 1 (1974): 37–63.

———. "Short Bull, Black Elk, Sword, and the 'Meaning' of the Ghost Dance." *Religion* 8 (Spring 1978): 171–95.

Parker, Lew. *Odd People I Have Met*. N.p., n.d. [1899].

Paul, Andrea I. "Buffalo Bill and Wounded Knee: The Movie." *Nebraska History* 71, no. 4 (1990): 182–90.

Pegler, Martin, and Graeme Rimer. *Buffalo Bill's Wild West*. Leeds: Royal Armouries Museum, 1999.

Pfaller, Louis. "'Enemies in '76, Friends in '85': Sitting Bull and Buffalo Bill." *Prologue, The Journal of the National Archives* 1, no.2 (1969): 16–31.

Phister, Lt. Nat P. "The Indian Messiah." *American Anthropologist* 4, no. 2 (1891): 105–8.

Pierson, Ruth Roach, and Nupur Chaudhuri, eds. *Nation, Empire, Colony: Historicizing Gender and Race*. Bloomington: Indiana University Press, 1998.

Porter, Bernard. *The Lion's Share: A Short History of British Imperialism, 1850–1995*. 3d ed. London: Longman, 1996.

Price, Catherine. *The Oglala People, 1841–1879: A Political History*. Lincoln: University of Nebraska Press, 1996.

Prucha, Francis Paul. *American Indian Policy in Crisis: Christian Reformers and the Indian, 1865–1900*. Norman: University of Oklahoma Press, 1976.

———. *The Indians in American Society: From Revolutionary War to the Present*. Berkeley: University of California Press, 1985.

Reddin, Paul. *Wild West Shows*. Chicago: University of Chicago Press, 2000.

Riney, Scott. *The Rapid City Indian School, 1898–1933*. Norman: University of Oklahoma Press, 1999.

Rosa, Joseph G., and Robin May. *Buffalo Bill and His Wild West: A Pictorial Biography*. Lawrence: University Press of Kansas, 1989.

Russell, Don. *The Lives and Legends of Buffalo Bill*. Norman: University of Oklahoma Press, 1960.

Shoemaker, Nancy. *American Indian Population Recovery in the Twentieth Century*. Albuquerque: University of New Mexico Press, 1999.

Shoemaker, Nancy, ed. *American Indians*. Oxford: Blackwell, 2001.

Sievers, Michael A. "The Historiography of 'The Bloody Field . . . That Kept the Secret of the Everlasting Word': Wounded Knee." *South Dakota History* 6, no. 1 (1975): 33–54.

Slotkin, Richard. *Gunfighter Nation: The Myth of the Frontier in Twentieth Century America*. New York: Harper Perennial, 1992.

Smits, David D. "Indian Scouts and Indian Allies in the Frontier Army." In *Major Problems in American Indian History: Documents and Essays*, edited by Albert L. Hurtado and Peter Iverson. 2d ed. Boston: Houghton Mifflin, 2001.

Standing Bear, Luther. *My People, the Sioux*. Lincoln: University of Nebraska Press, 1975.

Stanton, William. *The Leopard's Spots: Scientific Attitudes toward Race in America, 1815–59*. Chicago: University of Chicago Press, 1965.

Starita, Joe. *The Dull Knifes of Pine Ridge: A Lakota Odyssey*. New York: Putnam, 1995.

Stewart, Omer C. "Contemporary Document on Wovoka (Jack Wilson) Prophet of the Ghost Dance in 1890." *Ethnohistory* 23, no. 3 (1977): 219–22.

Swartwout, Annie F. *Annie Oakley: Her Life and Times*. New York: Carlton Press, 1947.

Sword, George. "The Story of the Ghost Dance." *Folk-Lorist* 1 (1892–93): 28–31.

Utley, Robert M. *The Last Days of the Sioux Nation*. New Haven: Yale University Press, 1963. 2d ed., 2004.

Vestal, Stanley [Walter Stanley Campbell]. *New Sources of Indian History, 1850–1891*. Norman: University of Oklahoma Press, 1934.

———. *Sitting Bull: Champion of the Sioux*. Norman: University of Oklahoma Press, 1957.

Walker, James R. *Lakota Belief and Ritual*. Edited by Raymond J. DeMallie and Elaine A. Jahner. Lincoln: University of Nebraska Press, 1991.

———. *Lakota Society*. Edited by Raymond J. DeMallie. Lincoln: University of Nebraska Press, 1982.

Walker, John, ed. *The North American Sketches of R. B. Cunninghame Graham*. Edinburgh: Scottish Academic Press, 1986.

Washburn, Wilcomb E. *The American Indian and the United States: A Documentary History*. Vol. 1. New York: Random House, 1973.

White, Richard. "Frederick Jackson Turner and Buffalo Bill." In *The Frontier in American Culture*, edited by James R. Grossman. Berkeley: University of California Press, 1994.

———. *The Roots of Dependency: Subsistence, Environment, and Social Change among the Choctaws, Pawnees, and Navajos*. Lincoln: University of Nebraska Press, 1983.

Wildhage, Wilhelm. "Material on Short Bull." *Native American Studies* 4, no.1 (1990): 35–42.

Wissler, Clark. *Indians of the United States: Four Centuries of Their History and Culture*. New York: Doubleday, 1951.

———. "Some Protective Designs of the Dakota." *Anthropological Papers of the American Museum of Natural History* 1, part 2 (February 1907): 19–53.

Wooster, Robert. *Nelson A. Miles and the Twilight of the Frontier Army*. Lincoln: University of Nebraska Press, 1993.

Yost, Nellie Snyder. *Buffalo Bill: His Family, Friends, Failures and Fortunes*. Chicago: Swallow Press, 1979.

Index

ς